WITHDRAWN

Discussion and Conference

Discussion and Conference

WILLIAM M. SATTLER

N. EDD MILLER

UNIVERSITY OF MICHIGAN

PRENTICE-HALL, INC.

Englewood Cliffs, N. J.

LIBRARY OF CONGRESS
CATALOG CARD No.: 54–11548

First printing .... September, 1954
Second printing .... August, 1955
Third printing .... May, 1956
Fourth printing .... March, 1959
Fifth printing .... August, 1961
Sixth printing .... June, 1962
Seventh printing .... April, 1964

PRINTED IN THE UNITED STATES OF AMERICA
21614—C

Preface

Our central aim in this book has been to show how group leaders and members can develop personal skills in discussion. Because the success of a discussion depends upon the actions of those in the group, it is proper that both leaders and participants develop a high degree of competence. To help them achieve this goal, we have tried to give a clear explanation of the principles that underlie cooperative face-to-face discussion. We have further listed and described suggestions that conferees should employ in a variety of situations. Although these suggestions are usually specific points of guidance, we believe we have given sufficient emphasis to the importance of good judgment on the part of leaders and participants. We have stated that the situation should dictate what conferees do and say in discussions. At various points in the book we have also stressed outcomes (both desirable and undesirable) of group meetings. This type of knowledge is very important to any person who desires to be an effective member of a group.

What we have reported has been drawn from many sources. First, we have been influenced by early writers (such as Dewey, Elliott, and Fansler) in the field of discussion; second, by recent writings and experimental studies in discussion and group behavior; and third, by our own experiences in teaching college and adult classes in discussion and conference.

Our use of materials of others has been acknowledged in footnote references throughout the book. We are grateful to these writers and to the publishers for permission to quote from copyrighted sources.

We are indebted to Gail E. Densmore, Chairman, Department of Speech, University of Michigan, for reading our manuscript in its early stages and for generously giving us the benefit of his suggestions and encouragement. We wish to thank Edward Stasheff, also of the Department of Speech, University of Michigan, for recommendations covering Chapter 17 on Radio and Television. William S. Howell, Department of Speech, University of Minnesota, has assisted us by reading and by commenting in detail upon our work. We gratefully acknowledge the help he has given us.

Mr. Dick Hansen, Associate Editor, Prentice-Hall, Inc., has also assisted us in many important ways. We are happy to record our expression of appreciation here.

W. M. S.
N. E. M.

Table of Contents

vii

PART II. PROBLEM-SOLVING

PART III. LEADERSHIP

PART V.   SPEECH AND LANGUAGE

PART VI.   PUBLIC MEETINGS

Appendixes

PART I

Fundamentals

1. Introduction to Discussion and Conference

If we were to ask whether you participate in discussions or conferences quite often you would probably answer, "I certainly do . . . and I spend much time doing it." Talking with others about problems you want to solve is far from unusual. And whenever the talking that you and others in your group carry on takes a purposeful and cooperative direction, your group meeting can be called a discussion or *democratic* conference. Meetings of this type can be seen in the hundreds of formally and informally organized groups and committees that are a part of our family, social, political, and business life. In fact, they seem to be as much a part of America as the automobile or the use of electrical energy.

Persons have been known to say, "My business is talking with people." This apparently is not always an exaggeration. The *Fortune* survey devoted to finding out how much time business executives spend in conferences shows these results: 19.6 per cent of the business executives interviewed reported that they spent "an hour or less" in conference per day; 69.5 per cent reported that they spent "several hours" per day; and 10.9 per cent reported that they spent "most of the day" in conference.[1] These statistical totals are impressive. They also suggest that persons other than executives probably spend more time in conference than they realize.

---

[1] "The Management Poll," *Fortune*, XXXIV (October, 1946), 14.

3

But certain important answers are not given in this report. For example:

1. Does *conference* mean casual conversation?
2. Does *conference* mean public speaking, persuasion, or order-giving?
3. Does a *conference* differ from a *discussion*?

For our purposes in this book answers to questions one and two are a categorical *NO*. The third question is less easily answered.

DEFINITION OF DISCUSSION AND CONFERENCE

There are three definitions that can be used to describe a conference and its possible relationships to discussion. The first definition is one that identifies a *conference* as any meeting, assemblage, or gathering of people, formal or informal. This would be a highly inclusive meaning. A second definition identifies a *conference* as a relatively small group meeting in which primary authority for decisions resides with the leader of the group or with select members of the group. Neither of these two definitions has important similarities to discussion. But a third definition interprets a *conference* as purposeful discussion by persons who engage in a cooperative search for answers to problems. Here there is an identity in meaning. Conference is understood as a synonym for *discussion*.

Socratic Discussions in Athens

In his *Memorabilia*, Xenophon gives us one of our earliest definitions of discussion when he says, "The very word 'discussion,' according to him [Socrates], owes its name to the practice of meeting together for common deliberation, sorting, classifying things after their kind." [2] This definition suggests that (1) discussion is an orderly intellectual process, (2) conducted by active and cooperative participants, (3) who are engaged in a search for previously

---

[2] Xenophon, *Memorabilia* (trans. E. C. Marchant), IV, V. 12. London: William Heinemann, 1923.

unknown answers to problems.   No person would wish to question this happy and ideal definition, and it is, moreover, one that Socrates had in mind when he talked about his dialectical method as a "friendly search."

Yet Socrates did not always carry on his question-and-answer discussions in the spirit of this definition.   His practice, as expressed in Plato's dialogues, shows that he followed at least three different patterns.

1. A cooperative search for "truth" as an unknown
2. Questioning designed to lead (guide) respondents to solve problems in the way Socrates wished to have them solved
3. Questioning designed to win an argument or to amuse listeners

The first method was often followed by Socrates when he discussed problems with his students.   In such discussions he seems to be what he professes, a "hesitating inquirer" honestly seeking a solution to a problem.   When he talked with the important citizens of Athens, however, he usually structured or guided the discussion in such a way as to gain verbal acceptance of a predetermined point of view.   He invariably said that he did not know the right answers to problems, but yet he was able to bring about admissions that were very damaging to his respondents.   Occasionally Socrates is reported as saying that his respondents refused honestly to carry on a discussion, and he therefore had no alternative but to depend upon questioning to refute them.   In this he did very well.   His respondents were usually baffled by his questions, and they found themselves unable to give sound reasons for their beliefs.   Socrates calls the third dialectical pattern a "corrupt" form of the true dialectical method, and he shows that it was a tricky procedure used by certain sophists who "dispute for purposes of contest."   Yet, in spite of all that he says, Socrates sometimes is guilty of the very practices that he condemns.

Some of the methods of Socrates—his use of questions to stimulate thinking and his insistence upon the testing of generalizations —are tremendously important.   We do not wish to minimize the stimulus toward rationality that stems from the conversations carried on by "the public talker" of Athens. Our own age, for example, owes a great debt to this early Greek thinker. But one further point should be remembered: *There is a difference between the Socratic ideal definition of discussion and some of his practices.*

Socrates is not alone in this apparent inconsistency. "Some people," said one business executive, "think that because a meeting is held in a room with the words 'Conference Room' printed on the door that the meeting will be a discussion or *democratic* conference." At least Socrates, to paraphrase his own doctrine, knew when a discussion was an ideal discussion and when it was not. This is less true of many people today.

Discussion Is Cooperative Problem-Solving

Our definition of discussion does not differ materially from the Socratic ideal. We define discussion as *reflective thinking by two or more persons who cooperatively exchange information and ideas in an effort to solve a problem or to gain better understanding of a problem.* Explicitly it means that:

1. All group members should have the opportunity to participate actively in the deliberations.
2. They should realize that they are searching for answers that have not been pre-determined.
3. They should engage in problem-solving (whether the purpose is to reach a specific decision or to improve understanding) in a careful, critical and reflective manner.
4. They should carry on deliberations cooperatively.

Group meetings that fail to conform to these requirements in minor respects may be called imperfect discussions. If however the violations are clear and persistent, the meeting is not a discussion at all. Howell and Smith refer to *pseudo-discussions* in this regard and identify types such as "advocacy cloaked in the discussion form" and "the discussion form used by status-dominated groups." [3] Briefly, then, command-and-obey performances and co-

---

[3] William S. Howell and Donald K. Smith, "Discussion Re-examined," *Central States Speech Journal*, V (Fall, 1953), 6–7.

ercion make a meeting something different from a discussion. Discussion is not only purposeful, but it is a democratic undertaking as well. It is, as Sheffield has said, "a face-to-face experience of an all-participant type." [4]

Conference Is an Exchange of Information and Ideas

A conference may be defined as a small *group meeting, normally not exceeding twenty persons, in which individuals exchange information and ideas for the purpose of solving a problem or for promoting better understanding of a problem.* By definition, then, a conference is not necessarily a cooperative undertaking, nor is critical (reflective) thinking necessarily stressed.

There are four classes of conferences that vary with respect to each other in the degree of freedom of choice that participants are permitted to exercise. They are identified in this relationship:

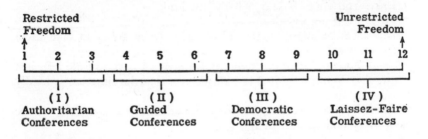

If we regard the extremes of "restricted freedom" and "unrestricted freedom" as numbers 1 and 12 respectively, it is logical to place democratic conferences in the range between 7 and 9 and guided conferences in the range between 4 and 6. All four of the types identified are popularly called *conferences,* but only the meetings in the range between 7 and 12 are within the area of discussion.

1. *The authoritarian conference.* Group meetings in which the leader or high status participants dictate decisions are largely an exercise in order-giving. In the following excerpt from the secret records of Hitler's daily military conferences, you will see that

---

[4] Alfred D. Sheffield, *Creative Discussion,* p. 20. New York: Association Press, 1927.

Hitler used the conference as a vehicle for communicating orders. Dictation is substituted for cooperation.

This *so-called* conference was held on July 26, 1943 between General Kluge, Commander of the Eastern Campaign, and Hitler. An apt title for the exchange of remarks might be, "Yes, you have no Panzers!"

Kluge: But I absolutely cannot spare any units until this operation has been finished. We'll see how we can manage things afterwards.

Hitler: You must see to it that you finish it as soon as possible. . . . You will have to give up a few Panzer—and a few Infantry Divisions—

Kluge: Not Panzer! I have—

Hitler: Yes, we'll pull them out and they'll be refitted in the West.

Kluge: But I can't do anything without Panzer Divisions!

Hitler: But certainly you don't care about that 'junk'. You can easily spare that.

Kluge: What junk?

Hitler: You yourself said "That's just junk."

Kluge: I did not say that!

Hitler: Yes, it slipped out. That's why we're going to take them away from you.

Kluge: No, my Fuehrer, I didn't mean that. I have so little left, just a little bit. What I wanted to indicate was that the situation is hardly tenable any more.

Hitler: Yes, you have no Panzers. That is why I say: they can be taken away and refitted in the West.[5]

2. *The guided conference.* In this type of conference the leader (and perhaps a few of the participants) knows the pre-determined conclusions that he wishes the group to reach. The leader is somewhat like Socrates in that he attempts to elicit the "right" answers by skillful questioning or subtle suggestion. And often the session is a recitation: If desired answers are not given by the group members, the leader supplies them. Within limits, this type of conference is useful in learning and training, but if the method is employed in problem-solving discussions the results are not likely to be favorable.

---

[5] Felix Gilbert, ed., *Hitler Directs His War*, p. 68. New York: Oxford University Press, 1950. Reprinted by permission.

The guided conference has been described as "a very elaborate series of devices for telling people something and making them feel at the same time that they are thinking it up themselves.   It doesn't work very well either.   A bit of oil now and then, of course, can be in order, but in this kind of manipulation the disadvantages outweigh the advantages." [6]   Two common weaknesses of the guided conference are: (1) participants usually resent manipulation by the leader; and (2) as a result, they tend to withhold their real feelings and ideas.   Thus in spite of the apparent smoothness of the guided conference, optimum results are not automatically attained.   *Remember:* A leader might prompt participants to express the statements that he wishes to hear, but these same participants may not honestly accept what they have themselves said. The strongly structured conference is ever subject to this danger.

3. *The democratic conference.*   In this type of conference we have the counterpart of discussion.   As Walser says, "We must want truth—more than fighting, more than tricky sparring for position and prestige." [7]   The freedom that is so largely absent in the cases of authoritarian and guided conferences emerges here as a primary feature.   This, then, is discussion.   Or to put the matter differently, discussion is a type of conference.

4. *The laissez-faire conference.*   In this, the "free rein" conference, the nominal leader places full responsibility upon the group members.   He does not advise, suggest, or direct attention to matters that should be considered.   But whether or not the laissez-faire group meeting is a true discussion depends upon the degree to which cooperativeness prevails in the group.   If the group members engage in a cooperative search for solutions and thus avoid manipulation and coercion, the laissez-faire conference is, of course, fully within the realm of discussion.

We have now named two types of conferences that can be called discussions and two types that are distinguished from discussion.

---

[6] "Problem for the Front Office," *Fortune*, XLIII (May, 1951), 152.   Reprinted by permission.

[7] Frank Walser, *The Art of Conference*, p. 9.   New York: Harper and Brothers, 1948.

Actually the label, discussion or conference, is less important than the meeting itself. But since both terms are used by varied groups and professions, we cannot arbitrarily deny the existence of either term. This is the test question to apply: *Is the meeting a free, cooperative and critical search for answers to a problem?* If you can answer "Yes," then dictation and manipulation are ruled out. It is in this sense that we understand discussion and conference in this book.

DISCUSSION RELATED TO DEMOCRATIC LIVING

If we as citizens do not believe in the "equal dignity and worth of all human personalities" we cannot have such a thing as discussion. This relationship between democratic principles and discussion seems to be perfectly obvious, and we subscribe to the belief that there is a correlation between the two. But our intention is not mainly to extol the American way of life. Our remarks here will be devoted to showing how discussion operates as an instrument for carrying out democratic ideals.

Discussion Helps to Achieve a Humane Civilization

What we know of past civilizations and the history of ideas tends to make us regard the freedom to think, to criticize, and to recommend as "human rights." This belief is common to our heritage. It has been nurtured in part by such writings as John Milton's *Areopagitica, A Speech for the Liberty of Unlicensed Printing Addressed to the Parliament of England,* published in 1644, and John Locke's *Treatises on Government,* 1685. These writers, and others, and especially the framers of the Constitution have shown that freedom is the best social order under which man can live.

Persons in a discussion practice the principles of freedom and toleration because they are encouraged to respect the points of view of everyone. This of course is often difficult to do. In general, however, people are willing to admit that a method of non-violence is a rational and humane way in which to resolve differences.

"In the end," says Morris R. Cohen, "there is no way in which people can live together decently unless each individual or group realizes that the whole truth and virtue is not exclusively in its possession." [8] What is called for in this case is mutual respect, tolerance, and a procedural plan that promotes cooperation among individuals who differ. Discussion emphasizes collaborative efforts rather than conflict. It is a procedural arrangement that encourages conferees to center their attention upon *what is right* rather than upon *who is right*. While there are many occasions when this goal is not attained, we seem to have no better alternatives open to us that so fully preserve the intellectual freedom and dignity of personalities.

What we have said should not be interpreted as a criticism of other verbal methods of resolving differences. We do not depreciate the importance of public speaking, persuasion, and debate. We believe that they are very valuable in any society that respects individual initiative and freedom. They represent, together with discussion, essential tools of a democracy.

Discussion Calls for Participation in Decision-Making

1. *Spectatorship differs from participation.* Being a spectator in a group meeting is different from being an active participant. The spectator does not help to formulate decisions, although he may occasionally have the chance to vote for or against a proposal. If he has not assisted in determining what proposals are to be voted upon, however, his level of participation is at best quite weak. And if he is not consulted at all, participation in decision-making is fully absent. The participant in discussion does not play such a passive role: he displays initiative by making his ideas known and he thus shares responsibility for whatever decisions are reached. He suggests, questions, clarifies, and evaluates in a way that distinguishes him from the passive spectator.

2. *Participation in decision-making is widely applied.* In a statement given more than twenty years ago, Elliott says:

---

[8] Morris R. Cohen, *The Faith of a Liberal*, p. 135. New York: Henry Holt and Company, 1946. Reprinted by permission.

Many believe that we have now reached the time when it is possible to move from a representative organization of life to a truly democratic form of group participation. Indeed, we are at the present time, in a very real sense, at the forking of the road. There are evidences in home, school, industry, and community life of the desire for such participation and definite demands have been made in various quarters. . . . We may move at the present time constructively into a more truly democratic organization of life; or we may return to a control more authoritative than in recent years.[9]

What results can we note?   Have our communities, industries, and schools encouraged participation rather than passivity on the part of individuals?   There are clear signs that this is true.   We have made gains in promoting the type of participation suggested by Elliott.   Organizations and businesses by the thousands that were once authoritarian in their controls are now learning the value of democratic participation.   In the Detroit Edison Company, for example, each level of supervision solves its own problems through discussion and group decision.   This practice of "true participation in decisions" has shown that *if employees are given a voice in what they do, their work will be done more efficiently.*[10]   In other words, productivity as well as employee morale seems to be related to freedom to participate in the solving of problems.   Other reports suggest that democratic participation has proved to be effective where it has been tried.[11]   In a number of other experimental cases, groups working under democratic conditions were more productive than workers under a system of autocracy.[12]   We know further that the junior boards and consultative committees used by schools, businesses, labor groups, and the government are a sign of interest in cooperative participation.

---

[9] Harrison S. Elliott, *The Process of Group Thinking,* p. 4.   New York: Association Press, 1932.   Reprinted by permission.

[10] "How Democratic Can Industry Be?" *Modern Industry,* XX (September 15, 1950), 67.

[11] See Stuart Chase, *Roads to Agreement,* pp. 123–135.   New York: Harper and Brothers, 1951.

[12] See John R. P. French, Jr., "Field Experiments: Changing Group Productivity," in James G. Miller (ed.), *Experiments in Social Process,* pp. 81–96. New York: McGraw-Hill Book Company, 1950.

GOALS IN DISCUSSION AND CONFERENCE

Decision-Making As a Goal

Some discussions are held in which the primary goal is to discover a superior solution to a problem. Other goals may be achieved, but *a good solution* is of first priority.

Can groups make better decisions than individuals? In answering this question one must remember that much will depend upon the problem to be solved and the competence of individuals and group members. As might be suspected, it is impossible to give an unqualified answer. We do know, however, that groups reach qualitatively superior answers with certain types of problems. This seems to be true in the case of *additive solutions* that involve a number of sequential steps, each of which must be correct, in order to reach a final correct answer. With these types of problems there is a tendency for members of a group to detect errors that the individual misses.[13]

A single person is often unable to discover all of the facts that have a bearing upon the problem to be decided. When this is true, reliance upon a decision by any one individual is likely to be hazardous. Group decision-making seems to be a better practice. In commenting upon this point, Benson Ford says: "You can't have people work wholeheartedly with you if you say 'Do it this way.' You've got to ask them their opinion, because often enough you might be in error. In a business as big as this one no one knows everything."[14]

And even when an individual does discover superior solutions he often must credit others with the help that they have given him. "No commander," says Dwight D. Eisenhower, "could normally take oath that a particular plan or conception originated within his own mind. Preoccupation with the concerns of his command are

---

[13] Marjorie E. Shaw, "A Comparison of Individuals and Small Groups in the Rational Solution of Complex Problems," *American Journal of Psychology*, XLIV (1932), 491–504.

[14] *Time*, LXI (May 18, 1953), 109.

such that it is impossible for any person later to say whether the first gleam of an idea that may have eventually developed into a great plan came from within his own mind or from some outside suggestion." [15] Many of us have probably had similar experiences. While a single person may have the responsibility for the success of a plan, it does not follow that he depends solely upon himself for all decisions. He almost invariably calls for ideas from his associates. The dictator, of course, is different, but his success in making correct decisions has proved to be something less than spectacular.

Learning As a Goal

Much of what we have said about decision-making discussions also holds true of discussions in which learning is stressed. Here, for example, is a report that concerns correction of errors of fact and errors of interpretation by group members:

> *Cairns:* . . . Do you think that the dialogue method we employ is more advantageous than the method of lecture by a single individual?
> *Van Doren:* Certainly I do. One man does not correct himself as readily as any one of us is corrected by the others.[16]

The soundness of Van Doren's answer here is, as always, dependent upon the qualifications of the persons in the group. Participants who discuss problems that they are not competent to discuss cannot give facts and interpretations that are needed by a learning group.

Motivation As a Goal

Less understood than either decision-making or learning is the motivational force that arises from taking part in a group discussion. In many cases motivation must be an outcome of a discussion if participants are to act in conformity with what they have learned and with the decision they have reached. "Experience is teaching

---

[15] From *Crusade in Europe,* by Dwight D. Eisenhower, p. 256. Copyright 1948 by Doubleday and Company, Inc. Reprinted by permission.
[16] Huntington Cairns, Allen Tate, and Mark Van Doren, *Invitation to Learning,* p. xviii. New York: Random House, 1941. Reprinted by permission.

us—slowly and painfully it is true—that people live only by ideals they themselves understand, and carry out effectively only such plans as they have had a part in framing," says Harrison S. Elliott.[17] The findings of the Conference Research Project at the University of Michigan substantiate the conclusion of Elliott. The survey reported by Martin Kriesberg of the conference practices of top-level executives in seventy-five businesses and organizations shows that seventy-nine per cent of the executives thought a conference would spur participants to execute the decision.[18]   In other words, while decision-making itself is of great importance, motivation to carry out decisions is also vital.

Experimental studies show how important discussion is in relation to motivation.   One of these studies conducted during World War II tested the degree to which housewives changed their buying habits by purchasing cheaper cuts of meat.   Three groups of housewives were given lectures which showed the relation of buying habits to the war effort, to nutrition, and to family economics. Three other groups discussed the problem under the direction of Mr. Alex Bavelas.   The housewives in these groups participated in the analysis of the problem and discussed the obstacles to a change in buying habits.   Only 3 per cent of the housewives who heard the lecture changed their buying habits.   On the other hand, 32 per cent of the housewives who participated in group discussion changed their buying habits.[19]

Interest in carrying out decisions is also related to how satisfied group members are with the decision that they have reached.   "All problems do not raise the issue of quality *per se* since the fact of co-operation and support of a plan may be more important than the nature of the plan.   The important thing is to get a plan that is

---

[17] Harrison S. Elliott, *The Process of Group Thinking*, p. 5.   New York: Association Press, 1932.

[18] Publication No. 5, Conference Research Project, sponsored by the Office of Naval Research.   See Martin Kriesberg, "Executives Evaluate Administrative Conferences," *Advanced Management*, XV (March, 1950), 15.

[19] Kurt Lewin, "Group Decision and Social Change," in Guy E. Swanson, Theodore M. Newcomb, and Eugene L. Hartley (eds.), *Readings in Social Psychology*, pp. 459–473.   New York: Henry Holt and Company, 1952.

acceptable." [20]   Decisions that persons do not genuinely endorse are likely to be meaningless.   But if the opposite is true, group members tend to execute decisions with enthusiasm and dispatch.

PERSONAL DEVELOPMENT THROUGH TRAINING IN DISCUSSION

Apart from the goals of decision-making, learning of facts, and motivation, there are certain by-products that should also result from experiences in discussions.   These include the many skills that go to make up effective leadership and participation.   To a large extent these skills are based upon the ability *to think critically* and *to maintain good interpersonal relations with others*.   Most of what we shall say in later chapters is directly related to these objectives.   It is important that you put forth your best efforts to develop effectiveness in thinking and human relations.   Serious weaknesses in either of these areas will limit your competence as a leader or as a participant.

---

[20] Norman R. F. Maier, "The Quality of Group Decisions As Influenced by the Discussion Leader," *Human Relations*, III (1950), 157.   Reprinted by permission.

2. Basic Principles of Discussion

In this chapter we shall describe six central principles that are important in any discussion situation. You should appreciate and understand these principles in order to gain optimum benefits from practice discussions in the early stages of your training. What you learn at this time will also prepare you for the more detailed information to be presented in later chapters.

An Informal Group Atmosphere Should Prevail

The words *atmosphere, climate,* and *tone* may be used to refer to the degree of formality or informality shown in group meetings. Of course these words often mean much more than this. They may, for example, be used to describe interpersonal relations, cooperativeness, and other features of a particular discussion. But here, for the moment, we are mainly interested in the effects of informality as opposed to formality in discussions. Interestingly enough, these effects often concern the other "atmospheric" matters we have mentioned.

In a survey conducted by the authors, it was discovered that students in discussions gave high rankings to four *wants* (*needs*) that are often associated with an informal group atmosphere. The students reported that in discussions they wanted (a) to be recog-

17

nized by others, (b) to be accepted and respected, (c) to feel secure, and (d) to feel free to participate actively. You should not expect to attain these goals *solely* because of informal relationships, but, on the other hand, you are more likely to reach them under informal conditions than you are in situations governed by rules and restraints that limit your opportunity to express yourself.

Highly formal discussions tend to make you feel that you are being subjected to a "strait-jacket" of restrictions. Your words, and those of others, are likely to be impersonal. When you use names, you are usually intent upon emphasizing the status of the person identified. And most important, you often conceal your real feelings about the problem discussed. *Caution* is the watchword. You may in fact become so intent upon observing proprieties that you find yourself unable to think about the issues of the discussion.

Communications Before the Discussion

It took Ralph Bunche five days to arrange a meeting between the Israeli and Arab representatives when he assumed his position as Security Council mediator in 1948. When the two groups did meet face-to-face, the chairman of the Israeli group extended his hand to an Arab representative, but the proffered handshake was not accepted. When Bunche observed the behavior of the Arab and his group, he postponed the conference that had been planned. Before the contending parties met again to negotiate their differences, Bunche arranged meetings between the groups in which at least minimum signs of recognition and courtesy were exchanged. In this extremely difficult situation, Bunche felt that interaction between the groups was important in order to create a favorable climate for the negotiations that were to follow. Much the same is true of any discussion. Even when conferees have no reason for interpersonal conflicts, pre-discussion meetings help to promote cooperativeness and teamwork.

You can do the following things when you are a member of a discussion group: (1) When possible, exchange communications with those in your group before your discussion takes place; (2)

be able to refer to others by name and know something about their background and interests; and (3) recognize that all persons in your group are co-equals. If you cannot easily remember the names of those in your group, write the names on the blackboard so that everyone in the group can see them. Or, better still, place name-cards before each participant.

Physical Arrangements for Discussion

Physical conditions, and especially the seating arrangements for conferees, are important in facilitating a desirable group atmosphere. When you plan seating positions for participants, you should try to achieve at least three objectives. You should provide for the comfort of participants, face-to-face vision, and visible signs of equality of status among members of the group. So-called *high prestige* persons should not be given preferred seating positions.

An informal group atmosphere is best promoted when the leader is seated with others. His position should of course be central to the group. But he should normally refrain from standing or from taking a position that discourages participation by group members.

1. *Values of semi-circle or circle plan.* If you arrange chairs, desks, or small tables in a circle or semi-circle each person can see all other participants. No person, at least in the physical setting, has a claim to status differential.

2. *Values of hollow square or "U" shape plan.* Chairs, desks, or narrow rectangular tables may be arranged in a square or in a three-sided "U" shaped position. As you can recognize, this plan possesses the major virtues of the circular seating pattern. Many times this arrangement is used by groups numbering twenty or more persons, and its limitations, if any, are due to the size of the group rather than to factors that concern effective arrangement.

3. *Limitations of rectangular plan.* Many groups make use of a long rectangular table with participants seated on all four sides of the table. It seems to be used frequently because schools and offices generally have such types of tables readily available. If the table is relatively short in length and the group is small, no serious obstacles will be encountered. But if a long table is required, par-

SEATING ARRANGEMENTS

1. SEMICIRCLE OR CIRCLE *

 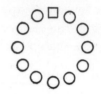

2. HOLLOW SQUARE OR "U" SHAPED *

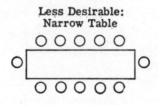

3. RECTANGULAR TABLE

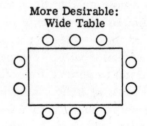

Less Desirable:
Narrow Table

More Desirable:
Wide Table

4. TEAM ARRANGEMENT

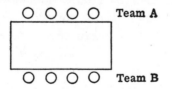

Team A

Team B

* Square symbol $(\square)$ refers to discussion leader.

20

ticipants will have difficulty in establishing face-to-face vision with persons to their immediate left and right.   And further, this plan encourages participant-to-leader communications rather than communications directed to the group as a whole.

4. *Limitations of team plan.*   Often groups are seated in positions that physically suggest competitive interests.   Individuals representing a clique, a department, or division sit on one side of the table, and "opponents" sit opposite to them.   Very frequently the groups may even sit in different parts of the room or at different tables.   A plan such as this accentuates differences, for factions usually feel that they must be "miles apart" in opinions or else they would not be seated in a "miles apart" fashion.

Pictures of labor-management conferences show that the parties to a conflict are usually seated opposite to one another.   Thus, officers from the C. I. O. might be seated as one independent unit, and representatives from U. S. Steel, Bethlehem Steel, and Inland Steel as other units.   These meetings are not meant to be true discussions; they are "bargaining sessions."   In spite of this difference, however, a variation in physical arrangements might be helpful in establishing a better climate for problem-solving.

Communications During the Discussion

What the leader of a discussion says and does greatly affects the tone of the meeting.   If you are called upon to lead a discussion group, bear the following suggestions in mind.   (1) Do not give lengthy lectures to the group; (2) address the members of the group by name; (3) use some open questions, directed to the group as a whole, which any person in the group is free to answer; and (4) think and express yourself in terms of "we" instead of habitually taking an "I" approach.   Suggestions one, two, and four also apply to what you say and do when you are a participant in discussions.

Group Unity Should Be Strong

Some of the suggestions we have given about creating an informal group atmosphere are closely related to the concept of group unity (or cohesiveness). The two principles are nevertheless not synonymous. Although informal group meetings often promote "bonds that unite," this result does not invariably happen. Sometimes, in fact, informal communications and actions are used as persuasive tactics by persons who seek selfish goals. Thus, group unity is not a mere show of friendliness and respect; rather it represents an honest respect for the group and the group's goals on the part of individual members.

One way of explaining group unity is to say that it is the result of all the forces that make a person value membership in a group. For example, group unity is strong if you and others in your group like one another, enjoy your relationships, feel that being a member of the group is an honor, and believe that the tasks performed by the group are important.[1] As you can see, cooperativeness and teamwork should grow out of conditions like these.

This description of the Board of Directors of the Standard Oil Company of New Jersey illustrates group unity in action:

They are undramatic, conscientious, and modest, and there is not a table pounder in all fourteen. They do not always agree, but they have the faculty, absolutely essential in modern industry, of getting together day after day on a variety of subjects, arriving at what the Quakers call the sense of the meeting, and coming to a joint decision.[2]

A complete explanation of the concept of group unity will be given in Chapter 12 where both the conditions and specific values of cohesiveness will be named.

FREEDOM OF CHOICE SHOULD BE STRESSED

The emphasis given to the idea of teamwork in group situations has led some people to say that originality and creative thinking

---

[1] See Kurt W. Back, "The Exertion of Influence in Social Communication," *Theory and Experiment in Social Communication,* pp. 21–36. Ann Arbor: University of Michigan Institute for Social Research, 1950.

[2] "The Jersey Company," *Fortune,* XLIV (October, 1951), 102–103. Reprinted by permission.

invariably will be sacrificed. If the individual sets group-conformity as the greatest goal, there is certainly some truth in this position. William H. Whyte, Jr., for instance, regards what he calls the "yen for consensus" as *the new illiteracy* in American life.

It is wretched advice that the healthy system is one in which the individual feels no conflict. Every great advance has come about, and always will, because someone was frustrated by the status quo, because someone exercised skepticism, the questioning, and the kind of curiosity which, to borrow a phrase, blows the lid off everything.[3]

This attack upon conformity is an important one. It is, however, not an indictment of decision-making by groups with a high level of group unity (cohesiveness) as we interpret the term. As a matter of fact, persons in cohesive groups contribute ideas without fear of reprisals from anyone, and more *different* points of view are usually expressed.

Range of Possible Choices

If you are aware of a wide range of possible decisions in a problem-solving discussion, you can be called a free agent. You are at least not imprisoned by a *one point of view* attack upon problems when this is the case. In this connection Perry says: "The extent to which a man is free, that is, exercises enlightened choice, depends in the first place upon the extent to which he is aware of the possibilities." [4] This statement is clearly worth a second reading because of its unusual importance to wise decision-making.

Some of the conditions that will help you to enlarge your range of possible choices are (1) education and learning, (2) mastery of emotionality and prejudice, (3) imagination, originality, and creativeness, and (4) freedom from authoritarian controls. Such conditions call for liberating influences that are opposed to propaganda, coercion, and force. These methods fail to promote open

---

[3] William H. Whyte, Jr., "The New Illiteracy," *Saturday Review*, XXXVI (November 21, 1953), 35. Reprinted by permission.

[4] Ralph Barton Perry, "A Definition of the Humanities," in T. M. Greene (ed.), *The Meaning of the Humanities*, p. 8. Princeton: Princeton University Press, 1938. Reprinted by permission.

inquiry: they tend to limit your attention to only one or two possibilities. For example, audiences at mass meetings, particularly
in a psychological setting such as Hitler designed, know only one
plan of action, and are therefore different from persons in a discussion who try to know many possible solutions to a problem.

Freedom to Express Choices

A businessman once said, "How can I get persons in conferences
to express their productive ideas instead of keeping them a secret?"
This question may be answered in many ways. Possibly, one of
the best answers was given by the very man who asked the question.
He finally said, "I'll have to stop doing the thinking for the persons
in the group."

In a discussion the leader should not limit freedom of speech
by insisting upon dictation. Compulsion, whether intentional or
otherwise, must be discarded if participants are to give their honest
opinions. The leader, and others as well, should try to increase
both the range of choices and the freedom to express ideas available
to every person in the group. Unless this is true the meeting is
not a discussion or a conference in the sense in which we would
like it to be. Participants are not free men; they are obedient
lackeys who echo the views of a master.

The arguments of J. S. Mill in favor of freedom of speech have
had much influence upon American life. Consider his four lines
of reasoning as a possible rationale for the principle of freedom:

First, if any opinion is compelled to silence, that opinion may, for
aught we certainly know, be true. To deny this is to assume our in-
fallibility.

Secondly, though the silenced opinion be an error, it may, and very
commonly does, contain a portion of truth; and since the general or
prevailing opinion on any subject is rarely or never the whole truth,
it is only by the collision of adverse opinions that the remainder of the
truth has any chance of being supplied.

Thirdly, even if the received opinion be not only true, but the whole
truth; unless it is suffered to be, and actually is, vigorously and earnestly
contested, it will, by most of those who receive it, be held in the manner
of a prejudice, with little comprehension or feeling of its rational
grounds.

And not only this, but fourthly, the meaning of the doctrine itself will be in danger of being lost, or enfeebled, and deprived of its vital effect on the character and conduct: the dogma becoming a mere formal profession, inefficacious for good, but cumbering the ground, and preventing the growth of any real and heartfelt conviction, from reason or personal experience.[5]

COOPERATIVENESS SHOULD BE STRESSED

We cannot presuppose that the human traits of assertiveness and aggressiveness will somehow magically disappear when you are a member of a discussion group. But you can change these drives. You can, as Shapley suggests, "substitute nonhuman enemies to fight" and thus reserve a place for cooperativeness in your interpersonal relations.[6] What this means is that you should be problem-centered—you should attack issues rather than persons in the group. Ideally, at least, you should derive so much satisfaction from trying to solve problems that you do not find it necessary to hate persons who disagree with you. This may be difficult for you to do, but it is a more productive scheme to follow than alternative forms of behavior.

"Individualistic" Points of View

T. V. Smith argues that in conflict situations an individual is unable to state the position of his opponents in a clear, honest and objective manner.

Half the aggressions of life arise from this social distance between private fancy and collective fact. Then there comes the day when we recognize that stubbornness in enemies is what we call character in friends. . . . When through a sense of humor or some other saving grace of modesty or tolerance, we wake up to the fact that the other fellow is probably as honest, as intelligent, and as patriotic as we, then we are on the road to another method of dealing with disputes. Waking up from our easy dream of omniscience, we are driven to acknowl-

---

[5] John Stuart Mill, *On Liberty*, pp. 101–102. Boston: Ticknor and Fields, 1863.

[6] See Harlow Shapley, "Must Men Fight?" *University of Chicago Round Table* (September 22, 1946), 15.

edge that the solitary way solves problems only for solitude. If disputes
are to be solved for company, then the company must be in on the
solution of them. Agreement without representation is about as fair
as taxation without representation.

*   *   *

The first conclusion we are likely to draw from the presence of real
and genuine conflict is that we cannot state fairly the other man's point
of view. We would have to make it our own before we could state it
fairly; and we cannot fully take his point of view when we are sin-
cerely of an opposing point of view.

*   *   *

The final proof that, in a disputed situation, we cannot state fairly
the other man's point of view is this: he cannot state fairly our point of
view. Every time he tries it, we see clearly that he is missing the point:
underdoing here, overdoing there.[7]

Here is a description of an experiment given by Carl R. Rogers
that you should try:

The next time you get into an argument with your wife, or your
friend, or with a small group of friends, just stop the discussion for a
moment and, for an experiment, institute this rule. "Each person can
speak up for himself only *after* he has repeated the ideas and feelings of
the speaker accurately and to that speaker's satisfaction."
You see what this would mean. It would simply mean that before
presenting your own point of view, it would be necessary for you to
achieve the other speaker's frame of reference—to understand his
thoughts and feelings so well that you could summarize them for him.
Sounds simple doesn't it? But if you try it, you will discover that it is
one of the most difficult things you have ever tried to do.[8]

An honest attempt to understand the ideas of another person from
his frame of reference will do much to put problem-solving on a
rational basis. To do otherwise is to suffer retaliation and recurrent
strife. The ambivalent struggle is between having your own way

---

[7] T. V. Smith, *The Legislative Way of Life*, pp. 11–13. Chicago: University
of Chicago Press, 1940. Reprinted by permission.
[8] Carl R. Rogers and F. J. Roethlisberger, "Barriers and Gateways to Communication," *Harvard Business Review*, XXX (July–August, 1952), 48. Reprinted by permission.

regardless of what others think, and getting along in a more peaceful fashion.

Levels of Cooperation

Conflicts that are resolved in discussions are depicted on this continuum showing five levels of cooperative action.

(1)	(2)	(3)	(4)	(5)
Silent Acquiescence	Opposition Followed by Agreement	Compromise	Shared Decision	Integration

Not included here are two other possibilities. The first of these concerns discussions in which consensus is not achieved—the discussion ends in disagreement; and the second, a happy but probably unusual situation, concerns discussions in which everyone in the group offers identical recommendations. Actually these possibilities do not have anything to do with cooperation, for in the one case we have a lack of cooperation and in the other adjustments are unnecessary because there are no conflicts. Thus, the five forms of cooperation are sufficiently inclusive to embrace the subject of settling differences in discussions.

1. *Silent acquiescence.* We are electing to define *acquiescence* as acceptance of a suggested solution even though the solution does not meet one's expectations. And further, this so-called "cooperative" act is performed by being silent, or at best, by saying very few words. The person who concurs by being silent may truly endorse a decision. Often, however, his apparent acceptance is a veiled form of opposition that he declines for one reason or another to express. But whatever the motives behind silent acquiescence, the persons who concur in this way are usually not interested in carrying out the decision of the group. Better results usually come from active participation, because the participant who expresses his agreement openly is better able to identify himself with the decision. He feels greater responsibility for the decision and the consequences that stem from successful execution of the decision.

2. *Active opposition followed by agreement.* In some discussions you might originally oppose a solution, and yet later endorse this solution. Many times your shift-of-attitude is genuine and sincere, because you recognize the solution to be superior to others. In still other situations you might be unable to gain group support for your ideas, and you might then be inclined to surrender your position in favor of the majority view. Now this surrender is believed by some persons to be a dishonorable act, and probably, under some circumstances this could be true. But on the other hand, in many practical situations the survival of the group is dependent upon agreement on some type of decision. You should remember in this connection that it is always possible that the solution you wish to have accepted might be less desirable than the solutions you are prone to reject.

3. *Compromise.* Cooperation through compromise is believed by many to be an unsatisfactory technique for resolving differences. Critics of this technique say that though the intermediary position represented by compromise results in an agreement, neither of the contending parties has accomplished his aims. The solution is merely a temporary one. In many situations the compromise represents only a lull in hostilities as can be seen in some cases involving labor disputes and international conflicts. What is needed, at least ideally, is a solution that satisfies the goals of all concerned.

But in defense of compromises, T. V. Smith says:

> True, when seen from the shining cliffs of perfection the legislative process of compromise appears shoddy indeed. But when seen from some concentration camp of the alternative way of life, the compromises of legislation appear but another name for what we call civilization and even revere as Christian forbearance. Compromise makes actual one great good, and it makes possible another great good. What it makes actual is self-expression through free speech and unhampered association. What it makes always possible is a scientific arrangement through which its gracious processes may be continuously improved.[9]

Full-scale agreement is doubtless better than compromise, but in some cases a compromise is better than no agreement at all.

---

[9] T. V. Smith, *op. cit.*, p. 92. Reprinted by permission.

And many compromises are honest endorsements of a decision in spite of failure to fulfill all desired goals.   Our Constitution, signed by thirty-nine delegates to the Convention, represented adjudication of differences by means of compromises.   Franklin, for example, urged every delegate to sign the document in spite of particular reservations.   He further added, "There are several parts . . . which I do not at present approve. . . ."

4. *Shared decision.*   Solutions to some problems can be called *additive* solutions because there are a number of parts that make up the whole.   For instance, in a discussion dealing with how to be a good leader, participant, or listener, you can see that many specific recommendations will be given.   If participants share in making these recommendations, no single person emerges as the author of the decision.   The final result is the product of the group. To a greater or less degree sharing is also present in other stages of a discussion such as recognition of the problem and description of the problem.

5. *Integration.*   A shared decision in which separate parts are brought together may be a form of integration.   Under some conditions it may also be a form of compromise.   We interpret integration to mean the discovery of a solution that fulfills the desires of all parties who have a conflict of interest.   Mary Parker Follett says: "When two desires are *integrated,* that means that a solution has been found in which both desires have found a place, that neither side has to sacrifice anything." [10]   In many situations intelligent living calls for solutions of this type.   Suppose, for example, that you want to spend a particular afternoon working on your correspondence, but one of your friends wants you to keep an appointment you have previously made.   What you really desire in this case is a time period that will permit you to complete your letters. And, assuming that you are able to change your plans, you might find that a different work period is equally acceptable or that the time of the appointment might be changed.   Thus the original conflict is not a *real* conflict.   So-called "incompatible" solutions are often

---

[10] Henry C. Metcalf and L. Urwick, ed., *Dynamic Administration: The Collected Papers of Mary Parker Follett,* p. 32.   New York: Harper and Brothers, 1942.   Reprinted by permission.

incompatible only because people fail to discover non-obvious ways of solving problems. To correct this tendency, you should seek to construct, to invent, to create solutions that differ from the stereotyped possibilities. If you try to discover non-obvious answers to problems, you can often resolve problems without introducing the elements of *winning* and *losing*.

Reflective Thinking Should Be Stressed

Definition of Reflective Thinking

Dewey has defined reflective thinking as "active, persistent, and careful consideration of any belief in the light of the grounds that support it, and the further conclusions to which it tends."[11] Certain important inferences are suggested by this definition that distinguish reflective thinking from many other forms of thinking in which we engage. Four characteristics that should be emphasized are: (1) The individual should give conscious and persistent attention to the perplexity that confronts him; (2) the thought process should be methodical and orderly; (3) facts and opinions should be evaluated objectively; and (4) the solutions to the problem should be judged in terms of their consequences, both probable and certain. These characteristics of reflection make it clear that emotion, bias, and uncritical acceptance of solutions are in definite contrast to reflective thinking.

Stages in Reflective Thinking

The reflective process is illustrated in the following description of a problem situation:

"That Tackhead" [12]

Senior counselors at our boys' camp are assigned eight young boys for whom they have direct responsibility. Actually this means that

---

[11] John Dewey, *How We Think*, p. 6. Boston: D. C. Heath and Company, 1910.

[12] Reported by William E. Merritt, M.B.A., 1951, School of Business Administration, University of Michigan.

each counselor has eight "problems" that vary in degree of importance. In my own case, the boy I shall call "Tackhead" gave me the most trouble. Before I continue, I should say that this name is really a good word; it is an "affectionate" term used by senior counselors to designate a particularly rebellious camper.

The boy in question was eleven years old and had a cleverly mechanical mind. He was, however, very much disliked by the other boys in the camp because he would not contribute to any group undertaking. Then, to add to his difficulties, the boy took great delight in throwing rocks at his fellow campers. It was soon apparent that I was his only friend. He followed me around like a sheep dog despite my efforts to discourage him.

The problem was inescapable, and I began to think about it seriously. I realized that the boy should learn how to make himself accepted among the campers. Something needed to be done to diminish his feeling of insecurity. Here are the possible solutions to the problem in the order in which they occurred to me: (1) Demand that he not follow me around and thereby force him into the company of the other campers; (2) Talk and reason with him and show him why he was being ostracized and how to avoid it; and (3) Try to interest him in sports and thus give him greater confidence in himself and common interests with the other boys.

I decided against keeping him away from me, because I knew he needed a friend. I couldn't reason with him because it would make him even more self-conscious. His troubles were so deeply ingrained that merely discussing them would not help.

So I tried athletics. The boy hated swimming. If he got wet above his ankles, he would run out of the water screaming and not go near the water the rest of the day in spite of the efforts of the swimming instructor. I began to take him down to the lake alone every day in the afternoon. Finally, after five weeks, he was floating. I never could teach him to swim, but after the sixth week of this treatment he was no longer throwing rocks. His pride in his floating was equaled by the surprise of the other campers at his accomplishment.

By the time he left camp (eight weeks), he even had a couple of friends. They astounded the boy's parents by telling him in front of them to "come back next year." Unhappily for his next year's counselor, that is just what he did.

You can easily recognize logically related stages or steps in the "Tackhead" problem: (1) The perplexity or problem was perceived; (2) consequences of the boy's behavior were known (effects); (3) probable causes of the effects were recognized; (4) conditions to be met by a good solution—*to become accepted by the group*—were identified; (5) three possible solutions were suggested; (6) the solutions were evaluated; (7) the solution that called for athletics was accepted as the most promising solution; and (8) a plan of action, namely swimming experiences, was designed and carried out.

The reflective process in this story of the eleven year old boy at the summer camp represents a continuity or progression from the problem to a plan of action.   It corresponds in most respects to the Dewey pattern of five separate steps in problem-solving:

1. A felt difficulty
2. Its location and definition
3. Suggestion of possible solution
4. Development by reasoning of the bearings of the suggestion
5. Further observation and experiment leading to its acceptance or rejection; that is, the conclusion of belief or disbelief.[13]

Reflective Pattern in Discussion

The logical pattern of reflective thinking has been widely applied both in discussion in college classes and in the decision-making conferences of business, educational, labor, and governmental groups.   In Chapter 7 we shall describe the reflective pattern fully.   At this time we shall merely outline the logical plan we recommend.

I. Recognition of the Problem
    A. Formulation of the Problem As a Question
    B. Definition of the Problem
II. Description of the Problem
    A. History of the Problem
    B. Effects of the Problem
    C. Causes of the Problem
III. Discovery of Solutions
    A. Conditions to Be Met by an Acceptable Solution
    B. Possible Solutions

---

[13] John Dewey, *op. cit.*, p. 72.   Reprinted by permission.

IV. Evaluation of Possible Solutions and Acceptance of Best Solution
    A. Evaluation of Possible Solutions
    B. Acceptance of Best Solution
V. Plan of Action
    A. Methods of Execution
    B. Action Group to Put Solution into Effect

RESPONSIBILITY FOR DECISIONS SHOULD BE SHARED BY ALL

Throughout this chapter we have in many ways shown that responsibility should be shared in a discussion. Neither the leader nor individual members of the group should by manipulation, dominance, or dictation, design solutions that fit special interests. As a matter of fact, a group meeting (under the guise of a discussion) should not be held if persons in the group are not given the opportunity to reach decisions under conditions of freedom. It is true that the decisions of some groups are advisory rather than final, but even in these cases conferees should have full freedom to suggest solutions and to share responsibility for recommended decisions.

Suggestions for the Leader

You will find it helpful to know some of the criteria of effective leadership that stress the sharing of responsibility. Within limits as imposed by the situation, you should apply these suggestions:
1. Encourage all persons in the group to participate.
2. Ask questions designed to obtain important information.
3. Encourage participants to offer many possible solutions.
4. Encourage participants to offer their true attitudes and beliefs.

Suggestions for Participants

The sharing of responsibility calls for active participation patterns rather than withdrawal patterns. It is difficult and probably impossible to give many hard-and-fast rules about participation. The four given here are offered as minimal suggestions:

1. Help to define the problem if clarification is needed.
2. Contribute factual information about the problem.
3. Listen carefully to the ideas of others and be willing to support the ideas that you believe to be sound.
4. Keep your preferences tentative at least until you fully understand all possible solutions to the problem.

The sharing of responsibility is usually causally related to two desired outcomes of discussions. A decision arrived at by a group as a whole will be more acceptable to that group than a decision dictated by one or a few members. Also, persons in the group will be more satisfied with their own behavior and the behavior of the other members. Happier interpersonal relationships are likely to result.

3. Problems for Discussion

In this chapter we are concerned with the selection of discussion problems by college groups, adult learning groups, and business groups. What we shall say applies both to classroom training discussions and to "true-to-life" organizational and business conferences. In either situation it is a matter of first importance to select discussion problems wisely.

What to Consider in Selecting Problems

Select Problems in Which You Have an Interest

When you take part in a discussion, you should be able to say: "I am interested in the discussion problem because I hope to gain more information about it and to discover ways in which the problem can be answered effectively." This goal is admittedly an ideal, but it is something more than an imaginary expectation. You should fully attain this ideal in most of the discussions in which you participate.

Two general classes of problems are likely to be especially meaningful to you: the immediate or "timely" problems and the "timeless" ones. The occurrences of the present—*the here and now*—have a great appeal to most of us. Thus, a polio epidemic, a threatened business recession, a political campaign, and an international crisis readily capture our attention. These problems are interesting to us not alone because they are current, but also because the events of the present often affect us directly. Our safety, economic prosperity, and hosts of other aspirations that we value may be affected by the way these problems are solved. But in addition to problems that have their inception in day-to-day events, most people also have an interest in problems that each generation must answer for itself. These include problems concerning government, social and business organization, ethics, religion, conflict, and personal and group goals. These problems also vitally affect our lives. They are meaningful even though they are not occasioned by a specific current crisis.

You might ask at this point, "Who decides what problems are of interest to the group?" As a rule, we believe that a system of sharing responsibility for choices is the best plan to follow. In other words, your group and your group leader should decide how selections are to be made. Sometimes your instructor or your group leader may find it necessary to make arbitrary selections, or, perhaps, you might authorize a sub-committee to choose problems for discussion. But in most cases it is better to choose discussion problems in a way that permits all persons in your group to participate. The reason is clear: You and your fellow conferees are likely to be more interested in problems when your group has taken the initiative to suggest possible problems and to make final choices.

Many business and industrial organizations encourage this type of group participation in the selection of problems for conferences. A group of supervisors, for instance, may be in a better position to choose problems than persons who are not in direct contact with the work in the various departments. For this reason it is common for higher levels of management to consult with first-line supervisors about the problems that they face. We are not arguing that all conference problems should originate with the group as a whole. We are saying simply that there seem to be advantages to group-originated problems, and that these advantages are often lost when problems are imposed upon a group.

Select Important Problems

A problem that challenges your interest is likely to be an important problem. Occasionally, however, you may feel impelled to select problems that are amusing but that have no importance aside from giving participants the opportunity to be funny. Thus, if you discussed "Is the moon made of green cheese?" or "Who put out the light?" you would be discussing problems designed solely for amusement. Although we believe frivolity and humor have their place, we do not believe you should spend an entire conference period with this object in mind. Problems that further your learning and understanding, and those that call for reflective thinking are much more desirable.

Select Problems That Can Be Investigated Prior to the Discussion

You will gain little if the problem you select is one that you are unable to investigate. We do not wish to discourage your originality in a discussion, but we believe that you should know relevant facts about the issue you plan to discuss. If the problem does not permit investigation and discovery of facts, you should ordinarily discard such a choice in favor of a problem that can be studied more fully.

You should also consider the time that is available for investigation of the problem when you make your selection. Some problems require weeks of study before one is qualified to become a helpful conferee. If you have only a short time in which to prepare for a discussion, it is undoubtedly wise to select a problem that can be investigated quickly or one about which group members are already well informed. *Remember:* Group members who do not know essential information about a problem can only "pool ignorance" when they give their contributions in a discussion.

Select Problems That Can Be Profitably Discussed in the Time Available for Discussion

Class discussions and business conferences are generally scheduled for specific time periods. It is thus not unusual for persons in conferences to say, "We have twenty minutes left in which to solve our problem." In some cases this time limit may be sufficient for a group to solve its problem effectively, but in others it encourages conferees to accept inferior solutions to problems. And in still other situations the group may not need all the scheduled period for purposes of discussion. It can be seen therefore that the "adjournment by the clock meeting" can be something other than a virtue.

When time limits for meetings are a practical necessity you should select problems that fit the time available. If you have only a thirty-minute discussion period, you should select a problem that you and your fellow conferees can handle effectively in the thirty minutes. This holds true of any of the conventional time periods for discussions: one hour, one and one-half hours, two hours. With especially general, and perhaps difficult problems, you should plan a series of conferences instead of blindly accepting the one-session plan. You might take up specific phases of the problem in your series of meetings. Thus, a *Problem Stage* and a *Solutions Stage* could be used for a two-session conference. Or, in unusual cases, you might want to have more than two group meetings. In any event, do not be oblivious to relationships between time matters and problem selection when you plan discussion meetings.

How to State Problems

The exact problem statement that your group formulates is equally as important as the selection of problems. A few rules about stating problems should therefore be remembered.

Phrase the Problem as a Question

Stating your problem in the form of a question is a primary requisite. *Reasons for this priority:* (1) The question identifies a specific problem; (2) motivates persons to seek answers to the problem; and (3) eliminates the habit of inactivity that topic statements tend to encourage.

On one occasion a member of a group suggested the topics of "motivation" and "leadership" as two possible discussion problems. When others in the group heard these two topics, they asked, "But where do we go from there?" In other words, these persons did not know how to handle the generalized topics given by their fellow group member. The topics did not identify a problem, and consequently, the group members had no guideposts to direct their thinking. As one participant said, "We could go on talking forever about motivation and leadership and never arrive at any answers." A perplexing situation, therefore, must be put into words by asking What? How? When? and the like. Until this is done, you are not likely to think as a problem-solver. In fact, it is commonly said that you do not think at all unless you ask yourself questions or are asked questions by others.

Phrase the Problem Clearly

If one or more of the words used in your problem question can be interpreted in several different ways, your group will need to spend time in deciding upon what the problem means. This may take longer than you expect. Sometimes your group may spend an entire discussion period without a definite understanding of the purpose of the discussion. The result will be high levels of individual dissatisfaction and "wasted motion."

A group that discussed, "What Attitude Should Our College Take Toward Religion?" found that it encountered difficulties in understanding the word "religion." Some participants thought the problem meant (1) the general attitude toward various religious teachings; (2) others thought the problem referred to student participation in the Y.M.C.A., Y.W.C.A., and church activities in the community; and (3) others thought the problem concerned courses in religion and a possible Department of Religion. Any of these three interpretations is defensible. Therefore, it would have been better to have included a specific reference in the problem statement.

Phrase the Problem Impartially

Questions that make either a false or doubtful presumption establish a bias for one position. Consider these questions: (1) What Course Changes Should Be Made in the Outdated Curricula of

Our College? and (2) What Can Be Done to Make Employees in the Advertising Department Interested in Their Work? In the first question you can see that the word "outdated" establishes a bias in favor of changing the curriculum. If the wording of the question is not challenged, few people would want to retain the curricula of the college as now constituted. The question is "loaded" in that it presumes as true the issue that should be decided in the discussion. In the second question the assumption is that all employees in the advertising department are indifferent toward the job they are doing. Although it is probably safe to say that some persons in almost any group should be more interested in their responsibilities, the question as phrased implies indifference on the part of all employees. In most situations this is not likely to be true. The question as stated is probably not a fair one. Since unwarranted assumptions in the phrasing of discussion problems are likely to condition the solutions given by conferees, deliberate attention should be given to the criterion of impartiality in the phrasing of problems.

Restrict the Scope of the Problem

A general question has the virtue of encouraging a high degree of freedom for the participants. At times, however, questions which are unrestricted in scope are not conducive to profitable discussion. They are likely to be discussed in a superficial way because the issue raised is too big for detailed consideration. Monroe C. Beardsley offers some advice on this point:

The first general rule for asking questions is that, when we are faced with a problematic situation, our questions ought to be just as specific as the situation permits. "What's the matter?" is the best we can do at times, but such a general question may send us beating about the bush. It is better to ask, "Which features of the American occupation policy in Germany have tended to make Germans unwilling to assume responsibility for self-government?" A question like this is manageable, and it may be enough to tackle at one time, though it is less ambitious than "What's wrong with our German occupation?" [1]

---

[1] Monroe C. Beardsley, *Practical Logic*, p. 524. New York: Prentice-Hall, Inc., 1950. Reprinted by permission.

The factors that should govern how inclusive a problem should be are the time available for investigation, the time available for discussion, and the interests of the group concerned. The highly generalized problem is often satisfying to persons who have much training and experience in the problem area. However, it is apparent that most persons will be more satisfied and more productive conferees if the problem is stated in a restricted form.

Examples: (1) When you have a discussion on curricular problems it is usually better to limit your discussion to a specific division of your school such as the College of Liberal Arts or the School of Business Administration rather than to include all divisions of your school in the problem statement. (2) When you discuss social problems or institutions, specify limitations. Thus, instead of asking, "What Does Congress Do?" you might ask, "What Legislative Programs Have Been Enacted in the Past Year?" (3) Similarly, in the case of business problems, you will get better results if you refrain from generalized discussions on such topics as absenteeism, motivation, and worker turnover. Specify "absenteeism in X Department"—"motivation for first-year employees"—"turnover among machine operators."

Kinds of Problems for Discussion

Problem statements can be classified according to the type of answers you give in a discussion. (1) If you ask, "What happened, is happening, or will happen?" you answer by giving *facts* or by predicting *future facts*; (2) if you ask, "How good or valuable is a certain idea, person or plan?" you answer by giving *value judgments*; (3) if you ask, "What should we do?" you answer by suggesting a *policy*; and (4) if you ask, "What steps will put the policy into operation?" you answer by devising a *procedure*. These four kinds of problems cover the field of problem statements in discussion.

Problems of Fact

Facts (*events, occurrences, characteristics, classifications*) in discussion refer to true reporting, and in a predictive sense, to the reporting of probable future occurrences. Thus, you should always ask, "Is the data that has been reported true?" Sometimes data can be checked and verified by repeating observations, but in many situations you will have to be content with reports based upon single occurrences.

You might ask, "Why should groups discuss questions of fact?" Here are two good reasons that justify the reporting of facts as a primary purpose of a discussion. In the first place, a single person is not likely to know all of the essential facts about a given situation, and therefore, it is important to have others make up for individual deficiencies. Secondly, facts must often be interpreted, clarified, and mentally tested. Individual participants will gain in these respects by contributions that others can give. These reasons are by themselves sufficiently important to make problems of fact fruitful questions for discussion.

These problem statements are illustrations of questions of fact:

1. What counseling services are available to freshmen and sophomores in our college?
2. What are the characteristics and skills of a competent discussion leader?
3. What are the techniques and methods used in propaganda?
4. What type of job instruction was used to train the employees who assembled the cooling unit?
5. What competitive conditions will our company face next year?

Problems one, two, and three concern *present* facts; problem four, *past* facts; and problem five, *future* facts. Principally, as you can see, these problems point toward increasing and clarifying knowledge and understanding.

Problems of Value

Edwin A. Burtt points out how problems of value are distinguished from those of fact:

Suppose we wish to compare Chicago and New York in various ways. Which is west of the other? Which is higher in altitude? Which is more northerly in latitude? Which is colder in winter? Which has the larger population? To these and a host of similar questions we can get answers that are definite and objective, so that whatever our partisan feelings may be about these cities, the way in which answers to these questions are to be reached and the validity of the results, are matters on which we easily find agreement. Such questions are, in short, questions of fact, and facts seem to have a compelling objectivity about them which forces our agreement. But suppose we ask the further question: Which is the better city to live in? Can we answer such a question so easily or confidently? . . . in a given discussion about the matter every fact introduced might be agreed upon without dispute, and yet diverse answers be given on the issue of evaluation. In short, this is a question of value, not of fact.[2]

Problems of value ask: *What is good? What is proper? What is better?* In short, whenever you express a choice or preference you make a value judgment. For example, in aesthetic questions you try to determine what is pleasing and in ethical questions you try to determine what is good. You transfer similar evaluative judgments to a great many other personal and social issues. It is clear that the words *good, right,* and *better* are very much a part of your active vocabulary.

Correctness, goodness, and degrees of preference are evident in these problems:

1. Is the pursuit of a college education a valid reason for military deferment?
2. Are objective examinations a better measure of learning than essay examinations?
3. What is the value of the Voice of America program?
4. How effective is our orientation program?
5. Is Jones a more valuable employee than Smith?

Many problems of value are related to policy-making because value judgments reveal our attitudes. And, in turn, our attitudes predispose us to act in a certain way and to believe in the soundness or unsoundness of a particular point of view.

---

[2] Edwin A. Burtt, *Principles and Problems of Right Thinking*, pp. 433–444. New York: Harper and Brothers, 1928. Reprinted by permission.

Problems of Policy

Problems of policy offer participants greater freedom in decision-making than is true of value judgment problems. "What should we do?" is a question that permits a person to offer a wide range of possible solutions. Problems of value, on the other hand, keep your attention centered upon assessment and appraisal of known possibilities. It is true that you evaluate solutions in questions of policy, just as it is true that you report facts in any good discussion, but in questions of policy you do more than report facts and evaluate. You also create. You try to discover answers to problems that are not limited to those revealed in the statement of the problem. You also indicate ways in which the policy selected by the group can be put into effect.

Problems of policy are usually the most useful types of problems that you can discuss. They not only give you a wide range of freedom in selecting solutions to problems, but they also pose a situation that calls for resolving the problem through action. Sample problems of policy are:

1. What solution should we recommend on the issue of foreign language requirements for college entrance?
2. What federal policy should we advocate in regard to assisting producers of farm products?
3. What federal tax changes, if any, should be made at this time?
4. What plan should the personnel office follow in allocating new employees to the fifteen departments of our company?
5. What should our company do to improve the executive development program?

Problems of Procedure

We are using the word *procedure* to mean the details or steps to be followed in carrying out a policy. Although it is true that a specific program of action is required if problems of policy are carried to the overt action stage, many decisions are limited to the development of a procedure alone. For example, sometimes you already know the policy your group wishes to follow when you begin your discussion. In such cases your problem becomes one of implementation. In still other cases you may not have jurisdiction over policy. Group discussions, in spite of this apparent limitation, may serve a highly useful purpose in delineating the exact program for execution of the policy.

Although procedural problems have some points in common with problems of policy, they are, as we have indicated, a distinct type of problem. For instance, when a sub-committee is given the task of carrying out a policy, it is often advisable for the members to pool their judgments about ways and means to put the policy into effect. The issue before the group is not "What policy should we approve?" but "How can the policy be carried out effectively?" Emphasis must be directed toward procedural suggestions that are likely to make the previously approved policy successful in operation.

AREA PROBLEMS FOR DISCUSSION

There are literally thousands of problem situations that you can use as questions for discussion. In making your selections you can choose problems that are limited to a single area, or you can choose problems from a number of different areas. Our own recommendation is that you should practice diversification in the choices you make. During your term of study in discussion, we believe you should discuss problems from several of the four areas identified below.

Personal Problems

By a "personal" problem we do not mean one that is meaningful only to yourself. Rather, we are thinking of problems that everyone faces in regard to goals, frustrations, tensions, and interpersonal relations. These problems can be called personal problems because each person must usually answer them for himself, but they also are problems that everyone faces. They could well point toward philosophies of living. These examples of personal problems should make our meaning clear on this point:

1. How can I improve my study habits?
2. What standards should guide me in the selection of my profession?
3. What does the word "success" mean?
4. How can I improve in interpersonal relations with others?
5. How do emotional tensions weaken my effectiveness?

School and College Problems

The examples of school and college problems that we shall give are probably sufficiently general to apply to most colleges. But you should not be content with these, because a problem is invariably more interesting if it refers to specific conditions that you face in your school. These examples should suggest other possibilities that are perhaps more relevant to your own situation:

1. Is the fraternity system a desirable feature of college life?
2. What should be the place of the Student Legislature in our college?
3. How can loyalty and enthusiasm for our college be shown?
4. How can instruction in classes be improved?
5. How can the residence hall system be improved?

Social and Political Problems

Many persons believe that problems of widespread social and political interest should receive most of your attention in a discussion group. Although this position is a debatable one, we are inclined to believe that there is merit in it. You are likely to gain valuable learning as well as experience in discussion methods if you select important social issues as your discussion problems. You certainly learn information by discussing other classes of problems, but a social issue has an importance that goes beyond the temporary problems that you face. Possibilities that we are giving to illustrate social and political problems are:

1. Can the Supreme Court decision outlawing segregation in the public schools be carried out successfully?

2. Should the voting age requirement be lowered?
3. How should the tariff issue be decided?
4. Do you think the United Nations is accomplishing its purpose?

Organization and Business Problems

Most organizations and businesses have many occasions for group discussions. The conferences, as we said in the first chapter, are held for purposes of decision-making, learning, or motivation, or perhaps for all of these reasons. Common problems faced by these groups are:

1. How can communication in Department X be improved?
2. What are the values and/or weaknesses of consultative decision-making?
3. Should a merit award system be inaugurated for hourly-rated workers?
4. What can be done to overcome resistance to change on the part of supervisors?
5. How can the business executive become a better problem-solver?

It is now common for business and industrial organizations to conduct training conferences for supervisory personnel. In other words, conferences in business are the direct concern of a great many people over and above those persons at the higher management levels. Regularly scheduled supervisory conferences are held by many of America's largest corporations. Maintenance problems, production problems, and personnel problems are area subjects considered by these groups. This, as you can see, means that one-way communication is being supplanted by face-to-face conference communication.

Conference problems designed for the training of personnel may emphasize the learning of facts or they may call for decision-making by conferees. The problem statements that follow are classified according to these two general purposes:

Training Problems That Stress Learning

1. What do the factors included in the Employee Progress Report mean?

2. What employee benefits does our company provide?
3. What should supervisors know concerning the union contract?
4. What production schedule does our company face?
5. What reports and records are needed by departmental managers?

Training Problems That Stress Decision-Making

1. How can supervisors develop understudies?
2. What can be done to achieve work simplification?
3. What techniques of job instruction should supervisors use?
4. What type of order-giving brings the best results?
5. How can supervisors practice preventive maintenance?

PROBLEMS USED IN RADIO PROGRAMS

The following list of some of the 1952–54 subjects used in radio network discussions and symposia should prove to be helpful to you when you choose discussion problems. We are giving the titles of the broadcasts in the form in which they were given in printed transcripts. No attempt has been made to restructure or to restrict the scope of any of the statements that appear.

University of Chicago Round Table (NBC)

1. How Effective Is the North Atlantic Alliance?
2. Crisis in Indo-China
3. The President's Economic Program
4. Sharing Our Atomic Secrets
5. Can Europe Unite?
6. Are the Community and School Failing the Unusual Child?
7. The Changing Role of Women in the United States
8. What Is the American Tradition in Foreign Policy: Ideals or Power?
9. Can Democracy Prevail in the Moslem World?
10. Jobs for Senior Citizens
11. New Facts on Medical Costs
12. Are Slum Neighborhoods beyond Control?

Northwestern University Reviewing Stand (MBS)

1. Do We Face a Teacher Shortage?
2. How Should We Encourage Democracy Abroad?
3. Can We Have Guns AND Butter?
4. What Does Alaska Mean to Us?

5. Are More People Turning to God?
6. Are We Outgrowing Our Highways?
7. What Is the Future of the White Collar Worker?
8. How Can We Get Economy in National Government?
9. What Can Talk Settle?
10. What Makes a Good Employee?
11. Do Labor's Demands Mean Inflation?
12. How Can We Prevent Family Failures?

Town Meeting of the Air (ABC)

1. How Can We Stay Alive on the Highway?
2. Should Congress Be Televised?
3. Will Universal Military Training Make Better Citizens of Our Youth?
4. What Is the Future of Japanese-American Relations?
5. Can We Afford a "Trade, Not Aid" Policy?
6. What Procedures Will Assure Effective Congressional Investigations?
7. Is Advertising Responsible for Our High Standard of Living?
8. How Can We Meet the Challenge of Juvenile Delinquency?
9. Who Should Judge the Fitness of Our College Teachers?
10. Is Industry Effectively Using the Liberal Arts Graduate?
11. What Makes Prosperity—Man or Machine?
12. Should Hawaii and Alaska Be Admitted to Statehood?

Problems Based Upon Articles and Books

A magazine article, a book, or perhaps certain chapters of a book may be profitably discussed by groups that meet to clarify and to evaluate the ideas expressed by a writer. This form of discussion is widely used by educational classes and study groups of all types, by training groups in business, and by joint labor-management groups.

The program sponsored by the Great Books Foundation of the University of Chicago is an example of discussion based upon specific books. This idea of reading books and discussing them on an organized basis was developed by John Erskine shortly after World War I for American soldiers in Europe. Since this time, a similar discussion program has been accepted by many of our colleges, and by organizations interested in adult education.   It has been strongly supported as an educational method by Robert M. Hutchins and Mortimer J. Adler.

The first year reading list recommended by the Great Books Foundation is reprinted here.   These books, in inexpensive sets, may be purchased from the Foundation or from bookstores.

1. The Declaration of Independence
2. Plato: *Apology, Crito*
3. Plato: *Republic,* Book I, Book II (through p. 368c)
4. Thucydides: *History,* Book I, chaps. 1, 2, 3, 5; Book II, chaps. 6, 7; Book V, chap. 17
5. Aristophanes: *Lysistrata, Birds, Clouds*
6. Aristotle: *Ethics,* Book I
7. Aristotle: *Politics,* Book I
8. Plutarch: "Lycurgus," "Numa," and "Comparison"; "Alexander" and "Caesar"
9. St. Augustine: *Confessions,* Books I–VIII
10. St. Thomas: *Treatise on Law (Summa Theologica,* Books I–II)
11. Machiavelli: *The Prince*
12. Montaigne: *Selected Essays*
13. Shakespeare: *Hamlet*
14. Locke: *Of Civil Government* (second essay)
15. Rousseau: *The Social Contract,* Books I–II
16. *Federalist Papers:* Nos. 1–10, 15, 31, 47, 51, 68–71 (along with the Constitution)
17. Smith: *The Wealth of Nations,* Book I, chaps. 1–9
18. Marx: *Communist Manifesto*

Any article or book may be chosen when you conduct discussions in which members read identical materials prior to the discussion. In order to give the discussion some degree of organization, however, you should plan to use questions about *content, evaluation,* and *application.*   For instance, you might ask: (a) What are the major ideas developed by the author?   (b) To what extent is there agreement or difference about the soundness of the ideas of the author?   (c) What consequences (applications) follow from acceptance or rejection of the views given by the author?   You may gain considerable knowledge by limiting your attention to what the writer said. But your gains will probably be greater if you also ask, "Is this true?"

CASE PROBLEMS FOR DISCUSSION

By a case problem we mean a *specific problem situation* or *critical incident*. Basic facts about the situation are reported in a way that permits others to gain a clear understanding of the issues involved. The group members then proceed to identify goals and solutions in much the same way as in any problem-solving discussion.

This case, for example, raises several interesting and important issues that are worth discussing:

Who Is Stupid?

Situation

Jane Robinson was a typist in a policy-writing department in the home office of a large insurance company. She was twenty years of age and had worked in this office for about nine months. She had proved that she was slightly above the average in quality and quantity of work. She was interested in her work and, all in all, was a valued employee.

On Tuesday morning at 10 A.M. her supervisor, Harry Wilbur, assigned an important policy-writing job to Jane. This particular task required about four hours of work. The job was not simple copy work, for Jane was expected to type the policy in spite of the confusing information supplied by the underwriter. Harry went over the assignment with Jane, explained the difficulties she would encounter, and made suggestions. He then asked, "Do you understand how to prepare the policy?" Jane answered affirmatively to this question. After Jane began her work on the draft of the policy, Harry on one or two occasions asked her whether she was getting along all right. Again Jane reported with a "Yes."

After lunch Harry did not again confer with Jane. He was particularly busy on this day. He was behind schedule, and he was also spending part of his time in instructing two new employees. He felt that he had too much work for which he was responsible.

Shortly before quitting time Harry began checking the important policy forms that Jane had completed. To his surprise he discovered that the forms were prepared incorrectly. He immediately announced in a loud voice that all twelve girls in the department could easily hear, "You weren't listening after all, were you?" He then walked to Jane's desk. Jane, who by this time was working on another assignment, now realized that Mr. Wilbur's outburst was directed at her. When the "weren't listening" statement was repeated to her, she replied by saying, "Don't you dare call me stupid!" Harry said that he didn't call her stupid. Said Jane, "When you talk as you do it means that you're calling me stupid."

Results

Jane returned to work on Wednesday and for the rest of the week did straight typing work. She felt that she had been badly treated, and as a result did not try to complete her quota of work. This continued for several weeks. Finally Harry talked with Jane and apologized for his actions. After this Jane's work improved.

Questions for Discussion

What mistakes did Harry Wilbur make in this situation? What mistakes, if any, can be charged against Jane? How could the problem have been avoided?

Instead of giving additional case problems in their complete form at this time, we shall summarize two situations that pose problems. You can easily add more details if you wish. The outlined cases should suggest problem situations that you have had and that you may wish to use for discussion.

Case No. 1

1. Mary was a member of a sorority whose constitution contained a "bias clause" restricting membership to persons of a specific race and religion.

2. She did not realize that this was true until after her initiation.

3. *Questions for Discussion:* Should she deny personal responsibility? Defend the restrictive constitution? Oppose it? Or, are there other possibilities that she should consider?

Case No. 2

1. John was the outgoing president of the Nineteen Club. He was a strong authoritarian leader and in the course of his administration had alienated many of the members of the club.

2. Howard, a very friendly and likeable person, was elected to succeed John as president. He was markedly different from John.

3. Howard did not want to cause such ill-feeling as had existed previously. Therefore, he was loathe to issue orders and demand action from the members.

4. The accomplishments of the Nineteen Club hit a new low under Howard's leadership, the finances dwindled sharply, and the members began resigning. By these standards Howard was less successful than was the authoritarian president.

5. *Questions for Discussion:* How could John have been a better liked president and yet kept the efficiency record he set? What behavioral changes on the part of Howard would have made him a more successful president?

When you discuss a case problem you should keep these five questions in mind: What are the facts? What is the exact problem raised in the case? What are the conditions that should be met by a good solution? How should this particular problem be solved—or how should it *have been* solved? How can future recurrences of the problem be avoided? If you discuss the case problems that we have given here, those given in Appendix A, or your own case problems, these questions should prove to be valuable.

4. Types of Discussion

METHODS OF CLASSIFYING DISCUSSION

There are a great number of types of discussion. Sometimes it is difficult to classify a particular discussion group as a certain *type*. Many discussions are combinations of a great variety of methods, arrangements, and techniques, and defy adequate classification. Hence, classifying discussion simply for the sake of making neat labels fit all kinds of discussion activity is a rather useless task. But classifying discussion with the aim of exploring some of the more important purposes and characteristics of discussion can be very worthwhile. Our purpose here is twofold: (1) to describe some of the many forms a discussion may take, and (2) to learn something about the multifold purposes of discussion.

It should be understood at the outset that when we talk about types of discussion, we are dealing, not with distinct categories, but rather with a continuum. By this we mean that it seldom happens that a given type of discussion is completely and recognizably different from all other types, but that a given discussion group tends to merge into and take on some of the characteristics of other types of discussion groups.

Specifically, we are dealing with two different continua in describing different kinds of discussion: one is a continuum showing discussion classified according to the physical arrangements, and the other is a continuum of discussion classified according to pur-

54

poses. The first continuum might look something like the following:

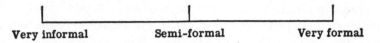

Very informal	**Semi-formal**	**Very formal**

On the "very informal" end of the scale we would expect to find such types of discussion as group conversation, some staff conferences, and so on to the semi-formal discussions typified by some round table discussions, and, beyond that, to the very formal discussions found, for example, in radio and television panel programs. The deciding element here is the kind of physical set-up to be found.

The second continuum showing differing kinds of purposes of discussion might look like this:

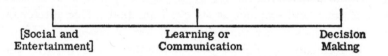

[Social and Entertainment]	Learning or Communication	Decision Making

Quite often social conversations develop into discussions or conferences having learning or decision-making purposes. Our attention in this book, however, will be centered on the more systematic discussion groups where the acknowledged purpose is learning, communication, or decision-making. It can be seen that even with this kind of classifying, many deficiencies appear. For example, one may well argue that a learning discussion or a discussion with communication as its purpose belongs at the far end of the continuum rather than decision-making conferences. Furthermore, it can readily be seen that the two continua presented here must always be considered together. The purpose of the discussion might determine the degree of formality; and the degree of formality might influence the purpose of the group.

With these admitted difficulties, let us turn our attention to a description of some of the more common types of discussion.

TRADITIONAL CLASSIFICATIONS OF DISCUSSION

Traditionally, discussion has been classified into these major divisions: the panel, the round table, the conference, the symposium, the dialogue, the lecture-forum.   Since these types are commonly referred to, let us examine each of them.

The Panel

Confusion sometimes arises over the use of the word "panel" in referring to a discussion group.   It has been used variously to describe an informal round table discussion, a committee, for example; a formal round table such as a radio discussion of a type similar to the Chicago Round Table; or a group of experts who take part in any kind of discussion, perhaps a group of speakers taking part in a symposium.   We may define it as a face-to-face discussion, generally informal in procedure, which is held before an audience, and employs as its chief method a free interchange of participations rather than prepared, formal speeches.   The degree of formality and the purpose of the discussion, whether problem-solving, information-sharing, information-giving, or something else, might vary considerably.   But in every case, the group would come within the limits of the definition given here.

Physically, then, a panel usually means that the members of the group are seated in such a way that communication can flow easily. A circular or semi-circular seating arrangement is best suited for this.   Members are quite often seated around a table.   This is true especially of radio and television panels.   But since many panels are presented before live audiences, a semi-circular arrangement is somewhat better as it enables the audience to see and hear with less difficulty.   Since there are usually no prepared speeches or order of speaking, the panel discussion generally has a leader whose function it is to introduce the topic for discussion, attempt to keep the discussion orderly and organized, and conclude the discussion.

The Round Table

Conducted essentially like the panel, the round table is usually a non-audience type of discussion. It tends to be much more informal than the panel discussion. Like the panel, it has a leader who encourages participants to engage in a free interchange of opinions and ideas. It is well suited for either decision-making or information-sharing.

The Conference

The conference may be defined as a special type of round table discussion. By and large, the word "conference" is used to refer to decision-making or policy-making groups, such as boards of directors, executive committees, and so forth. In recent times "conference" has been used to designate any one or all of the types of discussion carried on in business, industry, government, and other large scale activities. Hence, the word in this sense might refer to training "conferences" or policy-making "conferences" on a high level.

The conference is conducted like the round table. It is a non-audience type of discussion, usually without prepared speeches, which employs the procedure of free interchange of ideas, and is conducted under the direction of a leader.

The Symposium

A discussion in which the members of the group each deliver a prepared speech is generally called a symposium. In most cases, the group for a symposium is made up of from four to six members and a leader or chairman. By pre-arrangement, each member of the group has been assigned a particular phase of the discussion topic for his special consideration. This kind of topic division might be chronological, spatial, problem-solution, or any one of several other common methods of division of a subject. The time is usually divided equally among the participants, and each participant prepares and delivers a speech on his phase of the topic. The chairman's functions center around introducing the topic, introducing the speakers, and connecting the speeches of the participants with brief remarks.

Since this kind of discussion is a kind of public speaking situation, physical arrangements would resemble those of the usual speaker-audience setting. The speakers and the chairman are seated on the platform, or, at least, in front of the audience, and come forward to speak when their turns come. At the conclusion of the speeches, the leader usually summarizes the talks, and conducts the forum period if one is planned. The symposium, then, is usually more formal than a panel, and is better suited in most cases to informational rather than decision-making discussions.

Dialogue

This is a two-member discussion group. In actual practice, the dialogue is most often somewhat like an interview situation. One of the two participants serves for the most part as a questioner, and the primary role of the other participant is that of a respondent. One asks questions, the other provides the answers. Typical examples of this kind of discussion are to be found in radio and television interviews.

Obviously, this is somewhat less formal than a symposium, and provides many opportunities for a give-and-take kind of speaking. It is particularly well adapted to the informational type of discussion, when one of the two speakers is an authority on the subject under discussion.

Lecture-Forum

When the audience is given an opportunity to ask questions and/or make comments about the subject under discussion, we usually call this a forum period. When the stimulus for the forum period is provided by a single speaker, we label the activity a "lecture-forum." In addition to the speaker or lecturer, there is a chairman who introduces the speaker and who moderates the forum period which follows the speech.

It should be kept in mind, however, that any of the other types of discussion considered here and in the following sections may also have a forum period. We may properly refer not only to a lecture-forum, but also to a panel-forum, a symposium-forum, and a dialogue-forum.

DISCUSSION CLASSIFIED ACCORDING TO PROCEDURES AND PHYSICAL ARRANGEMENTS

Let us consider the term "physical arrangements" to mean not only the place where the discussion is held and the arrangement of the furniture for the group, but also the general arrangements and procedures for the discussion program. We can then identify seven features of physical arrangements and procedures which characterize certain types of discussion.

With or Without an Audience

Some discussions depend on the presence of an audience to accomplish their purposes. An explanation of a new policy in a plant may be presented by having several speakers talk on various aspects of the new policy. This kind of program, a symposium, could not take place without an audience. It would have no point unless an audience were present. On the other hand, the formation of the new policy by a decision-making conference group may be facilitated if no audience is present. The chances are that this kind of conference group would not operate very efficiently unless it operated in a kind of "executive session."

Face-to-Face or Co-acting

Most of the discussions with which we deal are face-to-face—that is, each member of the discussion group can see and talk directly to every other member of the group without physical effort. The typical co-acting situation is the speaker-audience arrangement. Here, a speaker (or a group of speakers) is the focus of attention, the stimulus, and the audience serves as a kind of respondent, usually a passive respondent.

The Radio or Television Discussion

The radio or television discussion is an audience type but the audience is not seen by the discussion group. The physical arrangements for these discussions involve all the technical apparatus, microphones, television cameras, and so forth. Different procedures are usually employed in carrying on this kind of program. Such factors as the role of the moderator, the timing of the program, the spread of participation among members of the group will differ simply because the program is a radio or television program. That is to say, that a discussion on the same topic by the same participants would be conducted in a different fashion if no cameras or microphones were present.

With or Without a Forum

We have already defined "forum" to be an audience participation period, questions and comments from the audience directed at the discussion group. Most public discussions, these days, include a forum period. The forum may be considered, then, as one of the aspects of arrangement for a discussion which might be a distinguishing characteristic.

Seating Arrangements

Some aspects of seating arrangements have already been mentioned, the presence or absence of an audience, the set-up for typical face-to-face and co-acting group situations, and so forth. Still other seating arrangements are possible. For example, a variation of the more usual seating arrangements is the arrangement used in committee hearings:

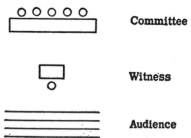

Committee

Witness

Audience

Type of Speaking

Discussions might also be differentiated on the basis of the kind of speaking done in the discussion. Some discussions call for the use of formal, prepared speeches, whereas others call for speaking that involves no formal preparation (social group conversation, for example). There are many variations between these two extremes.

Multi-arrangements

Some discussions involve the use of more than one set of physical arrangements. The popular student congresses, for example, involve arrangements for conducting meetings ranging from informal committees to formal parliamentary sessions. No single set of physical arrangements could be used to describe this particular kind of activity.

DISCUSSION CLASSIFIED ACCORDING TO PURPOSE

We mean by "purpose" the goal of the discussion group. It should be re-emphasized that many discussions have multiple goals, and it is not unusual for a single discussion group to have several of the purposes discussed in this chapter. This consideration of purposes, however, should help clarify some of the chief objectives of discussion groups.

Simple Problem-solving Discussion

Here, the primary objective of a discussion group is the reaching of a solution to a problem. The solutions may involve either overt action or simply a change in attitude or belief on the part of the group members. In solving a merchandising problem in connection with its business, a board of directors would be reaching a decision that would call for overt action, even though the action might be carried out by other people. A group of citizens discussing a neighborhood problem might reach a decision such as signing a petition or appearing before a city council meeting. In both cases, the decisions reached by the groups would call for observable action.

On the other hand, some groups discuss problems and reach solutions that do not involve any immediate, observable action. A neighborhood group that discussed the problems of American foreign relations and reached decisions about the kind of foreign policy we should have would not be involved in any overt action based on their decisions. Rather, the decision-making might influence and create attitudes or beliefs about American foreign policy. These attitudes and beliefs might be translated into action at some later time, but the action is not immediate. For the present, the action is cerebral, not physical.

Whatever kind of decision is reached, the functioning of this simple problem-solving discussion is always the same. The group begins with an unanswered question or problem and proceeds through a careful discussion of the problem to the reaching of an answer or solution to the problem.

Learning Discussions

It could be argued that all group discussions involve learning. Although this may be true, some discussions have learning as their ultimate, specific objective. Two kinds of learning discussions should be considered:

1. *Learning for the group members.* In many discussions, the objective is broadening the scope of information and knowledge of the people who participate. The education is for the group members. Good examples of this kind of discussion may be found in the many Great Books discussions carried on by neighborhood groups all over the country.

2. *Learning for an audience.* Some discussion groups have for their purpose spreading information and wisdom to audiences. Members of the discussion group are considered to be experts on the topic under discussion, and their function is primarily to increase the amount of knowledge of the people who listen to them. Expert opinion as well as factual material is presented in this type

of discussion. A great many radio and television discussions such as the University of Chicago Round Table, and the Northwestern University Reviewing Stand are of this type.

Communication Conferences

Some discussions have something akin to learning, communication of ideas, as their chief purpose. For example, a business staff conference might be assembled simply for the purpose of keeping the members of the firm informed about happenings in all parts of the business. No decisions are expected from this kind of group, nor any exploring of a problem for better understanding, but simply the exchange of information. Many times the exchange of information is general, but sometimes the conference method is used as a device for passing information from higher to lower echelons of the organization, or from lower to higher echelons.

Social Discussions

Some discussions have only a social objective. A group of people discussing the prospects of the local baseball team at a social gathering have no other objective than the social one. The same would be true if the topic were not baseball, but foreign affairs, or racial equality. Actually, this is a kind of enlarged conversation, a leaderless discussion aimed at nothing more than entertainment, but often resulting in learning, communication, or even decision-making.

Inquiry Discussions

A special type of discussion, developed in recent years, is the inquiry discussion. The purpose of the group is to gain information, and the chief methods used are observation and the interviewing of witnesses. We are all familiar with this kind of discussion as it appears in congressional and legislative committees. The same techniques can be, and are, employed in business conferences and in a great variety of other situations.

Training Conferences

These may be looked upon as a special type of the learning conference. Two important differences should be noted, however: (1) Most training conferences aim at training for a specific job, rather than a general broadening of information; and (2) Most training conferences include actual participation in the task about which the learning takes place. Hence, good examples of training conferences take place in situations that call for learning a highly specialized skill. Both talking and doing are part of many of these training conferences.

Bargaining Conferences

When members of a conference are divided into two opposing camps and the objective of the conference is to reach a suitable compromise solution, we are dealing with a bargaining conference. The best known examples of this type are labor-management bargaining conferences. The objective of these conferences is to bargain in such a way that the results will be mutually satisfactory.

Pseudo-Discussions

When the discussion method is used for the dissemination of propaganda, or when discussion groups are set up for the sole purpose of boosting morale by making participants feel they have had a part in reaching a decision already determined by others, then we are dealing with pseudo-, not real, discussions.[1]

SUMMARY

We have seen that it is difficult to classify discussion. Differences between types of discussion are sometimes minute and some discussions have elements of several types in them. In addition

---

[1] For a more complete explanation of this use of discussion method, see William S. Howell and Donald K. Smith, "Discussion Re-examined," *The Central States Speech Journal*, V (Fall, 1953), 6–7.

to panels, round tables, conferences, symposiums, dialogues, and lecture-forums, there are discussions which are classified according to their physical arrangements: (1) discussions with or without an audience, (2) face-to-face or co-acting discussions, (3) radio and television discussions, (4) discussions with or without a forum, (5) discussions classified according to seating arrangements, (6) discussions classified according to the type of speaking taking place in the group, and (7) multi-arrangements discussions. We have found it useful to distinguish these types of discussion according to purpose: (1) problem-solving discussions, (2) learning discussions, (3) communication conferences, (4) social discussions, (5) inquiry discussions, (6) training conferences, (7) bargaining conferences, and (8) pseudo-discussions.

PART II

Problem-Solving

5. Preparing for Discussion

IMPORTANCE OF THOROUGH PREPARATION

As much as any other single factor, the amount of preparation for a discussion is a determinant of the discussion's success. When the members of a group are ill-informed and poorly prepared on the subject being discussed, little can be expected by way of profitable exchange of information, or of high-quality solutions. A pooling of ignorance cannot result in anything more than a decision that reflects that ignorance. As Auer puts it:

Some discussion groups are ineffective because their members are poorly informed. If a group's thinking, as well as its speaking, is impromptu, the result is apt to be mere confirmation of prior judgments.[1]

Although many things that happen in a discussion may be viewed from a *group* standpoint, preparation for discussion is essentially an *individual* matter. For effective results, a group cannot afford to have a single "weak link." All members must be thoroughly prepared.

STEPS IN PREPARING FOR DISCUSSION

Our consideration of preparing for discussion will center around a chronological sequence of steps for the member to follow. Each

---

[1] J. Jeffery Auer, "The Citizen's Roundtable," *Adult Education*, XIII (February, 1949), 72.

of these is important, and each builds upon the one preceding it. Naturally, with experience in discussion, participants will find short-cuts and time-savers in following this pattern, but the fact remains that these five steps show the way to thorough and efficient discussion preparation.

The First Step: Organize Your Own Thoughts

1. *Think carefully and fully on the subject.* The chances are you would not be a participant in a discussion group unless you already knew something about the subject. Hence, the first step in every case should be a full and careful thinking about the subject, utilizing the information you already possess. This kind of personal stock-taking should be done on two levels: (1) Try to place the subject for discussion within a larger framework. If the discussion topic concerns the advisability of your community building a new court house, then you should take stock of your general information regarding such related matters as the status of the community's finances, the number of public buildings already in existence in the community, the general economic level of the people in the community, and other such related matters. It can be seen that these matters are not *directly* connected with plans for, or the advisability of, a new court house, but they certainly are essential parts of the general frame-work within which the specific court house proposal must be considered. (2) In addition, marshal your information regarding the *specific* topic for discussion. For example, in the matter of the court house, you would want to discover how much you know about such specific items as the probable cost of a new court house, the adequacy of the present court house in serving the community, the attitude of local public officials and of the community in general toward the new court house, and so on.

2. *List your stock of information and ideas.* After the mental compilation of information, take a pencil and a piece of paper and list the items of information you discover you already know. For the time being don't be too concerned with the degree of importance of this information. This listing may be part of your "full think-

ing" on the subject, or it may follow immediately after this first step.

3. *Organize your information.* When your array of information is complete, the next step is to organize this list so it will be more meaningful. Examine the list carefully. Decide which three or four or five items on the list seem to be of most importance. Then you will discover that many of the other items tend to fall rather naturally as sub-points or supporting material under the major ideas. More than likely, several items of information will appear to you as a natural group—all dealing with the same thing. Or, it may be, that some of the things you have listed seem now to be irrelevant or of such minor importance that they serve no useful purpose, they simply "clutter up" your stock of information. When you finish with this kind of organizing process, you should have a fairly good outline.

As an example of how this may be done, let us refer back again to our court house problem. Let us suppose we are dealing with a hypothetical county, let's call it Martin County. Our array of personal information about the subject might look something like this:

1. Martin County has a population of 92,000 people.
2. The county is largely a rural one, with two fair-sized cities.
3. The court house now in use was built in 1876.
4. The county officials say the court house is too small.
5. The style of architecture is not in keeping with other buildings nearby.
6. A proposal for a new court house was voted down ten years ago.
7. Smith County (the adjoining county) built a new court house two or three years ago.
8. Some people say that our tax rate will go up if a new court house is built.
9. The tax rate in this county is less than in many other counties I know of.

Admittedly, this is a small list, but it's large enough to illustrate our point about organizing a list of information. If we attempt such an organization, we could end up with some such arrangement as that shown on page 72.

I. What are the advantages and disadvantages of the present court house?
   A. It is old—built in 1876.
   B. County officials say it is too small.
   C. Outdated style of architecture.
II. What are the needs of the county with regard to a court house?
   A. Population is 92,000.
   B. This is a rural county.
III. What are the chief arguments for and against a new court house?
                              Against
   A. The proposal has been turned down once in recent times—ten years ago.
   B. The tax rate might go up if we get a new court house.
                               For
   A. Our neighboring county has a new court house.
   B. Our tax rate now is low (we could probably afford a new court house).

Naturally, there would be other ways of organizing this material, but this should give an indication of the procedure to follow in organizing your own ideas into a pattern of some sort.

4. *Discover the deficiencies in your preparation.* One of the chief advantages to organizing your ideas in the fashion described here is that it is revealing of your own deficiencies of information. A quick look at the outline above will show that there is need of much more specific information on such items as: the cost of a new court house, why the proposal was turned down ten years ago, in what particular respects the present court house is too small, the average income in the county, and so forth. To fill these "gaps" in information, we then would go to the second step in preparing for discussion.

The Second Step: Gather Additional Information

1. *Fill in the gaps in your stock of information.* By now you have probably demonstrated to yourself that there are additional things you should know about your subject. There are several places for gathering this additional information.

(a) *Observation.* Whenever it is possible, it is best to gather information first hand. If you can gather additional information by observing for yourself, this should be your initial step in supplementing the information you already have. In our court house example, an inspection of the court house would certainly give you valuable information regarding the condition of the building, whether or not there appears to be enough room to conduct the county's business properly, and other facts regarding the building and its use. Obviously, the information gathered in this way will be more precise and more meaningful to you than if it were to come from others. In addition, you can look for the *specific* items of information you need or want to have.

(b) *Interviews.* Where observation is impractical, or when you don't feel qualified to rely on your own observation, find people who are in positions to know more about your subject and interview them. Interviews have several advantages. They enable you to ask specific questions in a face-to-face situation; they are usually quick and to the point; they usually result in the acquisition of much useful information. For example, an interview with a county official would supply you with much information about the court house in a short period of time.

Sometimes interviews are out of the question. Authorities are not always readily available for interviewing. Consequently, we must look for information in other places.

(c) *Reading.* Probably the biggest single source of information on most topics will be met through reading in books, periodicals, newspapers, documents, and so forth. Let us consider briefly the matter of finding information by reading.

(1) *Reference books.* In gathering information on a subject, most of us turn first to standard reference works such as encyclopedias and dictionaries. This is a worthwhile practice for two reasons: first, we get a clear over-all view of our subject in such reference works, and, second, we get valuable leads on other sources of information. A third reason might be added in the case of special reference works like *The World Almanac.* We can get specific items of information quickly and with little effort from such a book. A trip to the library and a look at the shelves containing reference books will show the great number and wide variety of

reference works.   Among the standard reference works most frequently used are:

ENCYCLOPEDIAS: *The Encyclopaedia Britannica, The Americana.*
DICTIONARIES:*Webster's Unabridged* and *Collegiate, The American College Dictionary.*
BIOGRAPHICAL DICTIONARIES: *Dictionary of National Biography, Dictionary of American Biography, Who's Who in America.*
BOOKS OF STATISTICS AND FACTS: *United States Statistical Abstract, World Almanac.*

There are countless other reference books, many of them more specialized than these listed here.   The best advice is to ask the li-
brarian where information on a subject might be found in a reference book, and, more important from the standpoint of getting
acquainted with the books yourself, to browse among the reference
books found in your library.

(2) *Books.*   Additional readings or short bibliographies will be
found in many of the reference books.   These can be reading
guides for further pursuit of your subject.   But, more important,
learn to use the card catalogue in the library.   When you've located books that appear to have information you need, look through
them, find the more valuable ones and read them carefully.   It is
not necessary to read everything in every book on your subject,
although the more you read the better prepared you will be.   However, you should learn to use the Table of Contents and Index of
a book, in order to be able to get from the book the specific information you want.

(3) *Periodical literature.*   Books sometimes tend to be too
general for your purposes, or sometimes even the most recent book
on your subject is too old to give the particular information you
want.   So you would turn next to magazines and journals.   Just
as the card catalogue gives you a listing of books on a given subject,
so the *Readers' Guide to Periodical Literature* gives a listing of
articles in current magazines on your subject.   The *Readers' Guide*
categorizes articles, so that under a subject matter heading you could
find all the articles on your subject that have appeared in a certain
period of time, and you will also find the issue of the magazine in

which they appeared. Use of this *Guide* will save an enormous amount of time that otherwise might be spent in looking through magazines for articles on your subject.

(4) *Newspapers.* On local topics, topics of interest or concern primarily to your own locality, your local newspapers offer an excellent source of information. On topics of broader interest, other newspapers from other cities and areas might well be consulted to get differing points of view. Furthermore, just as the *Readers' Guide* is a time-saving index of magazine articles, so also is there an index of newspaper articles. *The New York Times Index* indexes and categorizes stories that have appeared in the *Times*. If a copy of the *Index* is available to you, and most libraries have copies, then much effort can be saved in finding a newspaper article on your subject. Even if a file of the *New York Times* is not available, finding the date of a certain story in the *Index* will give you a lead on when and where to look in your local paper. Often newspaper stories give much more detail than can be found later in magazines and books. Therefore, newspapers may often be an extremely valuable source of information.

(5) *Other publications.* In addition to the printed sources of information already discussed, there are other special printed materials which can give valuable aid in preparing for a discussion. There are many government publications on a great variety of topics; documents of a public or private nature; propaganda publications and publications by special interest groups. All of these often contain specific and detailed information about subjects not easily obtained elsewhere.

(d) *Miscellaneous sources of information.* Our processes of communication have improved vastly in the past few years. As a result, many of us have come to rely on the radio, television, and newsreels for a great deal of our information. These are good sources of information and certainly help fill in our general background of information. The obvious drawback, however, is that we count on these sources for specific information on a particular topic at a specified time. Thus, if we are interested in gathering more information about labor-management relations, it would be only coincidence if we were able to get the information we wanted by listening to the radio or by watching television tonight. But the fact remains that these means of communication should be considered important as suppliers of essential background information, and, occasionally, of the specific information we are looking for.

All of this might be summed up by saying: "Information is where you find it!" There are literally thousands of sources of information on most topics. We should avail ourselves of all those that are within our reach and for which we have time.

2. *Take notes on your information gathering.* Whatever your source of information, you should plan a system of note-taking. Taking notes is important for three reasons: (1) Notes enable you to put your information together better than if you relied on memory alone; with notes you may be sure of having a rather complete record of your new information; (2) Notes enable you to use your information carefully and accurately. You will be in a better position to report your information precisely in the discussion if you have kept notes. This is especially important if you are quoting someone for quotations should be accurate; (3) Notes provide a useful means of preserving information. If you are an active participator in many discussion groups, the information you use in one discussion may be useful at some later time in another discussion. A good set of notes will make the information readily usable at any time.

There are several rules about note-taking that may help make notes more valuable and more usable.

(a) *Be accurate.* If you are taking notes on an interview, be sure to get into your notes the exact information that was given you. If there is any doubt about what the person you are interviewing said, read your notes back to him and ask if they are correct. If your notes come from something you have read, be sure your quotations are correct. Check and re-check them for accuracy.

(b) *Be complete.* Be sure you get down all the information you might be able to use from the source. While there is always the possibility that you will get more than you will need, it is better to have too much rather than to have too little and be forced to spend valuable time in re-reading the same book or article you have already referred to once.

(c) *Keep a record of your source.* Just in case you might need to refer to the source again, be sure your notes indicate exactly where the material came from. If the source is a magazine article, your notes should tell you the author's name, the title of the article, the name of the magazine, the volume number, the year, and the page number or numbers where your information was found. In other words, you would want to keep the same kind of exact information that you would get for a bibliography.

(d) *Make your notes usable.* Making your notes usable involves two things: First, use a notebook or filing cards, or some device that will enable you to keep together notes taken from various sources, but dealing with the same subject. 3x5 or 4x6 filing cards are especially useful in this respect. They can easily be "shuffled" so that all the material relating to a given aspect of your subject can be put together. Second, your notes should be readable, and a system should be worked out for categorizing your information. If a key word or phrase is put on the note card indicating the subject matter of that particular card, then a quick glance will tell you whether or not the card has the kind of information on it that you might be looking for. These devices for making your notes usable are especially important if you plan on keeping the notes for use at a later time.

The following sample note card will illustrate at least one method of keeping notes:

PREPARING FOR DISCUSSION:
Baird, A. Craig. *Discussion: Principles and Types.* New York.
    McGraw-Hill Book Company, Inc., 1943. p. 42.
Preparation for discussion should involve six distinct phases: "(1) inventory of your general information and reflective thinking on the subject; (2) conversation; (3) auditing speeches; (4) reading and note taking; (5) construction of a bibliography or list of references; (6) assimilation and interpretation of ideas through outlines and, in some cases, written or oral composition making use of the material." [2]

[2] A. Craig Baird, *Discussion: Principles and Types*, p. 42. New York: McGraw-Hill Book Company, Inc., 1943. Reprinted by permission.

You will note that the top line gives a general heading for the material covered in the note; the second line gives the exact source of the information; and the third part of the card gives the information indicated by the use of quotations marks, in this case a direct quotation.

Now that you have listed and organized your own information and have gathered new information on the subject, you are ready to move into the third step in preparing for discussion.

The Third Step: Evaluate Your Information

You should be able to make a careful evaluation of the material you have assembled.   It is not enough simply to collect information; you should also be able to judge it according to worth.   Some items are bound to be more important and carry more weight than others. What we are suggesting here is that you should know something about the nature of evidence and some of the more common ways of testing it.   The ability to classify and test evidence is useful not only in preparing your own material, but also in judging the evidence used by others in a discussion.   So let us turn our attention now to the kinds of evidence and to some of the basic evaluative tests for these kinds of evidence.

1. *Facts.*   Facts are conditions or events that can be verified. If we were to say that you are reading these lines right now, that would be a fact, since it would be verifiable.   If you were told that there is a desk in the room next to you, that too would fall in the category of fact, since it could be demonstrated.   If we say that 1776 is the year of American independence, that would be a fact. Even though we ourselves could not verify that American independence came about in 1776, this fact could be established by other methods, documents, letters, diaries, and so forth.   Still, again, if we say that the population of the United States is 165,000,-000 people, this would be a fact, since it could be verified, not by our own examination, but by records and tallies in the Census Bureau.   These examples indicate that there are at least three kinds of facts: demonstrable, historical, and statistical.

(a) *Demonstrable facts.*   There are things, events, conditions, that can be experienced by us. By using our five senses we can satisfy ourselves as to the existence of a chair, a book, an automobile accident, a failing mark on an examination, or the absence of a classmate. These are facts that can be demonstrated. It is not always practical for us to collect our facts in this first-hand fashion, so we usually rely on the word of others to tell us about things which, under the proper circumstances, we might have experienced ourselves. We often get such facts from interviews, from books or magazine articles, from newspaper stories, or from other sources. For instance, George Amberg's book, *Ballet, The Emergence of an American Art,* tells us that part of the repertoire of the Ballet Russe de Monte Carlo is "Cappriccio Espagnol," with book by Leonide Massine, music by Rimsky-Korsakov, and choreography by Leonide Massine.[3] Now this information could have been secured first-hand by witnessing the ballet, but since we cannot do this we rely upon this book to transmit the fact to us. Thus, although most of the demonstrable facts that we will use in discussions come to us through other sources, it would have been possible (though not practical in many cases) to have secured them first-hand through personal observation and examination.

(b) *Historical facts.* Historical facts are those which are not verifiable by our own experience since they relate to events or things that have taken place in the past. We accept these events as facts largely on the basis of records which tend to verify them, records which are usually transmitted to us by a second party who has examined them. Thus, history books are accepted as factual because we accept the word of the author that his material is verified by documents, letters, diaries, and other records. When we read in Boak's *History of Rome to 565 A. D.* that Cicero was banished from Rome in 58 B.C.,[4] we accept it as fully as if we were able to verify it ourselves. In preparing for discussion, we nearly always rely on this kind of secondary source for our historical facts.

---

[3] George Amberg, *Ballet, The Emergence of an American Art,* p. 205. New York: A Mentor Book, The New American Library, 1949.

[4] Arthur E. R. Boak, *A History of Rome to 565 A. D.,* pp. 180–181. New York: The Macmillan Company, 1929.

(c) *Statistics.* Actually, statistics are a special kind of demonstrable fact. Theoretically, we could verify statistics ourselves, assuming we had the time, energy, and money to gather them or check them. Since we seldom have either the time or the desire to carry on this exhaustive kind of checking process, we accept statistics as surely as we accept demonstrable and historical facts. Naturally, as in the case of historical facts, we need to be careful about the source of our statistical information. However, second-hand reporting of statistics frequently gives the original source of the information. Our tests of reliability should then be applied to the original source of the statistics, since we usually assume the reporter would not alter the statistics. Where the original source is not given, however, we would test the reporting source. Examples of authors quoting statistics from another or original source might be found in many articles and books. For example, Backus, in her *Speech in Education,* quotes from the *White House Conference on Child Health and Protection, Special Education, Report of the Committee on Special Classes* in saying that among every 10,000 children with speech defects, 1029 stuttered.[5] Statistics are frequently used in discussions, and they serve as the foundation for much of the thinking that goes on in discussion groups. Hence, it is important that we know something about the testing of statistical material. The section that follows describes some tests that can and should be applied not only to statistics but to demonstrable and historical facts as well.

2. *Testing your facts.* Our chief concern here is setting up a series of questions that might be applied to facts in order to test their reliability. These tests should be used in gathering your information in preparing for discussion, but they also may be used in the discussion itself. As you listen to the facts used by other members of the discussion group, you should test them in light of these questions.

(a) *What is the source of the fact?* We have already indicated

[5] Ollie L. Backus, *Speech in Education, A Guide for the Classroom Teacher,* pp. 20–21. New York: Longmans, Green and Co., 1948.

how important this test is when applied to statistics. It is equally important when applied to demonstrable and historical facts. If the source is not a reliable one, then we should distrust the information; if the source is a reliable one, we can usually accept the facts without question.

(b) *Are the facts reasonable?* Are the facts in accord with our usual reasoning processes? If you were awakened in the morning and told that the sun was rising in the West, you would not accept this as a fact, since it would not be in keeping with the generalization you have made about the sun's rising in the East.

(c) *Do the facts agree with other facts?* Where two conflicting sets of facts exist, we tend to cast suspicion on both of them. If, however, one set of facts agrees fully with another set of facts, then we feel reasonably safe in accepting them as valid.

(d) *Are the facts acceptable to others?* This test might be labeled a kind of rhetorical test of facts. It has little to do with the ultimate reliability of the facts, but a great deal to do with the usability of the facts. If they are not acceptable by others in a discussion group, then as far as their use is concerned, they might as well be invalid. To be usable facts must also be acceptable.

3. *Opinion.* Now let us turn to the second major category of evidence: opinion. We have seen that facts deal with realities which are observable or verifiable by us or by others in whom we can place confidence. Now we are concerned with opinions, with statements which, by and large, cannot be verified since they express a judgment. The opinion may be supported by other opinions similar to it, but it does not express a fact or a reality. Opinions might be expressed by two kinds of people whom we can designate as ordinary witnesses and expert witnesses.

(a) *Ordinary opinion.* Ordinary opinions are those expressed by the layman, by a person who is not qualified as an authority on his subject. The opinion might be a very good one, and it might agree with the opinions expressed by authorities on the subject, but standing by itself it has little weight. Most of us, for example, would be able to give nothing more than an ordinary opinion on the constitutionality of a new law. We are not in a position to know all the facts, nor have we had the training or experience necessary to form an expert opinion on the subject.

One common mistake observed in many discussion groups centers around the use of ordinary opinions. Many people assume that because a person occupies a respected position he automatically becomes an authority on every subject. It is a mistake to believe that every statement made by a United States Senator, for example, is authoritative and expert. The senator would be an expert on matters he had studied and in which he had much experience, but his position does not qualify him on *all* subjects.

(b) *Expert opinion.* When the person making a statement is qualified because of his training, education, background, position, and other factors to know his subject thoroughly, then we usually consider him an expert or an authority. His statements may be used with much more reliance than those of the ordinary witness. What the expert says probably comes closer to a fact, to reality, than what the layman says. Thus, the quotation from Auer at the beginning of this chapter might be called an expert opinion. Professor Auer has studied in the field of discussion a good many years, he has had much experience with discussion groups, he is the author of many articles and several books on discussion. His training, education, background, position, and many other factors qualify him as an authority on discussion.

4. *Testing opinions.* Just as we set up a series of questions to be applied to facts, so we should have a series of questions relating to the use of testimony or opinions. Here again, these tests should be of use to you not only in preparing for discussion, but also in taking part in discussion. You should apply these questions to testimony used by other members of your discussion group.

(a) *Is the person quoted usually reliable?* If the authority has a dubious reputation for reliability and truthfulness, then we should be wary in using quotations from him. If his integrity is highly respected, then we may feel relatively safe in using him as an authoritative source.

(b) *Is the authority in a position to know about the subject?*

Here we would apply the tests already mentioned concerning the person's training, education, background, position, and, in general, whether he is in a position to really know thoroughly the subject he talks about.

(c) *Is the authority supported by other authorities?* As we did in the similar test about facts, we place much more reliance on an authority who is supported by other authorities. We are a little doubtful if he is the only person to take the position he takes.

(d) *Is the opinion expressed a reasonable one?* We are concerned here really with two interpretations of the word "reasonable." We generally have more faith in an authority who does not take extreme positions, who is reasonable in that sense. In addition, we want to know whether or not the statement made by the authority agrees with good logic, good reasoning processes. Do his inferences seem to be drawn fairly, with a proper regard to the available facts?

(e) *Will the authority be acceptable to others?* Again we must apply the rhetorical test of acceptability. If our authority will not be acceptable to the others in our discussion group, then it is profitless to use him.

As we have already said, a discussion member should prepare thoroughly, and part of his thorough preparation is his ability to evaluate the evidence he collects. Both facts and authorities should be examined carefully and critically before they become part of the member's "ammunition" for discussion.

The Fourth Step: Re-organize Your Information

Now that you have thoroughly investigated your subject and carefully evaluated the material you have collected, you are ready for the fourth step in preparation. Once again, take a piece of paper and list all the information you have available on your subject. This process is precisely like the method you used in the first step, except that now your array of items of information should be considerably longer and should cover the subject much more thoroughly.

After you get a complete list of all your information down on paper, re-arrange it again and organize it. Just as you did in the first step, find the major points in your list of information and organize the minor and supporting points under them. It may be that your plan of organization will be like the first attempt at organization, or it may be that with the new information you have you will want to change your organization. At any rate, your thinking on the subject will be improved if you can organize your thoughts as well as list them.

The Fifth Step: Construct a Discussion Outline

At the conclusion of the fourth step, you have an outline of your subject. The fifth step is a relatively simple one following that. The outline you already have prepared is probably a very complete one organized in terms of what seem to be the most important aspects of the subject, content-wise. Now re-arrange your material so it will fall into a pattern likely to be used in a discussion group. A good pattern to follow is the pattern for reflective thinking. This would mean that you would arrange your outline under some such headings as: (1) Definition and limits of the problem; (2) Effect-cause relationships; (3) Criteria for testing solutions; (4) Possible solutions to the problem; (5) Development of solutions; and (6) Means of putting solutions into effect.[6]

The discussion outline is a vital part of your preparation, since it crystallizes your thinking on the subject. In addition, it may, in most cases, be taken into the discussion with you. Used in the discussion itself, it will aid you in contributing fully and completely on the subject. You will have a constant guide for your participation. For this reason, and because the discussion outline may be referred to by others, it should contain sources of your information. Footnotes may be used, or the sources of your information may be listed at the side of the page opposite the appropriate items in the outline.[7]

---

[6] Chapter 7, "Reflective Thinking in Discussion," explains these headings in detail.

[7] Study the sample discussion outline on pages 329–333.

Summary

We have seen that careful preparation is an essential part of adequate participation in discussion. A five-step method of preparing for discussion has been suggested: Step one: organize your own thoughts; Step two: gather additional information; Step three: evaluate your information; Step four: re-organize your material; and Step five: make a discussion outline.

6. How We Solve Problems

In this chapter we shall describe common practices in problem-solving ranging from the mysticism of intuition to the more careful pattern of reflective thinking. To make our explanations of these forms of "thinking" as helpful to you as possible, we shall give many illustrative case reports. You should study the explanations and the case reports with care.

THE INFLUENCE OF INTUITION

"Intuition," says Durant Drake, "is not seeing with the eyes, or perceiving with any sense organ. It is strongly imagining that something is thus and so, with an accompanying conviction that it really *is* as we imagine it."[1] As defined here intuition represents a special avenue to "truth" that is known only to the intuitionist himself. It may be contrasted with decisions based upon observation, analysis of facts, and experimentation.

Intuition and Your Decisions

You have probably used the word *intuition* to refer to some of the decisions that you have made. Thus, you may have said, "I know that we will win the football game with X College but I haven't any reasons to prove my conviction." Or, if you do not use the word yourself, you have certainly heard others say, "I have

---

[1] Durant Drake, *Invitation to Philosophy*, p. 26. Boston: Houghton Mifflin Company, 1933. Reprinted by permission.

86

a premonition, a 'sneaking suspicion' that defies explanation." If these judgments are actually intuitive, the judgments are, first of all, regarded as true; and secondly, the person making the judgments is not able to advance evidence to support his conviction.

So-called *intuitive* judgments are popularly given about the character of people. A man might say, for example, "I can judge a person in ten seconds strictly on intuition." Apparently, then, the intuitionist makes his discovery through some super-rational faculty that is unrelated to previous knowledge and ordinary reasoning processes. But right here we might ask, "Is this true?" Do you successfully judge others in some mystical way? Drake punctures this view effectively when he shows that successful intuitions are really rooted in observations.

When we look, now, at the positive arguments offered for the intuitional method, we note the concrete successes of what is called intuition. But these successful "intuitions" reveal, in most cases, just the sort of world that ordinary knowledge and science reveal; they seem to be short-cuts to the same results, rather than a revelation of a different sort of world. And this is because what is called intuition is usually just the subconsciously reached or retained result of past experiences. Intuitions seem to well up out of some unknown deep; they are mysterious, inexplicable to the one who has them. But it is noteworthy that good intuitions come usually only to those who have considerable experience in the particular field where they appear. The man who is an "intuitive" judge of character is one who has known and watched many people; he cannot say how he reaches his swift judgments, but they are clearly the result of a long accumulation of observations. Valuable intuitions as to the disposition of troops come to the experienced general more often than to the inexperienced, valuable scientific intuitions to the man of long scientific training rather than to the tyro.[2]

Of course, the word *intuition* is often used to describe any sudden discovery or idea that occurs to a person. But if you use the word in this sense, your discovery is doubtless based upon prior knowledge. And what is more, the judgment you make must be

---

[2] *Ibid.*, p. 31. Reprinted by permission.

tested in the same way as any hypothesis is tested.   Unless you do this, your "leap in the dark" may fool you.   Intuition, even among women who are supposed to be especially endowed with it, is not a sure path to successful decisions.

Illustrative Case Reports

The illustrations we are giving here will help you to decide the worth of intuitive decisions.

1. The person who claims to have intuitive powers is likely to be most successful when he reports after-the-event happenings.   For example, "I had a premonition that I should not have taken the exam on Friday." . . . Or, "I knew by intuition that Donald would have an automobile accident today."
Question: Do persons like these also report their errors?

2. Suppose that in a discussion Miss Winters says, "I think course 129 in Department Y should be a required course for students in the College of Liberal Arts.   I know intuitively that it will be a good course for everyone."
Question: Wouldn't you insist upon proof in this situation?

3. In speaking about the differences between Adolf Hitler and Winston Churchill, John W. Studebaker said: "When I learned in 1940 that bricklaying was a favorite diversion of Winston Churchill I knew that Hitler was foredoomed; for the bricklayer works by a plumb line, not by intuition." [3]

4. Japanese-born, atomic physicist Hidehi Yukawa was awarded a Nobel Prize for his meson theory which he announced in 1935.   When asked how he conceived the idea, Yukawa said:

Well, it is very curious.   When one works in the daytime, it is easy to do your regular work.   You have your desk, your paper convenient. But it is hard in daytime to get something that is completely different from conventional notions.   So I used to work hard all day and get very tired and nervous.   Then I could not sleep at night.   Sometimes at night I thought of very interesting things.   Almost always, in the morning, these things turned out to be untrue.   But once in a while one of them was true and unusual.   This was the way, at night, that I thought of the meson theory. [4]

---

[3] "Bricks to Build Democracy," *Reader's Digest,* XLVI (April, 1945), Inside Back Cover.   Reprinted by permission.
[4] *Time,* LIV (November 14, 1949), 88.

Comments: Case 4 deserves further attention. Yukawa did not refer to his discovery as intuitive in nature, although some people might do so. He was, first of all, a competent physicist engaged in the solution of a problem. He had previously identified as many relevant facts as he could, and he had pondered their value. The result was therefore not something that cannot be explained on rational grounds. And, equally important, Yukawa tested his theory instead of accepting the theory without proof. In other words, his brilliant discovery is not intuitional in the usual meaning of the word. It is rather a high-order example of reflective thinking.

The Influence of Initial Choice

By an *initial choice* we mean your early reaction to a problem situation. You may have studied the problem thoroughly previous to making your decision. But after you have made your decision, you tend to disregard other possible answers to the problem. You exclude from your field of attention any direction, idea, or plan that is opposed to your initial choice.

Initial Choice and Your Decisions

You must necessarily make many quick decisions as contrasted with suspended or delayed judgments. If you didn't do this, the time you spent in deliberating would often spell disaster. In many practical matters you act speedily by following standards that previous learning and experience have proved to be sound. You follow principles, rules, or laws. If you know the right standards and if the problem can be correctly judged by these standards, you can pronounce decisions automatically.

Suppose, however, that you were given this problem.

Christmas Shopping with Dogs: On one of the busiest days of the Christmas shopping season of 1945, an attractive young woman entered a downtown store in Los Angeles. On a leash she had with her two retrievers, a spaniel, a bull-dog, and a St. Bernard. She insisted on bringing the dogs into the store, bought a highly colored sport-shirt and left, without offering any explanation. *What caused her behavior?* [5]

In the first place, there might be many causes for the behavior of this woman. Most persons, however, would connect the episode with Hollywood, and believe that the woman was an actress engaged in a publicity stunt. But the preferred solution is that the young woman was taking part in a radio program such as "Truth or Consequences" or "People Are Funny" in which prizes are given for unusual antics. Yet, as long as you center your attention exclusively on Hollywood, you will be blind to the preferred alternative of the radio program.

Norman R. F. Maier uses the words "direction in thinking" to explain the way in which persons attack a problem. He has shown that we are all likely to become so absorbed in a particular point of view, line of attack, or thinking pattern that we are "blinded" to new approaches to the problem. In one of his studies, a number of students were divided into control groups and experimental groups. The experimental groups were given a twenty-minute lecture on critical thinking designed to minimize the directional force of initial choices. Among the suggestions given were: (1) The difficulties you see are often controlled by your previous experiences with problems; (2) if you fail in your solution, try a completely different plan; (3) do not be a creature of habit and stay in a rut. The experimental groups of students in this study were much more successful in reaching correct answers to problems than were the control groups. Those in the groups who were given instruction in problem-solving made a 24.1 per cent higher score. [6]

---

[5] Max Black, *Critical Thinking*, p. 262. New York: Prentice-Hall, Inc., 1946. Reprinted by permission.

[6] Norman R. F. Maier, "An Aspect of Human Reasoning," *The British Journal of Psychology*, XXIV (October, 1933), 144–155; see also "The Quality of Group Decisions As Influenced by the Discussion Leader," *Human Relations*, III (1950), 155–174.

Illustrative Case Reports

In these case reports you will notice that initial choices may have the blinding effect of an "iron curtain"; and secondly, that non-obvious solutions to problems should be sought.

1. Abraham S. Luchins has done much experimentation with school children on the *blinding* effect of mechanical drill. He shows that first choice, mechanization, habit, or routine can make us blind to very simple solutions to problems. This tendency to persist in following initial choices is called *einstellung* by Luchins. It means the *set* or pattern that immediately predisposes us to act in a certain way even when other more acceptable solutions are possible. But like "direction," as defined by Maier, *set* blinds us to new possibilities.

Luchins asked students to find a four or five letter word in groups of letters without transposing the order of letters. The illustrative example was *M S A V R A E*—the word being MARE. The groups of letters were in some cases given to students orally, one group at a time. To some students Luchins gave this advice: "After you have solved the sixth problem, write 'Don't Be Blind' on your paper." Other students were not given special advice that might be helpful in overcoming *blindness*.

These letter groups have been used by Luchins (the letters E and C are symbols for *einstellung* and *critical test problems*, respectively):

1. E GZOQART GOAT
2. E BOUFLML BULL
3. E DZEPEWR DEER
4. E MPUALME MULE
5. E WIORLZF WOLF
6. E BXESALR BEAR
(Here some groups are advised: "Don't be blind.")
7. C TSINGREUR SING—TIGER
8. C HFOURESTE FOUR—HORSE
9. # GNEVERZOE EVER—GEEZE
10. C SOWRITNGE WRIT—SWINE
11. C CBALMUEAL BALM—CAMEL [7]

Persons who are fully victimized by blindness will answer *tiger, horse, geeze, swine,* and *camel* for problems 7, 8, 9, 10, and 11. In

---

[7] See Abraham S. Luchins, "Mechanization in Problem-Solving: The Effect of Einstellung," *Psychological Monographs*, LIV (1942), 25. Copyright, 1942, American Psychological Association. Reprinted by permission.

some cases they will say "number 9 should be GNEVERSOE and the answer is *geese.*" Still others report "geeze" and imply that the word is spelled correctly. While this simple test has been designed especially for school children in elementary grades, the power of *einstellung* is also operative with adults. The initial choice that works satisfactorily for the first six groups of letters tends to persist in letter groups seven to eleven, although a simpler solution is clearly presented in letters that consecutively produce four or five letter words.

2. The following report shows how a student group selected a non-obvious solution to a problem:

At the Third Annual *National Student Association Congress* held in Ann Arbor late in the summer of 1950, there was an observer representing the *Labor Youth League* present. He was there, like many other observers, just to sit in on the meetings.

The Congress discusses many topics which can be broken down into four main subjects: Educational Affairs, Student Affairs, Organizational Affairs, and International Affairs. It was the latter in which the member of the LYL was most interested.

Four facts of significance in this case were: (a) The LYL had been listed as a communist front organization. (b) At the time of the Congress in 1950 the United Nations troops were in about their worst position in Korea. (c) The LYL representative was of the opinion that the United Nations should not have troops in Korea. (d) The LYL representative was not a delegate to the Congress. He was an observer and could, according to rules of the Congress, speak before any of the committees, but he could not speak on the floor of a general meeting.

At the Executive Committee meeting just after the last regular committee meeting was held, this man from the LYL asked permission to speak to the whole group on the Korean situation. He claimed that he felt that it was necessary to speak to the whole group, and not just a committee. A serious problem presented itself. Should he be allowed to speak, notwithstanding the rules which he knew about?

This request was a well-planned idea by the LYL. Failure to permit the LYL member to speak would mean that the LYL could show that the Congress denied freedom of speech to their representative. But, on the other hand, if this person did speak, the newspapers might interpret the speech as a sign that the *Student Association Congress* favored the Communist position in the Korean War.

The two obvious solutions were clear: either permit him to speak, or deny him the opportunity. Both of these solutions were suggested. Then one member of the Executive Committee came up with what proved to be a better solution. His solution was to permit the LYL representative to have a stated time limit in which to give the speech. But there were two other special conditions of this solution. First, the press would be notified in advance; and secondly, listeners would remain passive during the speech.

The speech was then given, and the Congress proceeded to other business. Everyone was pleased with the decision except the LYL speaker who had spoken to the sleepy, indifferent audience. The news representatives reported that the *Student Association Congress did not* endorse the LYL point of view. *Life* magazine devoted several pages to the event and included pictures of the unresponsive audience.

3. Elmore Jackson, author of *The Meeting of Minds,* says:

One of the difficulties in international disputes is that occasionally people think there is only one way of getting the problem solved. I remember at the 1948 Assembly in Paris the lift which came in the negotiations when one of the American negotiators went before one of the Committees of the Assembly and said, "There are five different approaches we can take to solving this particular problem." At that time it related to the Berlin dispute. Just the idea that there were five different ways of approaching this problem, any one of which might lead to some agreement, was quite a new idea to a good many people there.[8]

Children are often more creative than adults. For example, on one occasion a teacher met Johnny, the ten-year-old son of his neighbor, about three-thirty in the afternoon. When Johnny told the teacher he was en route home from school, the teacher said, "But this is not the way home from school!" The boy smilingly replied, "Oh, I know I don't usually go this way, but there are a hundred different ways to go home from school." Perhaps the number *hundred* is extreme, but the idea suggested here is a good one. The usual route that Johnny took to go home did not operate to make him "blind" to alternative routes.

The Influence of Authority

Authority, including expert opinion, has been mentioned in the previous chapter in connection with preparation for discussion. Knowledge of what others report is valuable as one of the factors

---

[8] Elmore Jackson, "The Mediation of Labor and International Disputes," *University of Chicago Round Table* (September 28, 1952), 9. Reprinted by permission.

related to effective decision-making. Usually, however, it is not the whole story. Acceptance of the opinion of an "authority" because of the authority himself, rather than because of the evidence or reasons upon which the opinion is based, may be foolhardy. Few persons would recommend that we should accept the opinions of others uncritically.

Authority and Your Decisions

You have looked to authority for guidance on many occasions. As a child, your ethical, social, and political codes were in large part determined for you by your parents, teachers, and the various agencies of communication, newspapers, magazines, books, radio, and television. These sources also affect you at present, although you are now more critical than you were as a child. Nevertheless, the influences we have named probably control your decisions to a greater degree than you recognize.

It would be foolish for you to reject the influence of authority in fields in which you have no knowledge. That is, it would be foolish if the authority is a good one. If the "expert" meets the tests of a good authority, given in Chapter 5, you may be wise to follow his advice. What we are pleading against is "blind allegiance to authority." There are clear dangers to limiting one's attention to the opinions of others. If you do this, you destroy your own ability to create, to discover, to be original. You become a slave to the judgments of others.

Illustrative Case Reports

1. In the following paragraph, Carlson argues that people tend to believe what they are told without examining the validity of the statements:

But the daily press, and the radio, touch more human lives, adult and children, more often and for a greater time than does our effort at education from the kindergarten to the university. What kind of education do we get through these agencies? Is it science? Is it integrity? Is it learning how to get at the facts and prove them? No! It is just the old drive of education by dictation that started 'way back in infancy and carried through the churches and through the grade school and the high school, and, I am sorry to say, frequently into the college. It is not a matter of understanding or mastery.[9]

2. Albert Speer, the Nazi War Production Minister, in his defense statements shows how completely the German people became *uncritical recipients of orders:*

Hitler's dictatorship differed in one fundamental point from all its predecessors in history. His was the first dictatorship in the present period of modern technical development, a dictatorship which made complete use of all technical means in a perfect manner for the domination of its nation. Through technical devices such as radio and loudspeaker eighty million people were deprived of independent thought. It was thereby possible to subject them to the will of one man. The telephone, teletype, and radio made it possible, for instance, for orders from the highest sources to be transmitted directly to the lowest ranking units, where, because of the high authority, they were carried out without criticism. . . .

* * *

Earlier dictators during their work of leadership needed highly qualified assistants, even at the lowest level, men who could think and act independently. The totalitarian system in the period of modern technical development can dispense with them; the means of communication alone make it possible to mechanize the subordinate leadership. As a result of this there arises a new type [of man]: the uncritical recipient of orders.

We had only reached the beginning of this new development. The nightmare of many a man that one day nations could be dominated by technical means was all but realized in Hitler's totalitarian system.[10]

3. A group of students were discussing a problem concerning federal taxation. One member, Mr. A, was advocating a position that differed from the ideas of two members of the group. Moreover, his views were quite convincing to a number of others. Finally A was asked, "Have you read the text used in Economics 136?" When A answered "No," his two opponents replied, "No wonder you are suggesting such a silly idea."

. . . Today our government uses the tax plan recommended by Mr. A. The *appeal to authority* by A's opponents was nothing more than a logical trick.

---

[9] A. J. Carlson, "The Social Responsibility of Scientists," *The Authoritarian Attempt to Capture Education,* p. 73. New York: Kings Crown Press, 1945. Reprinted by permission.

[10] Quoted from *International Military Tribunal: The Trial of the Major War Criminals, Proceedings,* Vol. XXII, pp. 405–406. Nuremberg: Allied Control Authority for Germany, 1948.

Comments: Briefly, then, you should consider authority when you study a problem, but you should not become an addict to its power. Avoid, especially, what Speer referred to when he said "eighty million people were deprived of independent thought."

THE INFLUENCE OF TRADITION

Tradition finds its expression in the acceptance that people give to usual courses of action, custom, or habit. Often it cannot be differentiated from the influence of authority, for traditions are built in part upon the power that various authorities exert. Usually, however, people are unaware of specific authorities when their behavior is guided by tradition. They know only that the belief they propose to act upon is a generally accepted way of doing things in the society of which they are a part.

Tradition and Your Decisions

Many times you follow a traditional point of view because you know that the tradition produced successful results in the past. Tradition, one could say, has a presumption in its favor in such cases. If the tradition had not been a good one, many disastrous results would have taken place. And since the traditional beliefs have proved their pragmatic value, why change? "Why," say some people, "shouldn't we make traditional choices instead of following something new and different?"

Traditions do have values. But what we are trying to say is that a tradition should have more to commend it than successful results in some earlier period. It must also bring about successful results *today.* Jefferson said, "As new discoveries are made, new truths disclosed, and manners and opinions change of circumstances, institutions must advance also, and keep pace with the time." Even if traditions have proved to be good in the past, you must still determine whether *present conditions* are largely the same as those at the time when the traditions had their beginnings. Unless you do this, you may be making serious errors in the decisions you make.

Illustrative Case Reports

As you read these case reports, keep these questions in mind:
(1) Was the traditional solution the best solution that could have
been made when the tradition first began? and (2) Does the evidence based upon present conditions point to the soundness of the
tradition today?

1. [Tradition: Isolation] In 1939 the newspaper columnist Raymond
Clapper was severely criticized because his writings no longer supported
the isolationist point of view in international affairs.   Clapper's answer
was: "Yes, I have switched.   I try to learn from events.   Events have
not been consistent, so why should I?"

2. [Tradition: Usual Type of Harbors] In this illustration Dwight
D. Eisenhower suggests that unusual situations are likely to call for
non-traditional solutions:

We knew that even after we captured Cherbourg its port capacity and
the lines of communication leading out of it could not meet all our needs.
To solve this apparently unsolvable problem we undertook a project so
unique as to be classed by many scoffers as completely fantastic.   It was a
plan to construct artificial harbors on the coast of Normandy.
The first time I heard this idea tentatively advanced was by Admiral
Mountbatten, in the spring of 1942.   At a conference attended by a
number of service chiefs he remarked, "If ports are not available, we may
have to construct them in pieces and tow them in."   Hoots and jeers
greeted his suggestion but two years later it was to become a reality.[11]

3. [Tradition: Earth-Centered Universe] When Galileo (1564–
1642) perfected his telescope which would magnify to the power of
thirty-two, he reported that he had discovered the satellites of Jupiter.
The ancients who thought that the world was earth-centered were
interested only in seven planets.   A Florentine astronomer argued for
the traditional view in this manner:

There are seven windows in the head, two nostrils, two eyes, two ears,
and a mouth; so in the heavens there are two favorable stars, two un-
propitious, two luminaries, and Mercury alone undecided and indifferent.
From which and many other similar phenomena of nature, such as the
seven metals, etc., which it were tedious to enumerate, we gather that the
number of planets is necessarily seven.

---

11 From *Crusade in Europe*, by Dwight D. Eisenhower, pp. 234–235.   Copyright 1948 by Doubleday and Company, Inc.   Reprinted by permission.

Moreover, the satellites are invisible to the naked eye, and therefore can have no influence on the earth, and therefore would be useless, and therefore do not exist.

Besides, the Jews and other ancient nations as well as modern Europeans have adopted the divisions of the week into seven days, and have named them from the seven planets: now if we increase the number of planets this whole system falls to the ground.[12]

Comments: Perhaps we should say that change just for the sake of change is not the correct antidote to use in combating traditional types of decisions. Departures from tradition often meet with failure. All we can say is that in discussions, and elsewhere, you should try to improve upon traditional answers to problems. But these non-traditional answers must be examined carefully; they should not be approved unless evidence substantiates their acceptance.

THE INFLUENCE OF EMOTION

Emotions and Your Decisions

The emotions that ideas evoke (whether love, hate, fear, and so forth) may cause you to approve decisions without examining the facts involved in the situation. These decisions are said to show personal bias or prejudice. If the evidence about the problem is considered at all, it is usually slanted in favor of the position you wish to uphold. This is much like deciding which of two football teams should win a game before the game is played. Since you have decided upon the outcome of the game, the conclusion that can be drawn is that the game does not have to be played. Persons whose judgment is warped by strong emotion act in this way. They do not test decisions fairly.

Emotions do play a part in our thinking, and they can often be helpful. You should, however, learn to recognize your special wishes, desires, and attitudes. If you are aware of your tendency

---

[12] Sir Oliver G. Lodge, *Pioneers of Science,* p. 106. London: Macmillan & Company, Ltd., 1919. Reprinted by permission.

toward bias in a given case, you can check your decisions by insisting upon a careful and honest study of the facts. In this way you can avoid faulty judgments that emotionalism leads you to accept.

Unless you check your biases, you are likely to have an imperfect understanding of the problems you face. Your picture, or "structure" as Wertheimer says, of a particular problem will be false. You are then a victim of self-deception. You may even become an obsessive thinker whose vision is wholly controlled by his desires if your emotions are especially strong. In this way emotions can act as a "blinder," denying you the chance to know reality. All you know is your ego-centered picture of the problem. And this, as we have said, is often a false picture.

Illustrative Case Reports

In these reports problems are incorrectly understood because of the blinding effect of self-interest and related desires:

1. Let us suppose that two men are arguing about a proposal for increased taxation of incomes of more than $10,000. One of them is in favor of the new tax. He argues the case in its favor entirely on general grounds, with logical arguments as to its general economic effects. His opponent argues hotly against it with equally general arguments. Neither of them argues the question from any consideration of how the proposal would affect him personally, and both would indignantly repudiate the suggestion that the effect of the tax on themselves plays any part in determining their opinions about it. Yet, as onlookers, we are not surprised to learn that the man arguing for the tax has a smaller, while the man arguing against it has a larger income than $10,000. Nor are we likely to be wrong in guessing that these facts are much more important influences in determining the opinions of the two men than any of the logical arguments they bring forward so impressively.[13]

2. In my country [Belgium] I made an investigation about the emotional attitudes of high-school boys toward the Dutch people. I found that a lot of these boys manifested feelings of contempt and hostility toward our neighbors. Continuing this investigation, I was surprised to find that several boys mainly gave historical reasons to motivate their hostile feelings. It was because a hundred years ago the neighboring people tried to dominate

---

[13] Robert H. Thouless, *Straight and Crooked Thinking*, pp. 204–205. New York: Simon and Schuster, 1932. Reprinted by permission.

our country that the boys did not like them. On this basis all kinds of unfriendly traits of character were attributed to the Dutch people.

I talked about this question with the teachers and found that the course in history given to the boys ended with a vivid description of the revolution of our people against the Dutch a hundred years ago; but nothing was taught about the friendly relationships between the two peoples in the more recent years.[14]

The Influence of Personal Experience

Personal Experience and Your Decisions

Groups of college and adult business students were asked to rate the relative importance of a number of factors that are commonly said to be of value in problem-solving discussions. They were told to use this rating scale in recording their judgments about eleven factors:

1	2	3	4	5
Very Unimportant	Unimportant	Sometimes Unimportant; Sometimes Important	Important	Very Important

The highest ratings were given for factors closely identified with the problem, perception of the problem, facts, and goals sought.

Rating	Factor
4.9	Selecting the correct problem to solve
4.7	Stating the problem in a clear and unprejudiced form
4.8	Perceiving the problem objectively rather than in a strong self-centered manner
4.8	Knowing basic facts regarding the problem
4.8	Knowing goals or criteria by which to judge solutions

Other ratings were:

3.5	*Previous experience*
3.5	Willingness to break from routine

---

[14] Joseph Nuttin, "Emotions and World Problems," *University of Chicago Round Table* (October 31, 1948), 4. Reprinted by permission.

3.4   Knowing what experts (authorities) say
3.0   Persistence
2.2   Tradition
2.0   Intuition

The score of 3.5 suggests that personal experience is moderately important as an aid in problem-solving situations. Apparently, however, it is not a highly reliable guide.

One weakness of personal experience stems from incomplete and unreliable observation. You might think your experience covers a total situation, but in many cases it is selective and partial experience, and even what you actually observe has its limitations. Bacon, for instance, in speaking of *Idols of the Tribe*, mentioned the fact that "false mirrors distort observation." By this he meant that there is a tendency, often an unconscious one, that prompts people to make their reports of experiences bolster their preconceptions. When this occurs your inferences that are presumably rooted in first-hand observation become synonymous with your personal desires. You see what you want to see.

A second weakness of the influence of previous experience is that it may lead to purely mechanical responses when new situations are faced. You might reason that if item A is associated with item B in one situation, it will be associated in others. Many times this will be true, but the point is that it is not always true. You must not permit personal experience to condition your responses without regard for the complexities of the new problem you are trying to solve. The practice of associating previous successful answers to problems with new situations works only in cases when the new problem is the same as the old. When problems are different and you persist in making stereotyped decisions, you obviously will be making inferior decisions.

Illustrative Case Reports

The first case report we are giving shows that Hitler permitted personal experience to bolster his preconceptions. The second case is designed to illustrate how Kettering sought new discoveries instead of associating previous answers to problems with new situations.

1. Hitler's selective and unfair use of experience derived from books, magazines, and movies is the antithesis of the rules of good observation and interpretation. In the case that follows we find that the low value Hitler ascribes to the American soldier is conditioned by his delight in recalling the movie *Grapes of Wrath* which he is said to have seen several times.

The excerpt we are presenting is from one of Hitler's military conferences held on March 5, 1943. At this time the North African campaign was in a state of flux, but the German forces under Rommel were still in excellent positions.

The conversation opens with a statement by General Hewel in apparent reference to a failure in an engagement by the American II Corps. Hitler shows that he mechanically associates the American soldier with weakness and incompetence. His conferees reflect subserviency; Hewel, in fact, shifts his position from praise to that of disparagement for American soldiers. Note the interesting words:

Hewel: But the Americans do have good human material somewhere.
Jodl: Only superficially.
Hitler: Not as much as we have been told. It is concentrated in a few areas which are known to Europeans. . . . The farmers are terribly run down. I have seen photographs. You can't imagine anything as miserable and degenerate as farmers; a completely uprooted mob, wandering all over the place.
Christian: They have no spirit, no inner pride.
Jodl: They have nothing like that.
Hewel: Just look at their war posters. They are completely impossible.
Hitler: There is no doubt that of the Anglo-Saxons, the English are the best.[15]

2. The discoveries of the inventor-scientist Charles F. Kettering illustrate a type of problem-solving that goes beyond routine association based upon experience. His discovery of a new painting process for automobiles, for instance, was a departure from stimulus-response thinking that is geared to the acceptance of old ways of doing things.

In the earlier days of the automobile industry newly painted cars had to be stored for several days while the paint dried. People who based their direction in thinking upon experience apparently believed that whenever more cars were produced, more drying buildings would

---

[15] Felix Gilbert (ed.), *Hitler Directs His War*, p. 24. New York: Oxford University Press, 1950. Reprinted by permission.

need to be leased or built. But Kettering didn't think in this way. He discovered a new type of paint, a quick-drying lacquer that would harden in a few hours. Without the improved process, mass production of cars as we know it today would have been impossible.

This example shows that "bigger and better paint drying sheds" is an inferior decision to that given by Kettering, but merely following experience, accepting previous successful answers to the problem, would make it impossible for a person to come up with the Kettering solution.

The Influence of Reflective Thinking

Many persons believe that patterns of thinking such as those we have described control most of the decisions you and I make. George C. Lewis says that "we fear singularity more than error" and therefore we are influenced greatly by tradition, authority and the voice of the multitude.[16]   A. J. Carlson argues that the average man cannot protect himself from "plain and artistic lying" because he does not understand the scientific method.[17]   Rationalization, desire, and prejudice victimize most of us repeatedly according to the reports of James Harvey Robinson.[18]   Erich Fromm speaks of *modern man* in much the same light as Lewis, Carlson, and Robinson: "He conforms to anonymous authorities and adopts a self which is not his. The more he does this, the more powerless he feels, the more he is forced to conform. In spite of a veneer of optimism and initiative, modern man is overcome by a profound feeling of powerlessness which makes him gaze toward approaching catastrophes as though he were paralyzed." [19]

These conclusions by Carlson and others give us a dim picture of the popularity of reflective thinking. But the situation is prob-

---

[16] George C. Lewis, *The Influence of Authority in Matters of Opinion*, p. 10. London: Longmans, Green and Company, 1875.

[17] A. J. Carlson, "The Social Responsibilities of Scientists," *The Authoritarian Attempt to Capture Education*, p. 70. New York: King's Crown Press, 1945.

[18] James Harvey Robinson, *The Mind in the Making*, pp. 40–91. New York: Harper and Brothers, 1921.

[19] Erich Fromm, *Escape from Freedom*, pp. 255–256. New York: Farrar and Rinehart, Inc., 1941. Reprinted by permission.

ably not as hopeless as these writers seem to imply. We have already given a number of case reports in this chapter that illustrate "a critical open-minded attitude" on the part of problem-solvers. The case of Yukawa and his meson theory is one example. Other case reports that illustrate reflective deliberation, or some phase of reflection, are the National Student Association Congress case, the Elmore Jackson case, the Raymond Clapper case, the Artificial Harbor case, and the Kettering case. In each of these situations problems were solved in a way that is distinguished from intuition, initial choice, authority, tradition, emotion, and personal experience as described in this chapter. In other words, reflective thinking is not just a word. It is a method that is used efficiently in many situations.

Perhaps you have wondered exactly how all that we have said in this chapter can be applied in a discussion. We think that much that we have reported should prove to be very helpful. If we have done nothing else, we have in this chapter emphasized case studies that illustrate good and bad patterns in problem-solving. Details of application of reflective thinking to the discussion process will be outlined in the next chapter.

7. The Reflective Pattern in Discussion

The tendency to begin discussions by making decisions is quite popular. You would be unusual if you had escaped this practice of "thinking in reverse" in your experiences as a member of discussion groups. But reflective thinking, as you will recall from our earlier chapters, differs from this short-cut approach. It demands that you give your attention to five sequential steps in thinking. In other words, reflection is a more orderly process than the chance tactics followed in many problem-solving discussions. And further, it is a more logical process. Making a decision before identifying the problem and knowing the facts would be like buying a car without knowing whether you needed the car, or whether you could pay for it. The validity of your thinking in this case would certainly be questionable.

STEP ONE: RECOGNITION OF THE PROBLEM

Formulation of the Problem As a Question

As a rule, your discussion group should select and phrase the problem to be discussed several days before the date of your discussion. You should be able to do this in a short pre-conference meeting. Your problem, as we have said in Chapter 3, should be stated as a question, and it should conform to the criteria for phrasing problems for discussion.

The fact that your group has agreed upon a problem statement should not unalterably commit the group to this statement of the problem. In one discussion, for example, the group had previously agreed upon one problem statement, but at the time of the discussion they decided to change the statement. The first problem was, "What Is the Meaning of Propaganda?" The new statement that the group decided to accept was, "What Can We Do to Avoid Being Influenced by Propaganda?" The group liked this statement better; it posed the question that the members really wanted to answer. The discussion that followed was successful largely because the members felt they were tackling a challenging problem.

This example suggests that groups should try to pose the "right" question at pre-conference meetings. It implies, further, that a completely new problem should not be substituted at the time of the discussion, because participants will usually lack the information needed for a profitable discussion. Many times, however, changes in the phrasing of problems are important, and should be made. With the approval of the group, these changes may be introduced at any stage in the discussion.

Definition of the Problem

"People do not readily begin discussions," says Plato in the *Gorgias*, "by defining to each other what it is they are undertaking to discuss, and so cannot, after mutually learning and instructing, bring their conversation to an end." This point is well taken; everyone has had such experiences. The remedy here lies in getting agreement upon the meaning of the problem statement early in the discussion.

1. *Purposes of definition.* Basically, definitions should dispel differing private interpretations of what the problem means.

(a) *You should clarify vague and ambiguous words.* The meanings of some words differ both in denotation and connotation depending upon our education, experiences, and preferences, and upon the context in which they are used. A word is vague, for example, when it fails to reflect exactness. Thus, Max Black says "classes in speech" is vague because we do not know at what point a class becomes one in *speech* rather than in something else.[1] Similarly, the words *democracy, freedom, liberal,* and *socialism* are vague.   And any time you use the words *good, better,* or *desirable,* you must define them in order that others may know the standards you are using when you judge something to be good, or better, or desirable.

Ambiguity, on the other hand, means that a listener or reader may find it difficult to choose between alternative meanings of a word.   The speaker who said "the *Gettysburg Address* was a powerful piece of *propaganda*" was using the word *propaganda* in a non-moral sense.   But his audience elected to understand the word as something reprehensible and associated with evil practices.   The two interpretations were very different, yet the way in which the speaker used the word did not indicate which of the alternative definitions was correct.   In this case the audience followed the common connotation of the word, rather than the objective denotation that the speaker had in mind.

(b) *You should clarify unfamiliar words.*   Specialized vocabulary used by certain professions and groups is usually fully understood only by the people in these fields.   You should explain technical words whenever they are used in problem statements.

(c) *You should indicate the exact scope of the problem.*   Your definitions should make clear what is to be *included* and what is to be *excluded* in the discussion.   Suppose that you are to discuss a problem that concerns *general education, intercollegiate athletics,* or possibly *selective service.*   In each of these cases you should name the phases of education, athletics, or selective service that you intend to consider in the discussion.

(d) *You should depict the problem objectively.*   Selfish points of view are usually weakened by calm, straight-forward explanation of what the problem means.   The words "we" and "our" in problem statements, for instance, will be more likely to be understood from a group-centered point of view if participants pay attention to honest definition.   The time you spend on definition may

---

[1] Max Black, *Critical Thinking,* p. 169.   New York: Prentice-Hall, Inc., 1946.

therefore be very valuable, and, perhaps, indispensable to the success of your discussion.

2. *Types of definition.*   If you define *prejudice* by saying that it is "opinion formed without objective study and evaluation," your statement is a *logical definition.*   What you have said identifies *classification* (opinion) and *differentiation* (without objective study and evaluation).   In other words, logical definition places a word in a general class (*genus*), and then differentiates the word from other members of the class (*species*).

But important details often remain unknown when you use logical definitions.   You still need to know essential characteristics, elements, or qualities of the word *prejudice* as we have defined it. The *analytical definition* provides this information by naming the kinds of non-objective thinking that cause pre-judgments—authority, tradition, self-interest, and emotions of one kind or another.

When you show how a word developed and came to take its present meaning, your explanation can be called an *historical definition.*   Many times you will mention the derivation of the word, but it is probably more important for you to show the changes the word underwent as it developed its present meaning.   Even the term *federal taxation* has a different meaning today from its earlier meaning in our history.   These differences include changes in the purposes of taxation as well as in the kinds of federal taxation. Many times a definition of this type adds to the knowledge of individual participants and serves to broaden points of view more effectively than either a logical or analytical definition.

3. *Specific methods of definition.*   Common methods used in definition include the use of *examples, illustrations, analogies, contrasts,* and *testimony.*   The method you use is less important than the purposes you accomplish.   Your goal, as we have said, is to eliminate varied personal interpretations of what the problem means.

STEP TWO: DESCRIPTION OF THE PROBLEM

After you have agreed upon the statement and the definition of the problem, your next step is to present facts about the subject you are discussing.   Here you must try to avoid having opinions take priority over factual information.   Remember the question: "What are the facts?"   It will help you in any problem-solving situation.

History of the Problem

Reports about the history of a problem (as distinguished from present and predicted effects and causes) are important in some cases and unimportant in others.   Problems that call for quick action do not permit time for a consideration of historical background.   Problems that are new, or that have no extensive history (that is not already known by the conferees), do not require the reporting of past successes and failures.

In discussions where learning is especially stressed, some time should be spent in reporting the history of the problem.   A discussion on socialism would not be complete unless the ideas of Karl Marx were mentioned.   Similarly, a discussion dealing with work simplification would demand that you spend time in describing how your company and other companies have attacked this problem in previous years.   After doing this, you may logically proceed to present events relating to socialism, or to work simplification.

You will have to decide whether information about the history of the problem should be given a special position in the discussion.   With some problems the "historical" may be presented whenever it seems to be especially appropriate.   It may well be considered when you mention solutions, or when you evaluate solutions.   At other times, depending upon your problem, your historical information should be given when you begin Step Two in the reflective thinking pattern.

Effects of the Problem

You become aware of the existence of a problem because of certain known effects (*evidences, signs, symptoms*), or because of the probablity that undesirable effects will occur in the future. You should pose two questions, (1) "What effects show that a problem exists?" and (2) "How serious are the effects?" These questions concern present conditions or effects that have been observed by some person. Most effects reported in discussions are of this type although there are some occasions when you must name predicted effects.

1. *Reporting observed effects.* Specific instances, illustrations, and statistical data represent the usual ways in which you should report effects in a discussion.

(a) *Use specific instances.* Suppose that you were asked to give examples of the harmful effects that have resulted when political pressures were brought to bear upon colleges. You might do what Laird Bell did in a *University of Chicago Round Table* discussion when this subject was discussed. In this excerpt, he cites three specific instances:

> We see examples from time to time—witness Huey Long in the University of Louisiana. One of the most distressing things about Germany was the abject surrender of the German universities to the Nazis. We then heard of a Nazi scientist, and a Nazi truth, just as we hear now of a Soviet scientist and a Soviet truth. We hear of a scientist who recants from the beliefs he has developed in a lifetime in favor of the party line—and, if you please, on genetics.[2]

Specific instances are important in a discussion primarily because they make the problem more understandable. Secondly, they are usually interesting. And, third, as one type of factual data, specific instances represent a valid form of evidence if they are typical cases.

---

[2] Laird Bell, "What Should Society Expect from a University?" *University of Chicago Round Table* (March 20, 1949), 11. This quotation and others in this chapter from the *University of Chicago Round Table* are reprinted by permission.

(b) *Use illustrations.* If you describe a specific instance in considerable detail, it can be labeled an illustration. Thouless does this in the following case to show that emotional language may be dangerous to society:

We can take an example of a speech, a very good speech, made by one of the leaders during the last war. It ran like this: "Hitler and his Nazi gang have sown the wind; let them reap the whirlwind. Neither the length of the struggle nor any form of severity which it may assume will make us weary or will make us quit. These gangs of bandits have sought to darken the light of the world, have sought to stand between the common people of all the lands in their march forward in their inheritance."

That is what I mean by the emotional use of language. It does not convey any information; it just calls up strong feelings. And I have no quarrel with its use there; it happened during a war. If you have wars at all, you have to stir up people's feelings; and the use of emotional language is a way to do it. Such language makes men efficient soldiers, but it does not make them think sensibly. The real danger is going on using such language in peacetime to stir up hostile feelings against other nations.[3]

(c) *Use statistics.* Information regarding statistics and other types of evidence has already been mentioned in Chapter 5 when we described how you should prepare for discussions. A few points about statistics should nevertheless be mentioned here. The first of these is that while statistical reporting may not be as interesting as specific instances and illustrations, it is usually a more reliable method. And secondly, participants in discussions are prone to overlook the importance of statistics. One reason for this tendency is that it takes considerable effort to discover information that can be reported in numbers, degrees, or percentages.

The completeness represented in statistical reporting makes this method a requirement in virtually any discussion. In the following case, statistics should certainly not be neglected in describing the effects that reveal political apathy:

---

[3] Robert H. Thouless, "Emotions and World Problems," *University of Chicago Round Table* (October 31, 1948), 3.

Mr. Hicks: Wait a minute. How serious is this problem? What proportion of the potential voters are truants? How does it compare in this country with other democracies?

Mr. Finer: Roughly in this country something like 50 per cent of the eligible people vote at presidential elections. It has sometimes been as high as 76 per cent; that is the highest. And I think that it was in 1940. In congressional elections we have to reckon that some 90 per cent of the vote for the presidential election—not 90 per cent of the people but of the presidential voters—come out to vote. That compares with a steady vote of always over 70 per cent in the Western democracies—sometimes up to 75, and recently it was as much as over 80 per cent.[4]

The effects of the problem under discussion can be reported in ways that we have not mentioned in this chapter. The use of analogies and expert testimony have not been mentioned. But these forms of evidence and the inferences to be drawn from them are described in both Chapters 5 and 8 of this book. In this connection you should remember that analogies and expert testimony should be rooted in observation, specific instances, illustrations, and statistics, and therefore are simply vehicles for reporting the three kinds of observed effects we have mentioned.

2. *Reporting predicted effects.* Whenever you decide upon plans for tomorrow, next week, or next year, you must be able to identify future circumstances (causes) and the probable effects resulting from these circumstances. When you ask, "What products should Company X advertise during the month of March?" you must deal with predicted effects. Similarly, when you ask, "How can we control inflation, or deflation?" or "What is a good wartime tax program?" you must be prepared to name likely effects of future sets of conditions.

Causes of the Problem

You will find that it is difficult to distinguish causes and effects in some problem-solving cases. At times you will probably feel that you are going around in circles, because an *effect* in a chain of re-

---

[4] Granville Hicks and Herman Finer, "Political Apathy in America," *University of Chicago Round Table* (October 29, 1950), 6

actions may become a *cause* of still other effects.   Or, perhaps, causes and effects are so intermingled that you cannot readily isolate them.   This is true in the statement, "Today, out of General Electric's 226,000 employees, one in twenty is an engineer.   The new products you see are both the cause and effect of this engineering force."[5]   You can see that the double-edged way in which causation operates here is something of a logical puzzle.

But the difficulties you experience in reporting causes must not lead you to disregard them.   You must in fact redouble your efforts. If you expect to have control over future events, and you do when you have a discussion, you should know the factors that bring about the undesirable results you want to correct.

Suppose that you wanted to stimulate greater campus interest in student government activities carried on by the *student legislature*. After identifying effects (indifference by most students), you might logically search for causes of the indifference.   Perhaps the student legislature has little authority, perhaps its decisions do not vitally affect students, or possibly it fails to publicize the work that it carries out.   Before you prescribe remedies, you should know these causes for lack of interest in student government.   When you do, you can decide upon solutions that are designed to alter or remove the causes of your problem.

1. *Find the necessary causes or conditions.*   Sometimes you can discover the factor or set of circumstances that must be present in order to produce a certain result.   Thus, when you say that a minimum red corpuscle count in the blood stream is a requirement for good health, you have named a *necessary condition*.   There may be, and usually are, other necessary conditions for effects, either good or bad.   And the more necessary conditions that you know, the more likely you are to understand how to change unwanted effects.   It is perhaps true that in discussions you do not often think about causes as "necessary," but you may accomplish a somewhat similar result when you decide upon the *importance* of various causes of the problem.

---

[5] *Saturday Review*, XXXVI (June 13, 1953), 8.

2. *Find the probable cause.* Most factors that we call causes are probable rather than certain or necessary. They are true causes only under certain conditions, or we may add, "other things being equal." The four causes which follow are of this type: (a) The quality of instruction in our schools will be improved if schools are granted greater appropriations. (b) Credit restrictions will operate to decrease installment purchases. (c) Free competition in business results in lower prices. (d) Advertising programs will increase sales of products. These alleged causes (school appropriations, credit restrictions, free competition, and advertising) are generally said to be true only if they are not offset by other causes. It can be seen that the causes will not invariably produce the effects we have indicated. Circumstances like *poor teachers, increases in wages, war spending,* and *inferior products* can make our alleged causes quite meaningless. This must not deter us from finding causes, but it does suggest that we cannot place full reliance upon a single conditional factor.

3. *Find multiple causes.* Many of the problems we discuss in conferences are similar to the example we have given about the lack of interest in the work of the *student legislature.* You will recall that we suggested several contributing causes for the problem. This is also the case in a University of Chicago Round Table discussion on the question of "How Can We Get Better Law Enforcement?" The causes identified in the discussion included (a) public apathy, (b) insufficient funds for law enforcement agencies, (c) corruption of law enforcement personnel, (d) lack of clearly defined jurisdiction for enforcement agencies, and (e) lack of cooperation among enforcement agencies.[6] Here you see that the law enforcement problem is caused by many factors, and what is more, these factors vary from community to community. Statistical correlations will help to determine the relative importance of these causes, but it seems clear that a single solution will not adequately correct the situation. Thus, in this case, and in many class prob-

---

[6] See Rudolph Halley, Donald Leonard, E. W. Puttkammer, and O. W. Wilson, "How Can We Get Better Law Enforcement?" *University of Chicago Round Table* (March 11, 1951).

lems as well, identification of multiple causes is necessary if you expect to discover solutions that will work.

STEP THREE: DISCOVERY OF POSSIBLE SOLUTIONS

Conditions to Be Met by an Acceptable Solution

In the day-to-day decisions you make, the goals you expect to achieve have a bearing upon your choices. For instance, when you buy a particular pair of shoes, a dress, a car, or when you select a vacation site or elect to attend college, you should know the type of results you desire. You should at least decide upon the conditions that must be met by an acceptable solution. What are some possible conditions you might have in mind? *Economy, beauty,* and *serviceability* are possible conditions that you might want to satisfy when you make purchases. In the same way, you ought to know the standards by which to judge possible choices regarding your vacation, and your decision about college.

This case problem will further clarify what we mean:

Two boys were playing badminton in the garden. I could hear as well as see them from my window, although they did not see me. One boy was twelve, the other ten years old. They played several sets. The younger was by far poorer, he was being beaten in all the games.

I heard some of their conversation. The loser—let us call him B— became more and more unhappy. He had no chance. A often served him so cleverly that he could not possibly return the bird. The situation grew worse. Finally B threw down his racket, sat on a tree trunk, and said, "I won't play any more." A tried to persuade him to continue. No answer from B. A sat down beside him. Both looked unhappy.[7]

Now before you solve this problem, you should ask yourself the specific conditions of a wise decision. The condition chosen by the two boys was this: the game should be played in such a way

---

[7] Max Wertheimer, *Productive Thinking*, p. 127. New York: Harper and Brothers, 1945. Reprinted by permission.

that *both boys have a chance to excel.* You might of course select a different condition, but the one we have given seems to be reasonable.

Wertheimer, who observed this conflict between A and B, reports that after some discussion A's face lit up, and he said, "I have an idea—let us now play this way: let us see how long we can keep the bird going between us and count how many times it goes back and forth without falling. What score could we make? Do you think we could make it ten or twenty?" This solution was happily accepted by B, and the game was resumed. The arrangement permitted both A and B to excel, and was therefore attractive to both boys.

All that we have said here applies to problem-solving discussions. You should determine conditions of an acceptable solution, decide whether these conditions are realistic ones, and then list possible solutions for your problem.

Possible Solutions

1. *You should identify all possible solutions.* Instead of keeping your attention centered on only one or two solutions, you should try to think of many ways in which the problem might be solved. Keep a record of the possible solutions that occur to you as well as those suggested by other members of your group. As a rule you should complete the task of listing possible solutions before you begin to compare and evaluate solutions. Only in this way can you avoid the "blinding" effect created by the one-solution or two-solution approach in thinking.

2. *You should keep three types of solutions in mind.* Either a single solution, a combined solution, or a multiple solution may be suggested.

(a) *Suggest a single solution.* By a single solution we mean answers like "yes," "no," "correct," "incorrect," or a one-unit policy suggestion. Thus, when you travel from Detroit to Chicago, you might prefer to choose a specific type of transportation such as car, railway, or airplane. This type of single solution is often called for in discussions.

(b) *Suggest a combined solution.* The solution you offer may combine features of two or more single solutions.

Consider this illustration: A group of students was faced with the problem of deciding how the index for a university yearbook should be prepared. In the previous yearbook there were a large number of inaccuracies in page references as well as in the spelling of the twenty-five thousand names listed. The problem was therefore felt to be an important one. Two solutions were suggested: (1) The indexing system should be planned and executed by one person; and (2) the indexing system should be planned by one person, but because of the necessity of speed in completing the work, a group of students should carry out the project. The final decision agreed upon was one that *combined features of both of these solutions.* A student involved in this decision-making discussion described the combined solution by saying, "We decided that I should plan the system of indexing and use it myself for a limited period of time. Then I could pick out the flaws in the method I was using and correct them. After doing this, I could turn the job over to the staff and let them proceed." This solution proved to be satisfactory. "The indexing," we are told, "was completed in record time and with virtually no errors." [8]

(c) *Suggest a multiple solution.* If a problem has been caused by a number of distinct and separate factors, your solution may have to contain several parts. For example, a group discussing "improvement of the University Health Service" will probably suggest several solutions or ways to correct diverse causes. In fact, it is not unusual for solutions to contain a six-point, or even a nine-point, plan by which the problem should be attacked.

---

[8] Reported by Pauline Kurtz, Class of 1953, College of Literature, Science, and the Arts, University of Michigan.

STEP FOUR: EVALUATION OF POSSIBLE SOLUTIONS AND ACCEPTANCE OF BEST SOLUTION

Evaluation of Possible Solutions

A most important feature of reflective thinking is the habit of reserving judgment until all possible solutions are listed and understood. Each possibility should be carefully analyzed and mentally tested before you make your final choice. Many questions may properly be asked in the course of your examination of solutions. Among these are four questions that are probably fundamental.

1. Does the solution eliminate or modify in a substantial way the causes of the problem?
2. Does the solution eliminate or minimize the undesirable effects created by the problem?
3. Does the solution conform to the conditions to be met by an acceptable solution?
4. Does the solution show promise of creating other desirable rather than undesirable consequences?

If you can answer "yes" to the questions listed, it is probable that your solution is a good one. You cannot achieve certainty unless you have tested the solution in actual operation. Experimental verification prior to endorsement of a decision is clearly helpful and should be encouraged. In cases where this is not possible, you will need to depend upon mental experimentation (reasoning). What seems to be necessary is a high degree of predictive skill in answering questions that force you to anticipate consequences.

Acceptance of Best Solution

Acceptance of a solution means that at the *present time*, under *present* or *anticipated* conditions, a particular solution appears to be preferable to others. This implies that your solution is *tentative* rather than *fixed and final for all time*. The "best solution" is simply the one that meets the needs created by the problem more satisfactorily than any of the alternative solutions. It also means that there may be alternative solutions that are quite desirable, but that they are somewhat less acceptable than the choice you are making.

STEP FIVE: PLAN OF ACTION

Methods of Execution

Many groups that decide policy fail to give adequate attention to the action phase in decision-making. In the first place, the methods to be followed in carrying out a solution should be considered because often you do not know the weaknesses of a policy until you determine methods of executing the policy. You may discover that what appeared to be a good decision is incapable of being put into operation. If this proves to be true, the solution should be abandoned in favor of one that is possible of attainment. A second reason for identifying methods and procedures for implementing a decision is that unless you do so you may become content with "just talking" about solutions. This could be sufficient in some cases where learning and attitudes are concerned, but it does not suffice with most problems of policy. You should therefore identify the procedures, resources, and agencies at your command for placing the solution into operation.

Action Group to Put Solution into Effect

Responsibility for the details of a plan of action may be assigned to an individual or to a sub-committee appointed by your decision-making group. The members of your group might outline the general features of the plan of action, and they might also be called upon to appraise the action program of the sub-committee. It is presumptuous, and at times definitely unwise, for your group to design all of the details of a program for persons who must carry out your policy. Very often the persons who execute decisions are better qualified to devise a plan of action than are members of a policy-making group. Furthermore, motivation to carry out policies is sometimes contingent upon participation in the planning stages by those who put the policy into operation.   Those who are closest to the actual carrying out of a decision usually do their task with greater interest and efficiency if they are free to decide some actions for themselves.

8. Reasoning and Fallacies

Just as it is important for a discussion group to have sound evidence as the basis for its discussion, so it is equally important for a group to be able to draw valid inferences from its evidence. This process of drawing inferences we usually call reasoning; and errors in this inferential process, either intentional or unintentional, we call fallacies. Although we have already considered some aspects of reasoning processes, we are going to examine them systematically in this chapter.

PLACE OF REASONING IN DISCUSSION

Discussion, like other orderly, communicative, problem-solving activities, relies heavily on clear, valid reasoning. By and large, discussion members who know something about the rules of reasoning and the tests to be applied to reasoning, perform better than those who do not. As Walter points out, "recent experiments show that the person who has been taught the 'rules of reason' tends to be able to do a better job of critical thinking than those who have not." [1] Since discussion is an activity that depends on careful, critical thinking, it is important that discussion participants know something about these "rules of reason." Therefore, we will indicate in the following pages at least five justifications for dealing with reasoning at this point, five benefits that will accrue to a dis-

---

[1] Otis Monroe Walter, Jr., "Descartes on Reasoning," *Speech Monographs*, XIII (March, 1951), 51–52.

cussion group whose members know something about and apply the "rules of reason."

Good Reasoning Processes Make Material More Intelligible

Sometimes evidence alone is not enough. A set of statistics standing by itself, without any conclusions being drawn from it, is likely to have little meaning. To give meaning to evidence, it is usually necessary to draw conclusions from the evidence at hand. To make material intelligible, we need reasoning.

Good Reasoning Processes Make Material More Acceptable

We must always be concerned not only with making material understandable to others, but also with making it acceptable to others. The use of familiar reasoning patterns, the drawing of inferences or conclusions similar to those drawn by others who have thought through a problem carefully, the employment of careful thinking about evidence, all of these tend to make our evidence more acceptable to other members of our group.

Knowledge of Good Reasoning Processes Makes Better Listeners

By better listeners, we mean listeners that are critical and evaluative in their listening. If you, as a member of a discussion group know about the rules of reasoning, about tests to be applied to reasoning processes, about the detection of fallacies, then you are apt to be a critical listener. You are much less likely to take things at their "face value." Consequently, it is important for you to know about reasoning not only as a *contributor* to a discussion group, but as a *listener*.

Good Reasoning Hastens the Process of Reaching Group Decisions

Poor and fallacious reasoning can become like a detour on a highway. It takes you from the main thoroughfare, is sometimes uncomfortable, and certainly slows down your progress toward your ultimate goal. Group decisions can be reached much more quickly if the members of the group employ good reasoning processes.

Good Reasoning Enables the Group to Reach Better Decisions

In general better understanding will exist among the members of a group if the participants rely on good, clear thinking. This is true because material is made more understandable, and acceptable. The manner in which evidence is considered and used may well build a foundation to a super-structure of decisions. If the foundation is well put together, the super-structure will certainly be more stable, and the whole construction will probably be well built. Our chances of reaching good, high-quality decisions in a discussion are improved when the quality of the reasoning in the discussion is good.

It is not our purpose here to give a complete and thorough text on reasoning, but rather to cover the essentials of the types of reasoning most frequently encountered in discussion groups and most useful for efficient participation in them. What follows is a brief consideration of several common types of reasoning, of ways of testing these types of reasoning, and of some of the common fallacies that occur in discussion groups.

TYPES OF REASONING

First, let us examine the types of reasoning most commonly found in group discussion situations.

Generalization

A great deal of our conclusion-drawing is done through the process of generalization. This is often called induction or inductive reasoning. Briefly, this type of reasoning consists of drawing conclusions based on many specific instances. It is, in essence, the type of process public opinion pollsters use. By sampling opinions of a relatively small and carefully selected group of people, they are able to generalize, to make statements about opinions held by the American people in general. All of us use this type of reasoning so constantly that we are seldom aware of the process itself. We form conclusions about all kinds of things from politics to fraternity life on the basis of our observation of particular instances. In any discussion group we will find many examples of this kind of reasoning. Let us suppose, for example, that a group is discussing the topic, "Is political freedom possible under communism?" We might very well use inductive reasoning in a pattern something like this:

> Czechoslovakia, under communism, has no political freedom.
> Poland, under communism, has no political freedom.
> Rumania, under communism, has no political freedom.
> *Therefore*: Countries, under communism, have no political freedom.

Our example is formalized somewhat to make clear how this kind of reasoning operates. We can see from this that a series of individual cases are cited, all having common elements, and a general conclusion is drawn from the statements.

Tests for inductive reasoning. If nothing else, the experience of public opinion pollsters has shown us that inductive reasoning can sometimes go astray. Hence, it is important to be able to test the process of generalization. What are some of the questions we should apply to inductive reasoning?

1. *Is there a sufficient number of instances to justify the conclusion?* If we generalize from only one or two instances of a potential several hundred or several thousand, our reasoning is apt to go wrong. We might very well find ourselves guilty of "hasty generalization," or "jumping to a conclusion." Obviously, the greater the number of cases used in forming the generalization, the more reliable the conclusion would be.

2. *Are the instances typical?* Not only must there be a large enough group of specific cases, but the cases should be typical ones, if the conclusion is to be valid. For example, if the only dog you had ever seen was a toy poodle, any generalization you might make

about the size and general appearance of dogs would hardly be a reliable conclusion about the size and general appearance of the whole population of dogs.

3. *Can exceptions, if any, be explained?* This question is related to the preceding one. In other words, we might ask, can atypical instances be accounted for? The old proverb about the exception proving the rule applies here. But the word "prove" in the proverb has the meaning of "test." The exception does *test* the rule, since, if the exception cannot be explained adequately, the rule may not hold. If there are many exceptions, then the very nature of the generalization itself may change. As the number of specific cases increases, the "exceptions" might become the typical instances. Let's take a simple example. If we were to examine a few small fish, we might reach a conclusion which would state that all fish have gills by means of which they take in oxygen from the water. But if, in the course of gathering specific instances, we should come across a fishlike mammal, a whale, perhaps, then we would have to acount for the lack of gills before making our generalization. In this case, we could account for the apparent exception by discovering that, in many respects, the whale is not a true fish. Consequently, our generalization about fish having gills would still be justified on the basis of our accumulation of specific instances.

Deductive Reasoning

In a sense, deductive reasoning moves in the opposite direction from inductive reasoning or generalization. Whereas in generalization we reason from specific cases to a general conclusion, in deductive reasoning we move from a generalization to a conclusion dealing with a specific case. Thus, if we say that honorably discharged veterans of the Korean War are entitled to government aid for their education, and we know that John is an honorably discharged veteran of the Korean War, then we would know that he is entitled to the benefits of the G.I. bill. However, we very rarely go through such a detailed and elaborate step-by-step process in the actual presentation of inferences drawn deductively. In the

example cited above, we might say something like, "John's on the
G. I. bill; he's a Korean vet." Or, perhaps, "Since John's a Korean
veteran, he's on the new G. I. bill." In both cases, we would be
implying the generalization, the major premise, from which the
inference is drawn: "All honorably discharged veterans of the
Korean War are entitled to government aid for their education."

Deductive reasoning usually takes the form of a syllogism, which
includes a statement of a major premise, a minor premise, and a
conclusion. The first example, in which the reasons for John's
being eligible for the G.I. bill were given step-by-step, is an instance of a syllogism; the abridged versions which followed are
sometimes called enthymemes. This particular kind of syllogism
is labeled a *categorical* syllogism.

Another form of deductive reasoning is the *disjunctive* syllogism.
In this kind of syllogism the major premise offers two alternatives.
One of these is denied in the minor premise; the other is affirmed
in the conclusion. This is the typical "either-or" kind of statement.
Many families may be confronted with this kind of major premise
of a disjunctive syllogism:

> Either we get a new car or take a vacation. (A decision is made
> which affirms one of the alternatives and denies the other.)

The third kind of syllogism is the *hypothetical* syllogism. Here
the major premise offers a condition (or antecedent) and a consequent. The antecedent is affirmed or the consequent is denied in
the minor premise, and the conclusion then follows logically. For
example:

> If I study hard, I will make an A.
> I will study hard.
> *Therefore:* I will make an A.

You will notice that, in this case the antecedent or condition is
affirmed, and the conclusion then affirms the consequent. Again,
as in the other two kinds of syllogisms, we seldom follow each premise of the syllogism through step-by-step. We would be more apt

to say, "If I study hard, I will make an A; so I am going to study hard." Or perhaps, even more simply, "If I study hard, I will make an A."

Tests for deductive reasoning. Each of the types of syllogisms has a series of technical tests that can be applied to it to determine the validity of the syllogism. These tests may be found in detail in any text on logic.[2] The following tests of deductive reasoning, however, should be listed here:

1. *Is the generalization true?* Assuming that the inference is properly drawn, the conclusion can be no more valid than the major premise. That is, if the generalization with which the reasoning process starts is not true, or is only partially true, the chances of truth in the conclusion are only accidental. If other evidence, your own observation, and the observations of others tend to confirm the truth of the major premise, you are probably safe in drawing inferences from it.

2. *Does the specific case really apply to the generalization?* Is this application a fair one? To refer back to our earlier example, we should ask if John is really an honorably discharged veteran of the Korean War.

3. In the case of the disjunctive syllogism: *Are the alternatives mutually exclusive and all inclusive?* If they are not, then, in the first case we may be dealing not with two alternatives, but with one, and in the second case, there may be more than two alternatives.

4. In the case of the hypothetical syllogism: *Does the minor premise affirm the antecedent or deny the consequent of the major premise?* The conclusion cannot be considered valid unless the minor premise affirms the antecedent (thereby affirming the consequent in the conclusion) or denies the consequent (thereby denying the antecedent in the conclusion).

Causal Reasoning

When we are concerned primarily with establishing connections between causes and effects, we are engaged in causal reasoning.

---

[2] See, for example, Albert A. Bennett and Charles A. Baylis, *Formal Logic, A Modern Introduction,* Chapter VI. New York: Prentice-Hall, Inc., 1939.

There are three kinds of causal reasoning: (1) reasoning from cause to effect, (2) reasoning from effect to cause, and (3) reasoning from effect to effect. Let us consider each briefly.

1. *Cause-effect reasoning.* When a cause is known to us and we are concerned with predicting its probable effect, we are engaged in cause-effect reasoning. In other words, we reason from a *known* cause to an *unknown* effect. When the mother tells her child that he must wear his boots when he goes out to play in the snow or else he will catch cold, she is using cause-effect reasoning. Two other examples can be seen in this short paragraph:

If a parent continues forever to make choices for a child, the child will never be mature and will never be free. If the state is given power and responsibility to make choices for men, and thereby to save them from any result of making personal choices, the people never attain political freedom and moral responsibility.[3]

In short, given a specific cause (the parent making choices for a child) an inevitable result will come about (immaturity and lack of freedom).

2. *Effect-cause reasoning.* When the effect is known and we are trying to discover its probable cause, we are dealing with effect-cause reasoning. In other words, we reason from a *known* effect to an *unknown* cause. This is the type of reasoning process involved in a doctor's diagnosis, where the effects (symptoms of a disease) are known and the doctor discovers the cause (the disease). Similarly, in the following quotation, the effect (Hitler's fascism) was known, and the writer assigns a probable cause (Bismarck):

It was Bismarck who, as Chancellor of Germany after 1862, conceived the plan for the transformation of the freedom of the people into the collectivism of a state-controlled economy. Hitler was simply the heir of Bismarck, and Hitler's brand of national socialism—called *fascism* —was the economic program of Bismarck reaching its inevitable conclusion.[4]

---

[3] Russell J. Clincy, "What Does Freedom Mean to You?" *In Brief*, IX (September, 1952), 19.

[4] *Ibid.*, p. 5.

3. *Effect-effect reasoning.* When we reason from one effect of a cause to another effect of the same cause, we are concerned with effect-effect reasoning. Thus, if we assume that engaging in a war is a cause, one effect of this cause might be inflation, and another effect might be higher taxes. Both inflation and higher taxes, then, are effects. Given one effect (inflation) we might predict the other (higher taxes).

Tests for causal reasoning. Since all three kinds of causal reasoning are concerned with the connection existing between a causative factor and an effect, the following tests will apply to all three kinds:

1. *Is there a logical connection between cause and effect?* Just because one event precedes another does not mean that it causes the other. There must be a stronger connection between the two events than a simple chronological or sequential connection.

2. *Is the cause sufficient to produce the effect?* Sometimes we tend to assign immense effects to supposed causes that are too inconsequential. Frequently, a single cause may produce several effects; and, on the other hand, a single effect may have multiple causes.

3. *Are there intervening factors which might prevent the effect arising from the cause?* Thus, if we are exposed to a disease, but take precautionary measures to prevent the disease from developing, we have intervened in the normal cause-effect relationship.

Reasoning by Analogy

A fourth kind of reasoning involves a comparison. The assumption is made in reasoning by analogy that things that are alike in some respects, will be alike in other respects. If we know that City A has a population of approximately 100,000, that it is located in the mid-west, that it is a state capital, and that it has a good airport; and if we know that City B also has a population of 100,000, is also located in the mid-west, that it, too, is a state capital, but we do not know whether or not it has a good airport, we would be fairly safe in reasoning by analogy that it has an airport comparable to that of City A.

Analogies are generally classified as being either *literal* or *figurative*. The literal analogy compares two things in the same class. The example given above about Cities A and B would be a literal analogy, since the comparison or analogy is drawn between two things in the same category. Sometimes we draw analogies between things in different classes, and when we do, we are using a figurative analogy. The following quotation illustrates a figurative analogy in which statecraft is compared to science:

Just as in science we cannot advance except as we take over what we inherit, so in statecraft no generation can safely start at scratch. The subject matter of science is recorded observation of the external world; the subject matter of statecraft is the soul of man, and of that there are records—the records of which I refer to here.[5]

Tests for reasoning by analogy. There are at least three questions that should be asked about analogies:

1. *Do points of similarity out-weigh points of difference?* This is a test to be applied to literal analogies. Since no two things are exactly alike, it is inevitable that there be some points of difference. However, do these differences out-weigh the similarities that exist between the two items being compared? This question should be considered not only from a quantitative point of view, but also from a qualitative one. As Graham points out:

Many similarities do tend to increase possibility to a certain extent, absence of differences combined with it is significant, but for dependable proof, for high-degree probability the important thing is not number of points—there may be many and still false analogy—but the *essential* or *non-essential* character of those points. The vital thing is to find similarity in essence, not accident. To show essential qualities repeated is to have high degree proof for inference by analogy.[6]

2. *Is there substantial identity of principle in the two instances?* This is a test for figurative analogies. It has essentially the same

---

[5] Learned Hand, "The Future of Wisdom in America," *The Saturday Review,* XXXV (November 22, 1952), 55. Reprinted by permission.

[6] Gladys Murphy Graham, "Analogy—A Study in Proof and Persuasion Values," *The Quarterly Journal of Speech,* XIV (November, 1928), 540.

purpose as the test just discussed, determining the "alikeness" of the compared items.

3. *Can outstanding differences be explained?* Where differences seem to be important, they should be explained. Upon close examination, the differences may turn out to be, as mentioned above, *non-essential*.

4. *Is the analogy relevant?* This question applies especially to figurative analogies. Sometimes two things are compared which are so entirely different that no true analogy really exists.

FALLACIES

A fallacy is an error in reasoning, a mistake in the process of drawing inferences and conclusions. In the course of discussing the types of reasoning, we have already seen many of the types of fallacies that can arise. There are others that should be considered.

Ambiguity

Sometimes members of a discussion group use words or language structure which are ambiguous. A discussion participant who referred to someone orally as a "democrat" might be using an ambiguous word, provided it were not clear in context. This would be so, since the hearer would have no way of judging whether or not the person referred to was a member of the Democratic Party, or one who believed in a democratic form of government. This and other kinds of ambiguities will be discussed in more detail when we consider the use of language in a discussion.

Begging the Question

When a discussion participant asks a question that contains its own answer, he is "begging the question." If a participant in a discussion on the status of intercollegiate athletics were to ask another participant: "Don't you believe that this mal-practice of recruiting is bad and should be abolished?" he is answering his own question. If it is agreed that recruiting is a "mal-practice," then it also would be agreed that it is "bad" and more than likely that it should be "abolished."

Ignoring the Question

When a discussion participant talks on something that is really irrelevant and beside the point, he is ignoring the question. Again, if we were having a discussion on the status of intercollegiate athletics, and a participant talked at length about the most exciting high school football game he had ever seen, he would probably be guilty of ignoring the question. What he would be saying would be dealing with athletics in a general sort of way, but would probably have little bearing on the specific aspects of the problems confronting intercollegiate athletics.

Appeals to Passion or Prejudice

This is actually another manifestation of the fallacy of ignoring the question. In this instance, the speaker talks away from the subject at hand, or at least away from the reasoning processes at hand, and makes appeals to the group's established prejudices.

Appeals to Tradition or Custom

The discussion participant who says that no matter how logical or reasonable a point of view might be, it nevertheless is not in keeping with the long-established traditions of the group, is using this kind of fallacy. For example, a member of a discussion group talking about intercollegiate athletics might be guilty of this fallacy if he ignored the arguments being presented and built his observations only on the glorious football tradition of his *alma mater*. He would be saying that intercollegiate athletics cannot be changed, because they have been as they are now for so long they have become traditional.

Non-sequitur

Fallacies of *non-sequitur* ("it does not follow") are those that arise when a speaker draws an inference that by the rules of logic cannot be drawn. One of the most common forms of this fallacy has already been mentioned in our discussion of cause-effect reasoning.   This is the fallacy of *post hoc ergo propter hoc,* or "after this, therefore because of this."   When a speaker assumes a causal connection between two events simply because of a time connection between them, he is engaged in the use of this fallacy.   If a black cat crosses in front of you on your way to school, and then you make a poor grade on an examination the next hour, it would be fallacious to lay the blame on the cat.   Simply because two things happen in a sequence does not mean that they are logically or causally connected.

PART III

Leadership

9. Styles of Conference Leadership

Over a period of years you have doubtless had experiences with a variety of types of conference leaders. In these instances the leader may have been authoritarian, strict supervisory, democratic, or non-directive. In fact, at some time or other you have probably been each of these types yourself. Few things are clearer than the fact that styles of leadership in conferences, as well as leadership in life generally, differ markedly from one another.

STYLE ONE: AUTHORITARIAN LEADERSHIP

The leader in a conference who is an authoritarian dictates both the way in which the conference is conducted and also the decisions that are reached. This leader represents one extreme in the control *versus* freedom continuum depicted here:

(1)	(2)	(3)	(4)	(5)
Authoritarian Leader	Strict Supervisory Leader	Democratic or Cooperative Leader	Non-Directive Leader	Leaderless Group

Control - Freedom

At the extreme opposed to authoritarianism, we have placed the group in which there is not a designated leader present. Leader-

137

ship is expected to arise in the leaderless group, but the members are free to make plans and decisions without guidance from a pre-announced conference leader. The remaining styles of leadership (indicated as numbers 2, 3, and 4) represent gradations of difference in direction by leaders.

In our explanations of styles of leadership, you will notice that control by the leader may take two directions. A leader may control or influence *procedure* by deciding the phases of the problem that will be discussed, the order in which these phases will be considered, who is to speak and under what conditions, and similar matters about "how" the discussion is to be conducted. Control over *content* is the second direction that leadership may follow. Here the leader makes decisions about the subject that is discussed such as the exact interpretation of the problem, the evidence or facts, and final conclusions. In short, the leader decides what is "right" and "wrong" about substantive phases of the discussion. As you probably suspect, the styles of leadership we have named in the continuum show varying degrees of influence on the part of the leader in regard to these two types of control.

Attitudes and Beliefs of the Authoritarian Leader

The authoritarian leader is so obsessed with the desire to influence that he tends to place all people into two classes: those persons *with* power and those *without* power. In a conference this leader understands his role to be one of domination, and his associates in turn are expected to play the part of subordinates. Almost invariably, conferees in the group do not feel that they are equal partners in a group undertaking. The authoritarian personality makes this difference in status very clear.

1. *He refuses to share leadership with others.* In a survey conducted by the authors of the *wants* or *desires* that college students hope to satisfy when participating in a discussion, it was discovered, among other things, that: (a) participants wish to be members of a cooperative group, and (b) they wish to excel and to be helpful. This second aspiration means that participants in a discussion wish to exert leadership influence. Whereas they do not wish to depose

the designated leader, they nevertheless refuse to believe that as participants they must entirely refrain from offering direction and guidance to the group.

The democratic or cooperative conference leader believes that he should share directive influences with others. The authoritarian leader, on the other hand, cannot accept a plan of shared dependence. If he did, he would feel that others in the group would be increasing their power fields, and that he, *the leader,* would be losing power. The authoritarian is particularly concerned about loss of control; he is ever mindful of maintaining his status and power.

2. *He believes that the end justifies the means.* The German philosopher Immanuel Kant (1724–1804) said that *we must treat every man as an end and not as a means.* An act, says Kant, is not good because of its results, but because it conforms to an inner sense of duty that could be accepted as a universal moral law. An authoritarian personality is little concerned about persons as ends in themselves; his primary interest is in using others as pawns for some result that he seeks. This same distinction between means and ends is also true of governments. In speaking before the Congressional Atomic Committee in 1947, David E. Lilienthal said that any form of government that exalts "the state as an end in itself" will control individuals without regard to an ethical standard. Thus, Goering was able to conclude, "Say what you will about Hitler, but don't accuse him (or me) of being *moral!*" [1]

3. *He insists that his ideas are always correct.* The authoritarian leader does not seem to be satisfied unless he has won every point, major and minor. He aggressively pronounces judgments on almost any subject, and in so doing, "talks down" possible opposition. He could not succeed as well as he does if he did not have coercive methods to enforce his decisions, but as Machiavelli (1469–1527) says in *The Prince,* the authoritarian leader controls through fear: "One ought to be both feared and loved, but as it is difficult for the two to go together, it is much better to be feared

---

[1] G. M. Gilbert, *The Psychology of Dictatorship,* pp. 293–294. New York: Ronald Press Company, 1950.

than loved, if one of the two has to be wanting." Fear of consequences is the force that makes others echo the views of the autocrat. He alone can be "right"—or in different words, *justice resides
with the strong.* Even a "loyal opposition" is incompatible with
authoritarianism.

Authoritarian Conference Techniques

The studies by Lewin, Lippitt, and White of styles of leadership in clubs of ten-year-old boys effectively show both the leadership methods and results of autocracy. The children were engaged in mask-making, model airplane building, and soap-carving
under varied types of adult leadership: democratic, autocratic, and
laissez-faire. The leadership principles employed by the autocratic
leader included a number of inflexible rules: (1) the leader should
determine policy; (2) he should dictate steps of procedure in such
a way that future direction is always uncertain to the group; (3)
he should assign working partners in the group; and (4) he should
not reveal standards of judgment when he criticizes or praises the
work of the boys. Some of the effects of autocratic leadership
upon the behavior of the boys included loss of initiative, in-group
hostility, and both aggressive and apathetic reactions toward the
leader. The boys working under autocratic leadership were both
less productive and *less pleased with their experiences* than were
the democratic groups.[2]

How does a conference leader exercise a high degree of procedural and content control? To answer this question, we observed a series of conferences led by authoritarian leaders and
recorded the conference techniques commonly used. The authoritarian, we found, does these things:

---

[2] See Kurt Lewin, Ronald Lippitt, and Ralph K. White, "Patterns of Aggressive Behavior in Experimentally Created 'Social Climates,'" *Journal of Social
Psychology,* X (May, 1939), 271–299; Ronald Lippitt, "Field Theory and Experiment in Social Psychology," *American Journal of Sociology,* XXXXV (July,
1939), 26–49; Kurt Lewin, *Resolving Social Conflicts,* pp. 74–83. New York:
Harper and Brothers, 1948; and Ronald Lippitt and Ralph K. White, "An
Experimental Study of Leadership and Group Life," in *Readings in Social Psychology,* Guy E. Swanson, Theodore M. Newcomb, and Eugene L. Hartley
(eds.), Revised Edition, pp. 340–355. New York: Henry Holt and Company,
1952.

Procedural Control

1. He gives many orders and directives about how the conference is to be conducted.
2. He specializes in questions directed to specific persons such as, "Jones, give us your report . . . ." He uses open questions that any person in the group may answer much less frequently.
3. He interrupts conferees very often.
4. He keeps the group in a "strait-jacket." Conferees are not permitted to initiate conversation on related phases of the problem unless the transition to the new phase happens to suit the authoritarian leader's purpose.
5. He lavishes praise upon those who are especially obedient.
6. He sometimes deliberately encourages irrelevant discussion prior to announcing a particular decision.

Content Control

7. He arbitrarily decides what problems are to be discussed, including the exact problem statement.
8. He uses many questions that are "slanted" in order to give conferees a tip regarding the "right" answers.
9. He is quite willing to draw unfair inferences from the data others have given.
10. He approves and disapproves the views given by group members with a "You are right" and "You are wrong."
11. He occasionally attempts to prove his beliefs by saying that a "high authority" believes as he does. In doing this, he is likely to talk in paragraphs while others are required to present their remarks in a few short sentences.
12. He makes many forceful summaries with little or no effort to discover whether the group as a whole concurs.

Participants subjected to such leadership have said: "The leader's attitude discouraged participation and I, as a group member, would rather just agree on the surface than incur some critical remark." . . . "I resigned myself to the obvious conclusion that the leader was going to make all decisions no matter what I might say." . . . "The leader showed open signs of friendliness, but we soon learned we were being betrayed." . . . "He cut us off a lot." . . . "As group members we argued among ourselves at times when there was little reason for heated differences." . . . "We were denied the opportunity of a group decision." . . . "He was the master and we were the slaves." . . . And, finally, one member said: "I felt the impulse for open warfare (commonly known as the urge to kill) whenever the leader monopolized so much of the time in defending conclusions that were unacceptable to everyone but himself."

STYLE TWO: STRICT SUPERVISORY LEADERSHIP

Attitudes and Beliefs of the Strict Supervisory Leader

The strict supervisory leader represents a milder form of autocracy than that which we have just described. He is likely to be more considerate and friendly than the authoritarian. Sometimes he can be called paternalistic, because he has a sincere interest in helping persons in his group without any thoughts of personal gain. *His major weakness:* In his efforts to promote efficiency, the strict supervisory leader relies heavily upon order-giving. Group members are thus unable to make decisions of their own.

There are two kinds of strict supervisory leaders. In the first type the leader keeps his guidance centered upon both procedural and substantive phases of the discussion. Sometimes, however, the strict supervisory conference leader limits freedom only in regard to procedure. This second type of direction is to be preferred over the first, but weaknesses still remain. With either type, the participants in the conference are "kept in line" quite closely; they are expected to follow directions slavishly.

1. *He believes strongly in personal responsibility.* The strict supervisory leader is likely to feel that he is more capable than the participants in the group. And, following this assumption, he feels that the sharing of responsibility is both unnecessary and unwise. Instead of saying, "this is our problem," he says, "this is how we should attack the problem" . . . "and this is what I think about it." Creativeness, initiative, and interdependency are neatly throttled.

2. *He is committed to pre-determined conclusions.* Like the authoritarian leader, the strict supervisory leader is accustomed to think in dichotomies of "right and wrong," "proper and improper." Since problems are thus packaged and labeled, the leader has only

to transmit his answers to the group.   Honest two-way communication in which participants freely offer suggestions cannot be encouraged.   In this respect the supervisory leader may be contrasted with the cooperative-democratic leader who earnestly seeks new and better solutions to problems.

Strict Supervisory Conference Techniques

In a conference the supervisory leader shows that he believes *talk by others* is a great waste of time.   He, of course, does not apply this belief to himself, for the supervisory leader cannot maintain his role unless he does a great deal of "telling."   Common techniques used to limit freedom for others include these actions:

1. He does not give participants the opportunity to suggest and to select the problems to be discussed in a conference.
2. He is likely to become a lecturer rather than a leader who elicits ideas from the group.   As a case in point, the strict supervisory leader usually introduces the problem in great detail, giving, apart from information, his own conclusions.
3. He expects all contributions from members of the group to be leader-directed statements.   Interaction among group members is at a minimum.
4. He passes judgment, offers advice, and summarizes frequently.

Persons in conferences under the leadership of the strict supervisor, as we have described him, are more likely to be *spectators* than *true participants*.   They do not actually share views with one another.   The information discussed in the conference is heard by the group members, but it is doubtful if they will be sufficiently interested in the information to remember it.   It is even less likely that as spectators they will feel impelled to act in accordance with what was said in the conference.   Gordon W. Allport in drawing a conclusion from experimental studies on motivation and learning says: "Such findings add up to the single proposition that people must have a hand in saving themselves; they cannot and will not be saved from the outside." [3]   The leader we have described fails

---

[3] Gordon W. Allport, "The Psychology of Participation," *Psychological Review*, LIII (May, 1945), 123.

to permit participants to play a vital part in offering and evaluating ideas. They are not honestly consulted either in the planning of the conference or in deciding its "announced" outcomes.

STYLE THREE: DEMOCRATIC OR COOPERATIVE LEADERSHIP

Attitudes and Beliefs of the Democratic Leader

The authoritarian and strict supervisory leaders, as we have seen, depend upon techniques that limit freedom of choice for participants. Both in procedure and in content these leaders establish controls that keep participants within confined bounds. The democratic leader, on the contrary, has an affirmative approach to problems and to participants in a discussion. Instead of saying, "You can't do this," the democratic leader says, "You can, if you wish." Instead of one-man control, we have a system of pluralistic control. Under these conditions, each participant is encouraged to be as valuable to the group as he can, for he is limited only by his interest, ability, and knowledge. Thus, the democratic leader has a liberating effect on others that cannot possibly arise from the types of restrictive leadership we have previously described.

1. *He is interested in having all participants show initiative.* The eminent biologist A. J. Carlson has said: "In my judgment, as I know biology, as I know the history of man, anything that decreases the responsibility of the individual is unbiological and will injure man in the long run." [4] If we apply this idea to discussion we might say that if participants are not permitted to be imaginative, inventive, or creative, two results follow. First, the participants will not feel a responsibility for conference decisions; and secondly, they will not learn how to master problems and thus improve in personal competence. Under restrictive leadership the

---

[4] A. J. Carlson, "The Social Responsibility of Scientists," in *The Authoritarian Attempt to Capture Education*, p. 71. New York: King's Crown Press, 1945. Reprinted by permission.

leader benefits from experiences in initiating and influencing, but the group members gain much less.   In contrast to this, we find that under democratic leadership the participants in a discussion have a chance to experience what it means to influence rather than merely to acknowledge the influence of the leader.

2. *He realizes that conference decisions should be understood as group achievements.*   For best results, group members should feel that they have shared in making the decisions agreed upon in a conference.   In other words, we may say that the decisions reached are not to be regarded as personal triumphs for the leader or for any particular participant.   The group members are the important persons, perhaps more important than many of us realize.   When seventy-five experienced conference leaders in executive positions were asked to identify the most important factors that lead to successful conferences, they listed "well-prepared participants concerned with the problem" as the number one factor.[5]   This conclusion is neither surprising nor does it in any way detract from the leader's importance in the group.   It is well understood that in a democratic society the leader cannot speak with finality for the group unless he has been asked to do so.   Similarly, in a discussion ultimate authority resides with the group members.

3. *He believes that intra-group communications are important.* The autocrat understands communication as a stimulus emanating from himself and directed to the group or, very often, to particular persons in the group.   But all statements *by participants* are expected to be directed *toward the leader.*   This pattern of communication does not provide for interactions among the group members, and, as a result, the group members are not likely to work together as a team.   In the diagram on page 146, the *A pattern* of communication is preferable if cooperation is our goal.   The arrows show the direction of contributions to be toward the group or to persons within the group.   In the *B pattern*, intra-group communication is absent.

---

[5] Martin Kriesberg, "Executives Evaluate Administrative Conferences," *Advanced Management*, XV (March, 1950), 16.

Pattern A

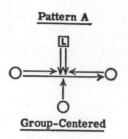

Group-Centered

Pattern B

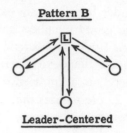

Leader-Centered

There will of course be times when a participant in a democratic group will direct his statements to the leader. Yet, it is important to realize that the participant will not direct all his statements to the leader. Most of his contributions will be directed toward the group as a whole, with occasional remarks addressed primarily to a particular person or persons.

4. *He is interested in having participants satisfy personal needs.* Participants in a group naturally wish to count for something; they desire recognition, acceptance, and the opportunity to talk freely about the problem. The directive leader, as we have seen, sets up barriers that block fulfillment of many personal desires. In addition to procedural and substantive dictation, the restrictive leader blocks goal satisfaction for participants by establishing himself in a position of supreme importance. With the cooperative-democratic leader, however, conditions are different. A spirit of co-equality is paramount. Personal needs of participants are more likely to be achieved under such conditions.

Democratic Conference Techniques

To be an effective democratic conference leader is not, as some persons believe, a task with few responsibilities. Autocracy can rely upon threats, actual or implied, to enforce decisions. But the democratic (or cooperative) leader must be sufficiently competent to win the support of group members by (1) being personally acceptable to the group, (2) promoting cooperation within the group, and (3) assisting the group members to reach sound answers to problems. No dictator in a conference has ever had such important responsibilities.

We shall give a detailed explanation of the techniques of the democratic leader in Chapter 10, "Leadership Functions in Discussion." Since this type of leader is ordinarily the ideal, both in discussion and in other group situations, you should understand his duties and techniques quite fully. It is for this reason that we shall explain the leadership functions in discussion in a separate chapter.

Style Four: Non-directive Leadership

Some persons believe that our experience with directive types of conference leadership, including the procedural direction of most democratic leaders, has not been very successful. To be sure, exponents of non-directiveness approve many of the attitudes and methods of the democratic leader, but there seem to be some important differences. For instance, the non-directive leader usually invites the group members to suggest the phase of the problem to be considered in starting a discussion; he permits group members to decide when a particular topic has been discussed at sufficient length; and he encourages group members to make their own summaries in a discussion. In each of these three respects the ordinary democratic leader assumes responsibilities that the non-directive leader prefers to leave with the group.

Of course, the non-directive leader can be called democratic, but, as we have shown, he is less likely to perform procedural duties for the group than the typical discussion leader. In leading a discussion, the non-directive leader may accomplish the same ends as the democratic leader we have in mind, but he does so in a more indirect and subtle manner. In spite of similarities between the two styles of leadership, there are some differences. Both reflect democratic procedures: non-directiveness however calls for greater permissiveness by the leader than that extended by the discussion leader described earlier in this chapter.

The following description of leadership by Lao-Tzu is an excellent illustration of the effects of non-directiveness:

A leader is best
When people barely know that he exists

Not so good when people obey and acclaim him
Worst when they despise him
"Fail to honor people,
They fail to honor you";
But of a good leader who talks little,
When his work is done, his aim fulfilled,
They will all say, "We did it ourselves." [6]

This leader gets things done, but the group does them.   And what is more, the leader's direct procedural influence is held to a minimum.

Much of what we know about non-directive leadership in conferences is patterned after techniques used in permissive styles of teaching, some types of employee counseling programs, and client-centered therapy in dealing with persons who have emotional problems.   The doctrines have probably been best stated in the writings of Carl R. Rogers, Executive Secretary of the Counseling Center, University of Chicago.   The basic hypothesis that underlies non-directiveness as a method is that the individual has "the capacity, latent, if not evident," to understand his problems and to solve them.[7]   If this is true, the leader's task is largely one of creating conditions that help group members to talk freely about the problem.   Above all, the leader must, particularly by his friendliness and patience, encourage participants to give their true beliefs rather than those which reflect outward desires to conform.

The primary aim of the non-directive leader is to help group members learn to guide and direct themselves:

1. He is informal and friendly in his manner.
2. He shows that he has confidence that the group members can solve the problem under consideration.
3. He is an especially good listener: he does not offer judgments, give advice, take sides, or analyze the problem for the group.

---

[6] Witter Bynner (translator), *The Way of Life According to Lao-Tzu*, Saying 17.   New York: The John Day Company, 1944.   Reprinted by permission.
[7] Carl R. Rogers, "Client-Centered Therapy: A Helping Process," *University of Chicago Round Table* (August 12, 1951), 12; see also Carl R. Rogers, *Client-Centered Therapy*.   Boston: Houghton Mifflin Company, 1951.

4. He shows awareness of what the group members have said whenever he poses questions that redirect the conversation.
5. He tries to use questions that are based upon what the group members have said. These questions may be called "turn-about" questions since they invite the group members to think further about the ideas they feel are important.
6. He makes the group members realize that they may make any progress they wish toward solving the problem during the discussion period. Pauses in the discussion, for example, do not alarm the non-directive leader.

Although the skillful non-directive leader places heavy responsibility for the success of the discussion upon the group members, he is not a *laissez-faire* leader. Apart from the friendliness and forthrightness that he encourages, his questions that are centered upon what the group members have either *stated or implied* help the group to carry on a profitable discussion. He does, therefore, affect the direction of the discussion even though his guidance is unobtrusive and largely stimulated by the group itself.

What follows from this? Will the group always need the leader? The answer, say some people, is "No." The leader may have done such a good job in training group members to exercise initiative, to cooperate, and to think critically that he will have "worked himself out of a job." Many people believe that this goal is both desirable and attainable.

Style Five: The Leaderless Group

When an acknowledged leader is not present in a group any one of a number of things might happen. Under some conditions anarchy may prevail, but in other situations a high level of cooperativeness may characterize the work of the group.

Anarchy and the Leaderless Group

By anarchy in a discussion situation we mean the failure of group members to agree upon the rights and responsibilities of one another. This so-called "right of nature" means that each participant might choose to carry on a battle with every other participant. In this battle of words there are no rules or accepted patterns of conduct. Every person is a "blocker." The result is chaos, confusion, and disorder. It is, as Hobbes has said, "a condition of war of every one against every one."

Cooperation and the Leaderless Group

But many leaderless groups are just the opposite of the anarchical type. Participants without a nominal leader can share leadership in a discussion quite effectively if they individually accept responsibility for decisions and actions. When responsibility is distributed equally, the group members are given the opportunity to practice self-direction in a way that is not possible under restrictive styles of leadership. If participants respect one another and if they have had training experiences in shared-leadership, they should be able to work together happily and productively.

Whether the leaderless group discussion is as desirable as it is sometimes said to be has not yet been proven. The success of the group will depend to a large degree upon the type of persons in the group. The participants may be both competent and cooperative. On the other hand, it is not reasonable to assume that persons will automatically become ideal participants simply because a nominal leader is not designated. For example, the authoritarian personality is not always to be found in the person of the conference leader. He is often a group member. When this condition exists and when other conditions fall short of the optimum, an assigned discussion leader seems to be required. In short, leadership that arises in a leaderless group may be restrictive or unwise leadership.

Maier and Solem conducted a study in which groups with a democratic leader and leaderless groups with a silent observer were given a mathematical problem to solve. After an eight minute discussion period, 83.6 per cent of the persons in the "leader" groups gave the correct answer to the problem. Correct responses in the "leaderless" groups were given by only 71.6 per cent of the persons. In explaining this result, the experimenters reported that democratic leaders encouraged the expression of minority opinions and that in many cases the minority opinions proved to be valid answers. Under the system of chance leadership in the "leaderless" groups, minority views were often given little attention. The democratic leader proved to be a great asset in this study because he made it possible for all points of view to have a hearing.[8]

Evaluation of Members in the Leaderless Group

The leaderless group discussion has been given a special application for the purpose of testing the abilities, traits, and skills of participants. According to Ansbacher, the systematic use of this technique in evaluation and testing programs was first carried out by J. B. Rieffert, director of German military psychology from 1920 to 1931.[9] It was used in Great Britain in 1942 by the War Office Selection Boards, and later by the Civil Service Selection Board. In the United States the assessment staff of the Office of Strategic Services has also used leaderless group discussion.[10] Today this type of discussion is used in the selection programs of some business, industrial, and governmental organizations. Ordinarily it is called the Group Interview Test, and, at times, the Speech Performance Test.

---

[8] Norman R. F. Maier and Allen R. Solem, "The Contribution of a Discussion Leader to the Quality of Group Thinking: The Effective Use of Minority Opinions," *Human Relations*, V (1952), 277–288.

[9] L. Ansbacher, "The History of the Leaderless Group Discussion Technique," *Psychological Bulletin*, XXXVIII (September, 1951), 383–391.

[10] A. G. Arbous and Joy Maree, "Contribution of Two Group Discussion Techniques to a Validated Test Battery," *Occupational Psychology*, XXV (April, 1951), 73.

10. Leadership Functions in Discussion

The husky dog teams that pull the sleds owned by Eskimos in Alaska or in Greenland make an interesting study in leadership. To achieve coordinated effort, the huskies are each given a specific position in the team. Some are "lead" dogs, and others have "followership" positions. After experience in either status the dogs not only become adjusted to their positions, but they jealously guard against changes in the functions that they have learned to carry out.

This leadership-followership pattern may be the best way to achieve efficiency with dog teams, but it is not fully applicable to discussion. When it is practiced with humans, it leads to what Norbert Wiener calls "the inhuman use of human beings." Although the leader in a discussion performs duties that tend to distinguish him from others in the group, he does not insist upon a personal monopoly over these duties. The line of distinction between the leader and the participants is thus much less rigid in a discussion than it is in the case of the huskies.

THE PROBLEM: GOALS AND MEANS

As a discussion leader your primary problem can be simply stated. In general terms it is: "How can I be an effective leader?" What we shall say about goals and means will help you to answer this question.

Your Goals in Leadership

You should have three basic goals in mind when you assume the role of leader:

1. The purpose of the discussion should be achieved (*attainment*).
2. The group members should have respect for you as a person and have confidence in your ability and skill (*satisfaction with leadership*).
3. The group members should feel that their experiences in the discussion have in general been satisfactory (*satisfaction with experiences in the discussion*).

These are optimum outcomes. In some cases the particular problem that is discussed or the participants in the group may adversely affect the goals. And, at times, these factors will off-set the desirable effects you are trying to attain. Normally, however, your effectiveness in leadership can be fairly appraised by the degree to which you attain the goals we have named.

Your Means in Leadership

The personal traits of a good discussion leader are sometimes described as avenues (means) to success. We are told, for example, that the leader should be a brilliant thinker; he should be friendly and considerate; he should be confident and emotionally stable; he should be able to adapt to varied conditions in a discussion; he should, in short, be a competent and likeable person. This list of personal qualities is not without value. What advice of this type fails to do however is to tell the leader what he should do in order to attain the ideal. In other words, lists of desirable personal qualities leave some important questions unanswered.

We believe that the twelve leadership functions we shall describe in the following section are a better set of means than the personal traits of the ideal leader. These functions are "things to do," *responsibilities* or *duties*. If you execute these functions when they are required and to the degree that they are required, you will have properly fulfilled your role as leader. We think, further, that by carrying out these responsibilities properly you will usually attain the basic goals of leadership. And finally, effective execution of the leadership functions is an indication that you possess many of the admirable personal traits that leaders are said to possess.

TWELVE LEADERSHIP FUNCTIONS

Try to Get General Participation

In one group discussion in which a record of frequency of participation was kept these results occurred: Participant A spoke 22 times; B and C spoke 16 times each; D spoke 3 times; and E made 1 contribution. This disparity in frequency of participation is striking, but similar results are not unusual in discussions. It is clear in this case that conferees A, B, and C monopolized the discussion and thus it was probably difficult for conferees D and E to have a chance to speak. Other possibilities such as lack of interest, lack of preparation, fear, or resentment on the part of D and E may also help to explain the disparity in contributions. But whatever the cause, a competent leader might be able to change the pattern of participation by providing D and E with opportunities to contribute. Unless this is accomplished, the discussion is a meeting in which there are three featured performers and two spectators.

We suggest that you try to bring about two conditions in the group in order to change the behavior of "monopolist" and "silent" members. The first of these is that group members should understand that discussion is a cooperative activity; responsibility should be shared by all persons. This condition of a good discussion is related to a second, namely, feelings of "group belongingness" by all, by the talkative persons as well as the reticent. Habitually quiet persons are likely to speak freely if they feel that there are bonds that unite them with the group. And this, in turn, is often a favorable influence in changing the behavior of compulsive talkers. If the compulsive talker feels that he is accepted and respected, he may not feel that he must impress others by stealing the show.

But many times the conditions that tend to promote general participation are not fully realized. When this is true, you might have to resort to one or more of the following techniques:

1. Arrange the seating positions of active members (if you know who they are) in a way that does not place them in a small self-contained group.
2. Summarize contributions by active participants very briefly, and ask for comments from others.
3. Reward reticent persons by showing that what they have to say is important to the group.
4. Enlist the help of others in getting reticent persons to contribute.
5. Refer directly to inactive members and ask for their ideas. Many times a general question is better to use when you do this than a specific one.
6. Tell monopolists, usually in private, that they could be more effective if they shared speaking opportunities with others.
7. Tell monopolists directly that others should be given opportunities to speak.

Simply getting people to talk does not mean that important things are being said. *Frequency of participation, therefore, is not an index of quality.* Thus participants should not be expected to speak the same number of times in a discussion. As a rule, however, you should be interested in controlling extreme differences in frequency of participation by the members of the discussion.

Try to Promote Group Cohesiveness

We have previously defined cohesiveness as the forces acting upon participants to cause them to want to be identified with the group and to work cooperatively with one another. We shall also discuss this doctrine in detail in Chapter 12, "Interpersonal Relations: Group Unity." Refer to Chapter 12, pages 189–201, for suggestions about what you can do to develop a cohesive discussion group.

Obtain Essential Information

Persons in a discussion sometimes talk about almost everything except facts or evidence. They may do this even when they have important factual data in their possession. When this is true you should deliberately try to get group members to share information with others. Ask for examples and statistics in order that you are sure that everyone understands the problem discussed. Two further suggestions are:

1. Try to determine when information is especially needed in the discussion. Remember that facts may be needed in all stages of the discussion. They should not be reserved solely for the *description of the problem* stage.
2. Try to distinguish facts from opinions in the contributions that are given in a discussion.

Encourage Opinion or Solution-Giving

In many discussions opinions are freely given. As a matter of fact, a discussion may be largely made up of opinions with little emphasis upon evidence. While we oppose over-emphasis upon opinion-giving, opinions or solutions are vital to a good discussion. You should encourage many opinions both from the active members as well as from less active members.

It is especially important to get group members to suggest non-obvious answers to the problem. To do this you might ask, "Are there other possibilities that should be mentioned?" Unless you do this, the group members might be content with stereotyped solutions.

Stimulate Critical Evaluation

Participants easily become interested in answers to problems, but they may not be disposed to test the answers suggested. Information on the idea of testing was given in Chapter 7 where we described the reflective pattern in discussion. See especially phase four in the reflective pattern called *evaluation of possible solutions and acceptance of the best solution* for details about critical evaluation.

Check Irrelevant Contributions

In the average discussion some of the contributions given may be statements that have little relationship to the problem under discussion. If these irrelevant contributions assume great importance in the discussion, the goals of your meeting will probably not be accomplished. When this is the case, you should be prepared to check irrelevant statements. You can keep group members problem-centered by saying:

1. "That's a new direction to our thinking. Can we delay talking about it until we have more discussion on . . . ?"
2. "Aren't we failing to stay with our problem?"
3. "What we have been saying in the last few minutes doesn't affect the problem we must solve. Will it be agreeable if we center our attention on . . . ?"

The attitude you reveal when you check irrelevant statements is probably more important than the words you use. Courtesy and friendliness will help to make your suggestions acceptable to the discussion group. A strong supervisory system of control over the relevance of contributions will do the opposite.

As a rule you should not make split-second decisions in identifying irrelevant comments. A fair degree of patience is desirable because (1) the information that you think is irrelevant may actually prove to be valuable, (2) the person who gives irrelevant material may correct his own error, and (3) the group members should be given time to judge the relevancy of statements. Remember that you need support from others in the group when you decide that one of the members is not sticking to the point. And remember also that participants often enjoy making a few irrelevant comments. In very many discussions the participants will quickly get back to the problem at issue without specific advice from the leader.

Clarify Contributions When Necessary

Lasswell has said, "If modern semantics has taught—or reminded us—of anything about language it is that what usually passes for communication is a thickening fog of mis-, non-, and partial understanding." [1] To meet the barriers to communication that are suggested on page 158 often calls for specific actions by the leader.

[1] Harold D. Lasswell, "The Clarifier of Public Discussion," *Quarterly Journal of Speech*, XXXIV (December, 1948), 453.

1. You can ask the participant whose ideas are not clear to describe his views more fully. "Tell us more" is often a good expression to use to combat ambiguity.
2. You can ask for restatement either from the participant who offers the vague contribution or from others in the group.
3. You can give a restatement and say, "Is this what you mean?"

One especially important suggestion has been given by Carl R. Rogers when he says we should *listen for understanding* before we evaluate statements. "It means to see the expressed idea and attitude from the other person's point of view, to sense how it feels to him, to achieve his frame of reference in regard to what he is talking about." [2] As discussion leader you should try to promote this attitude of listening for understanding. While this responsibility under ideal conditions should be shared by everyone in the group, there are many times when you must check the evaluative tendencies of participants in order to insure understanding. Hosts of unnecessary verbal battles can be avoided if you take time to find out what others really mean by their statements.

Encourage Differences As Well As Consensus

It has been said that "where all persons think alike, no one thinks very much." In some discussions this seems to happen. Polite agreement characterizes the meeting as everyone guards against taking issue with the ideas of anyone else. This way of reacting ordinarily shows that participants are not giving their real convictions, or else that they are placing an undue premium upon conformity. In the first instance participants will probably feel indifferent toward the values of the discussion. When absolute conformity is stressed above all else, the decisions reached are likely to be inferior decisions.

One good way to encourage true expression of ideas is to find out in what respects participants agree with one another and in what respects they disagree. In other words, keep in mind the principle of degree. Agreements and differences do not have to be

---

[2] Carl R. Rogers and F. J. Roethlisberger, "Barriers and Gateways to Communication," *Harvard Business Review*, XXX (July–August, 1952), 47.

absolute or one hundred per cent.   "In some respects" or "in part" are terms that you can try to get participants to understand when superficial agreements or violent disagreements occur too frequently in the discussion.   To be sure, consensus should be achieved whenever possible, but such agreement is most meaningful after honest differences have been adjusted.

Be Personally Neutral

If you are not impartial in a discussion it may be difficult for you to carry out your duties fairly.   For example: Will you as a partisan leader encourage participation by those who oppose your ideas? Will you give as much emphasis to the ideas of the opposition as you give to your own?   Will you be able to clarify and to summarize objectively?   Clearly, it is doubtful if you can execute these leadership functions with justice toward all persons in the group unless you remain impartial.

Neutrality does not mean that you cannot report facts, interpretations of facts, and possible solutions.   Some leaders give these types of contributions to stimulate interest or to be sure that important matters are considered.   Whatever the reason, however, you must clearly show that what you say is offered for consideration by the group.   Your statements must in no way commit you to partisanship in the discussion.

Try to Change the Behavior of Troublesome
Participants

The person who said that "the problems on the conference table are really not as difficult to deal with as the persons seated around the table" was probably thinking about conferees who make problem-solving unduly difficult.   These so-called "troublesome" participants destroy cooperative efforts and in turn block progress in a discussion.   Sometimes there are several such persons in a group; in other cases, there are none.   But most discussion leaders realize that troublesome persons are present in groups often enough to make it necessary for special precautions to be taken.

The very least that can be done about troublesome participants is to recognize their existence. Thus, in Chapter 14 we shall identify a list of fifteen types labeled as follows: (1) silent, (2) monopolist, (3) beside-the-point, (4) attention seeker, (5) orator, (6) fearful, (7) isolate, (8) "yes-yes," (9) executive complex, (10) know-it-all, (11) logic machine, (12) emotional antagonist, (13) contrary, (14) clown, and (15) dictator. We have referred to three of these types earlier in this chapter. The "silent" and "monopolist" members were mentioned in connection with the first leadership function (general participation). Similarly, the "beside-the-point" member as a disturbing force was depicted in our explanation of the sixth leadership function (irrelevant contributions). You will find specific suggestions about the other types (numbers 4 through 15 above) in our explanation of undesirable role patterns given in the fourteenth chapter.

Get the Main Phases of the Problem Considered

If you leave participants entirely to their own resources, they may spend an unnecessary amount of time upon certain phases of the problem. Your cues for suggesting a new phase of the problem for discussion are: (1) when enough information has already been presented, (2) when participants begin to repeat information, or (3) when participants engage in much aimless, gossip-like conversation. Your goal should not be to eliminate all non-purposeful conversation. But in order to achieve the purposes of the discussion, you must try to avoid having purposeless talking assume primary importance. When this threatens to be the case you must be prepared to say, "Let's take up the causes . . . the advantages . . . or the consequences, good and bad." Your group should not stop on "dead-center."

Summarize or Chart the Progress of the Discussion

Summaries should provide an answer to the question, "What have we accomplished?" If the participants can answer this question for themselves, a summary may be unnecessary. When they cannot, an effective summary is needed.

The following suggestions should be remembered: (1) The

number of summaries should be limited. Four summaries in a one hour discussion are usually enough. (2) Summaries should set forth basic ideas rather than details. (3) Summaries should be short—fifty words or less may be all that is needed. And (4) summaries should fairly represent what was said in the discussion.

Summaries can either be orally stated or they can be listed on a blackboard or chart. While the leader usually gives the summaries in a discussion, the task is sometimes assigned to a specially designated recorder.

LEADERSHIP FUNCTIONS AND THE PARTICIPANTS

Participants in a discussion often perform some of the twelve leadership functions. "When I do," said one student, "I don't feel like a puppet. I'm not especially happy if the leader pulls all the strings." This attitude may not be typical of all participants. It does, however, suggest that there are at least two ways in which leadership functions can be carried out.

The Leader Who Performs Responsibilities Without Assistance from the Group

This leader may be called a "strong procedural leader" because he executes all of the leadership functions himself. In some respects, therefore, he is similar to the strict supervisory leader described in Chapter 9. Because he is loathe to accept assistance from group members in procedural matters, a fixed position of responsibility separates participants from the leader. The lines of responsibility are clearly drawn. Participants are either discouraged or directly blocked when they try to penetrate the area that the leader regards as his personal domain.

In practice full-scale monopoly over leadership functions does not characterize the methods of most discussion leaders. It is somewhat inconsistent to encourage freedom in decision-making, and yet completely deny others any opportunity to give procedural suggestions. Thus, in most cases, gradations of difference distinguish various discussion leaders. The absolute dictator over procedure is likely to be regarded as a petty or misguided person. In an extreme form he may be just as out of place in a discussion as the leader who controls what is said about the discussion problem.

The Leader Who Shares Responsibilities with the Group

As we have said, most discussion leaders are willing to have participants be helpful in giving procedural suggestions. What it amounts to is this: If participants do not give procedural assistance when it is needed, you, the leader, must ask for suggestions from the group or else offer suggestions yourself. But you are not expected to have the discussion bog down while waiting for help from group members. Perhaps this practice is followed by some highly permissive leaders, but the discussion leader in the average group will act more quickly. The leader we have in mind does not monopolize the leadership functions, but neither does he relinquish the responsibilities associated with leadership.

Alfred W. Storey conducted an experimental study to determine the reactions of participants in a discussion to "strong-procedural" and "responsibility-sharing" styles of leadership. In both cases the leader maintained a neutral position and could therefore be called a "democratic" leader. But the strong-procedural leader personally performed all leadership functions such as encouraging participation, goal-setting, and summary-giving. The responsibility-sharing leader, on the other hand, encouraged group members to carry out these duties. The summary of some of his findings show that:

There were no significant differences between members of both styles of leadership groups with regard to satisfaction with the way the leader lead the discussion, or liking the leader as a person.

*   *   *

However, members of responsibility-sharing leadership groups were significantly more satisfied with the way the groups proceeded to their decisions and with the decisions reached. . . . Members of responsibility-sharing leadership groups were significantly more satisfied with what they said . . . and with what they did . . . during the meeting.

Also, they were significantly more satisfied with their feeling of being accepted by other members of the group.[3]

In this study the responsibility-sharing leader proved to be the superior type largely because the participants valued their own part in the discussion more highly than they did when under the strong-procedural leader. However, the preference is not absolute. This might lead us to conclude that neither of these leadership styles in their extreme is the ideal pattern to follow in a discussion. Under most conditions it seems logical that the leader who strikes a balance between the two styles of leadership, as tested in this study, will be the most effective leader. A leader, for example, can carry out some duties personally, and share others with participants. The conditions that he faces will have a bearing upon which practice he follows and the degree to which he follows either style of leadership.

EVALUATION OF LEADERSHIP

Ratings indicating how effective you have been as a discussion leader may be given by the participants in your group, by your training leader, by observers, and of course, you may rate yourself. Appraisals may be made in several ways:

By a Single Rating

Here we mean some type of rating of your general effectiveness as a leader. You might use this scheme:

1	2	3	4	5	6	7	8	9	10	11
Highly Inferior		Below Average				Above Average			Highly Superior	

---

[3] Alfred W. Storey, "A Study of Member Satisfaction and Types of Contributions in Discussion Groups with Responsibility-Sharing Leadership," Unpublished Ph.D. Dissertation, Department of Speech, University of Michigan, 1954, p. 36 and pp. 53–54.

Some groups might prefer a five-point rating scale with descriptive labels of poor, fair, adequate, good, and excellent. In other cases, letter grades may be used.

By Rating Leadership Goals

Earlier in this chapter we listed three desirable outcomes that should be sought as the final results of a discussion. We said that the purposes of the discussion should be achieved, the group members should be satisfied with their discussion leader, and the group members should be satisfied with their experiences in the discussion. Because these outcomes are measures of effective leadership, ratings on these factors should be especially meaningful to the discussion leader.

By Written and Oral Criticisms

Here is a sample of a written critique prepared by an observer:

In leading the discussion on freshmen and sophomore requirements, Don did quite well. First of all, he showed that he was well prepared. This was evident when he straightened out disagreements. One time he asked the group to see what the college catalog actually said, although I am sure he already knew the correct information. His leadership was democratic; he let the other members of the group pretty well run the discussion, interrupting, however, when the discussion bogged down into irrelevancies. Several times he accepted suggestions from the group as to direction of the discussion. The discussion ended on a good note—everyone except Dick was well pleased with the decision. But Dick was given enough opportunities, and I don't believe he was terribly disappointed. If more time had been available, Dick's solution might have been incorporated with the majority view or he might have been induced to change his mind.

But Don should give answers to these questions: When the Diane-Howard debate developed, why didn't he intervene more quickly and strongly to lead the discussion into new channels? Why did he give the "I think" (his solution) and lose his leadership to Jerome for a while?

A critique like this one tells the leader many things that he cannot get from numerical rating plans. This also applies to oral criticism. The latter may, in fact, be better because the leader has a chance to tell observers why he acted as he did.

By Rating Leadership Functions

Effective leadership in a discussion arises both from what you *choose to do* and from what you *choose not to do*. For example, it may be unnecessary for you to take specific action to encourage general participation in one discussion, yet, in other discussions this may be very important. Three choices are open to you: (1) You might fail to perform leadership functions that are needed; (2) you might offer the direction that is needed and refrain from carrying out unnecessary actions; or (3) you might persist in executing leadership functions that are not required. What this means is that your techniques of leadership should be conditioned by the specific situation that you face.

Since the discussion leader should be credited for perceiving which leadership functions need to be executed in a given discussion, he should be judged on each of the twelve functions. A rating scale that shows the three choices that are open to the leader might follow this pattern.

Function: Try to get general participation

1	2	3	4	5	6	7	8	9	10	11

Fails to Meet   Effectively   Exceeds
Needs of   Meets Needs   Needs of
Situation   of Situation   Situation

Here the mid-point represents the optimum level of direction by the leader.

This system of rating does have a relativistic basis, but in this way the situational factors you meet in an actual discussion are taken into consideration. Static and inflexible rules in a discussion imply that all discussions are alike. Anyone who has acted as a discussion leader knows that this is not true.

11. Leadership and Stages in Discussion

The assembly line process used in manufacturing permits standardization. Both the number and the types of operations to be performed by workers, as well as the sequence of the operations, are repeated again and again. The thousands of new cars that come from the assembly line only minutes apart from each other prove that standardization is successful. No one questions the wisdom of this step-by-step process in the manufacturing field.

In a discussion there should also be definable stages or steps that can be recognized. These stages, however, are quite different from the pattern of operations in the mechanical assembly of a product. In discussion the stages are not always constant. They are usually general rather than specific operational techniques, and all of the stages cannot be given a static time-order position. Yet, "pattern" in discussion is nevertheless important. A discussion leader should avoid the "strait-jacket" agenda of the assembly line leader, but, on the other hand, he must also avoid extreme forms of disorganization.

How to Plan Before the Discussion

Be Well Informed

You are not expected to be the world's greatest subject-matter expert when you lead a discussion, but neither should you be totally ignorant of information about the problem. Most persons find that a fair degree of familiarity with the problem to be discussed is a form of insurance that cannot be overlooked. Occasionally experienced discussion leaders who are especially competent persons are effective leaders in almost any situation. Whenever possible, however, even such persons try to familiarize themselves with at least a minimum of facts and principles. Skill in leadership is not adversely affected by knowledge about the subject that is discussed.

Prepare an Agenda or Leader's Outline

After you have studied the discussion problem carefully, you should prepare an agenda or leader's outline that you can refer to during the discussion. This outline may range from a simple list of six or eight questions to a much more detailed list. We shall explain types of questions you may wish to plan and structural patterns in discussion on pages 173–180 of this chapter.

Consider the Knowledge, Interests, and Abilities of Group Members

It would be ridiculous to assume that the knowledge, interests, and abilities of group members are matters of no importance to you. All of these factors will affect your planning. They have a bearing upon the structural pattern you intend to employ in the discussion, the type of questions you intend to ask, and the tentative time schedule that you assign to the main divisions of the discussion.

Plan Time and Place Details

Here are a few questions you should be able to answer affirmatively: Have you told all of the participants about the time and place of the discussion and the problem to be considered *several days prior to your meeting?* Have you checked to see whether suitable types of tables and chairs are in the room where your meeting is to be held? Have you made arrangements for the use of a blackboard, chart pad, posters, slides, or films if you intend to employ any of these visual techniques? These elements of planning are minimal requirements. You may have to do much more than we have suggested in order to be certain that you are not leaving too many details to chance.

How to Start the Discussion

Avoid Two Common Errors

Well-intentioned leaders who feel that they are performing a valuable service for the group sometimes start a discussion by giving an extended lecture about the problem, its history, causes, and importance.   In other cases the leader who begins with a long lecture may not be so well-intentioned but may be interested in controlling the thinking of the group members.   In either instance, however, the detailed introduction is usually an unwise choice.

A second error is committed by the lazy or pessimistic leader who says, "Well, there isn't much that we can do to solve our problem." Opening remarks of this type do not motivate participants to try to solve the problem.   Participants are likely to feel that the problem is a fruitless one that cannot be solved, or perhaps that the problem is not worth solving at all.   When the leader reveals indifference or despair in his opening remarks, the outcomes of the discussion are likely to match the expectations suggested by the leader.   A more positive approach is preferable in getting the discussion off to a good start.

Know the Characteristics of an Effective Introduction

The general purpose of your opening remarks should be to stimulate thinking and participation by members of the group.   To attain this goal, keep these ideas in mind: (1) Limit the length of your opening remarks (usually a two-minute introduction is a maximum—sometimes, in fact, a half-minute introduction is most appropriate); (2) try to make your remarks interesting; (3) strive for clarity; (4) imply or state that the problem is an important one; and (5) show that responsibility for decision-making resides with the group.   These characteristics of a good introduction become recognizable to others both through your manner of speaking and through the words you elect to use.

Plan a Particular Type of Introduction

There are a great many ways in which you can begin a discussion. The problem situation, including the time and place of the discussion and the persons in the group, has an important bearing upon the appropriateness of your introductory remarks. You should therefore have reasons for choosing a particular type of introduction.

1. *Begin by stating the problem directly.* Many times the best introduction is one in which you do no more than state the problem under consideration. For instance, you might say, "Our problem today deals with advancement opportunities for file clerks. We have tentatively agreed upon this problem statement: 'What plan for promotion should be established for our file clerk employees?' " After you have stated the problem in this manner, you can then ask a question to elicit clarification or information about the problem.

2. *Begin by stressing the importance of the problem.* Occasionally you may wish to emphasize the importance of a problem. Dr. Clayton G. Loosli does this in the following example:

Dr. *Loosli:* Today we are going to talk about the common cold. Before this year is over most listeners of this program will have suffered from at least two colds, and many will have had influenza. These and other infections of our respiratory systems are without doubt the greatest cause of illness today; and, of these infections, the common cold ranks first in prevalence. Perhaps in this country alone there are as many as three hundred million colds per year, involving some one-and-a-half-billion-odd days of actual illness. It has been estimated that from 40 to 50 per cent of all days lost by children in our schools is due to colds and their complications. It has also been estimated that the annual bill to the American people for the common cold is as much as three billion dollars annually, in work time lost, drugs, and medical bills.

Obviously, then, the common cold is a major medical problem.[1]

[1] Clayton G. Loosli, "The Common Cold," *University of Chicago Round Table* (March 4, 1951), 1. All quotations in this chapter from the *University of Chicago Round Table* are reprinted by permission.

3. *Begin by stressing recency.* Since current events have a strong interest to most of us, you might wish to refer to some immediate facts about the problem in your opening remarks. Here are two good examples of this type of introduction:

(a) *Mr. Shapiro:* Newspapers, this past week, have carried headlines that consumer prices have reached all-time highs. Wholesale prices have recently turned upward. Many people are saying that the settlement of the steel strike is going to result in higher prices. These and many other bits and pieces of economic data have again turned attention to a revival of inflationary pressures. . . .[2]

(b) *Mr. Eby:* The eyes of the entire nation are on the city of Chicago and what it does about crime. The election of its county sheriff is interesting everyone. Papers throughout the whole nation are writing stories about the election; and we in Chicago are naturally concerned about this election too. . . .[3]

4. *Begin by using historical references.* Sometimes references to the origin of the problem are especially suitable in an introduction. Ogburn and Dorfman use this type of introduction in the examples we are citing:

(a) *Mr. Ogburn:* The ideas of Sigmund Freud flashed like a meteor through the intellectual sky about a half a century ago. His impact upon civilization was almost unparalleled. The nearest illustration of which I can think to compare with Freud are the ideas of Karl Marx or the ideas of Charles Darwin. . . .[4]

(b) *Dr. Dorfman:* Almost two years have now elapsed since the announcement of the discovery of the effects of ACTH and cortisone on rheumatoid arthritis. During this time many patients have been treated with these drugs, and experiments have been conducted in attempting to understand their action better. It has been clear to everybody that they represent a very major change in our entire thinking about disease. . . .[5]

---

[2] Eli Shapiro, "What Are the Prospects of More Inflation?" *University of Chicago Round Table* (August 24, 1952), 1.

[3] Kermit Eby, "How Can We Control Organized Crime?" *University of Chicago Round Table* (November 5, 1950), 1.

[4] William F. Ogburn, "Is Freud Up to Date?" *University of Chicago Round Table* (April 15, 1951), 1.

[5] Albert Dorfman, "Stress and Disease," *University of Chicago Round Table* (December 10, 1950), 1.

5. *Begin by stating major issues.* The issues are the vital questions to be answered in a discussion. When you are certain that you can select the correct issues, you may wish to follow the practice illustrated here:

Miss Mentschikoff: As everybody knows, the President has seized the steel industry because management refused to accept the recommendations of the Wage Stabilization Board, and this refusal led to a strike order by the union. The validity of the President's action is now pending before the Supreme Court.

Apart from the labor issues involved, two constitutional issues are presented. The first is whether in seizing the steel industry the President has acted within the scope of his constitutional power. The second is, if the President has acted unconstitutionally, should the Supreme Court, by affirming the injunction issued by Judge Pine, review and repudiate the President's action? [6]

6. *Begin by using contrast.* The use of a striking contrast is an especially interesting way to begin a discussion.

(a) *Mr. Wirth:* We are in the midst of the greatest boom in the history of our national economy. In education, by contrast, we are in the midst of what can be described only as a bust. . . .[7]

(b) *Mr. Wirth:* "Warlike" and "peace-loving," "free men" and "slaves"——these are the words which are used to divide the peoples of the world. We Americans and our friends, of course, are good; our enemies are evil.[8]

7. *Begin by using a quotation.* Unusual or thought-provoking quotations may also be used.

(a) *Mr. Smith:* "If we could know where we are and whither we are tending, we could better judge what to do and how to do it." That, ladies and gentlemen, is Abraham Lincoln, the third of the great secular trinity of American heroes. . . .[9]

---

[6] Soia Mentschikoff, "The Constitutionality of the President's Seizure of the Steel Industry," *University of Chicago Round Table* (May 18, 1952), 1.

[7] Louis Wirth, "Equality of Educational Opportunity," *University of Chicago Round Table* (December 26, 1948), 1.

[8] Louis Wirth, "What Do Americans Believe About Their Fellow-Men?" *University of Chicago Round Table* (February 18, 1951), 1.

[9] T. V. Smith, "Lincoln and Democratic Morality," *University of Chicago Round Table* (February 10, 1952), 1.

(b) *Mr. Johnson:* In 1931 Republican Editor William Allen White wrote to Democratic Editor Josephus Daniels: "I have been reporting political conventions now since 1896 and trust I will die at it. A national convention is really the greatest show on this continent, combining for me all the thrills of a prizefight, a bullfight, a gladiatorial exhibit, and a house afire." . . .[10]

8. *Begin by using true-to-life portrayal.*   In a discussion on the subject of narcotics, the recorded statements of a sixteen-year-old girl dope addict were used to open a discussion presented on the *Northwestern University Reviewing Stand.*   She reported: "My boy friend and I decided we didn't have enough money to buy dope, and we decided to try breaking into a home in our neighborhood to see if we could steal money. . . .   I was arrested and sent away for several months. . . .   I returned home. . . .   I started on heroin. . . ."[11]

9. *Begin by using role playing.*   The aim in role playing is not to achieve the true-to-life effect we have just mentioned.   Role playing is a simulated enactment of a situation by persons who may or may not have previously experienced the roles that they portray before the group.   Suppose your discussion problem is: "How approachable are supervisors?"   You might introduce the problem by depicting a supervisor who shows that he is indifferent toward an employee in a conversation on the job.   Or you might depict a scene in which supervisor-employee relationships are revealed as friendly and sincere.   As you can see, the depiction of scenes about supervisor-employee relations may be an interesting way to start a discussion.   There may, of course, be other values.   Both observers and role players sometimes learn something about the problem that they did not formerly know.[12]

---

10 Walter Johnson, "Can the Republicans Defeat the Majority Party?" *University of Chicago Round Table* (July 6, 1952), 1.

11 "Can We Stop the Traffic in Narcotics?" *Northwestern University Reviewing Stand* (July 1, 1951), 3.

12 Some groups have been successful in using role playing at any stage in the discussion.   When a strong conflict arises in the discussion, for example, an imaginary enactment of a scene that illustrates the conflict may cause partisan group members to be more objective when the discussion is resumed.

If you make use of role playing, you should follow these suggestions: (a) The scenes that are depicted should be unrehearsed by the role players; and (b) the scenes should be brief, perhaps only a few minutes in length. As soon as the problem situation has been illustrated by the role players, you should interrupt them and begin your discussion proper.

10. *Begin by using visual aids.* Films, slides, or charts may make an otherwise abstract problem easier to understand. Like some of the other types of introductions we have described, visual aids also represent a departure from the normal practice followed by most discussion leaders. Because this type of introduction is a non-typical way to start a discussion and because it has other values as well, it should perhaps be used more than it is at the present time.

STRUCTURAL PATTERNS FOR THE DISCUSSION

The preparation outline or agenda that you prepare is likely to determine the actual structural pattern of the discussion. You cannot, of course, predict the exact pattern of organization that every discussion will take. Occasionally the participants may prefer a different structural plan, or you may discover that a pattern different from the one you previously planned should be followed. In any event, we think you should do considerable thinking about the logical pattern of the discussion before the discussion is held.

Plan by Using the Reflective Pattern

In Chapter 7 we described the pattern of reflective thinking in detail. As a rule, we believe you should follow this pattern closely when you plan your leadership outline. You should design questions that might be asked in the discussion in terms of the major divisions of the reflective pattern.

To illustrate this type of leader's outline, we are reprinting an outline used by a leader in a class discussion on "independent-affiliate" relations on a college campus. You should study the outline carefully.

Problem: How Can Better Relations between Independent and Affiliate Groups Be Secured? [18]

I. *Recognition of the Problem*

   A. *Formulation of the Problem as a Question*

      1. Should there be any changes in the statement of the problem?

      2. Should the problem be limited in any way?

         (a) Does it apply to our campus rather than to colleges generally? (Problem limited to campus.)

         (b) Does it apply both to fraternity-independent men relationships and to sorority-independent women relationships? (Problem limited to fraternity-independent men relationships.)

   B. *Definition of the Problem*

      1. What do we mean by "relations"—"good," "bad," and "better"?

      2. Are we agreed upon our interpretations of "independent and affiliate groups?"

      3. Should we define the functions of the Inter-Fraternity Council (IFC)?

      4. Should we define the functions of the Inter-House Council (IHC)?

II. *Description of the Problem*

   A. *History of the Problem*

      1. How was this problem handled in the past?

      2. Were these solutions satisfactory?

      3. Are conditions today different from those that existed earlier?

   B. *Effects of the Problem*

      1. What attitudes and actions are exhibited by independent men toward fraternity men?

         (a) Friendliness? (b) Reprisals? (c) Tension?

      2. What attitudes and actions are exhibited by fraternity men toward independent men?

         (a) Friendliness? (b) Reprisals? (c) Tension?

      3. What symptoms have been noted by the Fraternity Adviser and by the Dormitory Adviser?

      4. How serious are the effects that have been given?

      5. Are the undesirable effects off-set by desirable effects?

      6. Are the undesirable effects likely to become even more serious unless good solutions are discovered?

---

[13] Based upon an outline prepared by F. M. Scherer, Class of 1954, College of Literature, Science, and the Arts, University of Michigan.

C. *Causes of the Problem*
1. What are the primary causes of hostility between independents and affiliates?
2. What are the related or secondary causes of the problem?

III. *Discovery of Solutions*
A. *Conditions to Be Met by an Acceptable Solution*
1. Should both the independent and affiliate systems be preserved?
2. Should the problem be resolved at the student level or at the University administrative level?
3. Should more wholesome social relationships be an important feature of possible solutions to this problem?

B. *Possible Solutions*
1. In the area of coordination and government:
(a) Status quo? (b) Eliminate all organization? (c) Supervision over IFC and IHC by the Student Legislature? (d) Supervision over IFC and IHC by the Student Affairs Committee? (e) Supervision by the faculty? (f) Joint Action by the IFC and IHC?
2. In the area of social relationships:
(a) Abolish fraternities? (b) Disperse dormitory system? (c) Use objective descriptive literature; *e.g.*, Oxford Book proposal? (d) Integrated intramural sports program? (e) Integrated social program?
3. Are there other alternative solutions?

IV. *Evaluation of Solutions and Acceptance of the Best Solution*
A. *Evaluation of Solutions*
1. What are the merits and weaknesses of the six solutions in the area of coordination and government?
2. What are the merits and weaknesses of the five solutions in the area of social relationships?
3. What are the points of agreement and points of difference that we have in this discussion?
4. Will the solution we recommend be a multiple solution?

B. *Acceptance of Best Solution (or Solutions)*
1. Will the solution we have accepted change present undesirable effects?
2. Will the solution we have accepted correct the causes of the problem?
3. Will new undesirable effects result?
4. Does the solution we have accepted conform to the conditions to be met by an acceptable solution?

5. Should we do some preliminary testing before endorsing the solution?

V. *Plan of Action*

1. What groups and individuals must carry out the solution we have endorsed?
2. What recommendations, if any, should be given to the groups and individuals who will put the solution into operation?

This leader's outline based upon the reflective pattern proved to be a very good one in a real discussion. These pointers will further indicate how the leader used his outline:

1. Questions listed under "formulation of the problem as a question" were answered in a pre-discussion session.
2. More time in this discussion was devoted to effects of the problem than to either history or causes.
3. The leader did not dictate solutions, but he found that classifying solutions under "coordination and government" and "social relationships" helped to achieve clarification.
4. The leader found that it was unnecessary to ask some of his planned questions and that some questions that he did not plan were asked either by himself or by others.
5. The leader was so familiar with his outline that he did not find it necessary to refer to the outline repeatedly. He realized that if he kept his eyes glued to the outline, the preparation that he did would be a liability rather than an asset.

Plan by Using the Modified Reflective Pattern

By modified reflective pattern, as we are using the term here, we mean only minor changes in the full-scale reflective process. The pattern can be outlined in this way:

Step 1. Giving the Facts of the Problem
Step 2. Setting Goals
Step 3. Proposing Solutions
Step 4. Testing Solutions
Step 5. Reaching a Decision

This pattern differs from the full-scale reflective process in these respects. The *description of the problem* stage is here labeled "giving the facts" and appears as the first stage in the discussion rather than as the second. Giving history, giving effects, and giving causes are all grouped together as "facts." This does not mean that these factors that are telescoped are unimportant. Actually effects and causes will be reported in the discussion, but such information will not always be classified as "effects" or "causes." Second, "setting goals" is listed as stage two in the discussion and includes formulating the problem as a question, defining the problem, and establishing the conditions of a good solution. Third, specific attention is not given to the *plan of action* stage as listed in the reflective pattern described in this book.

What this means is that there are some sequential changes in the stages of the modified reflective plan, and that there are fewer details given. But basically the plan is a sound one. There are few, if any, weaknesses in this type of structural design, and possibly some special advantages.

We are reporting a case problem titled "Teaching My First Class" that you may wish to discuss in groups of six or eight using the modified reflective pattern as the structural plan for your discussions. After your discussions, report your reactions *pro* and *con* to the modified reflective pattern.

Teaching My First Class [14]

Last semester I was a student teacher at Tappan Junior High School. I had three classes including one class in ninth grade English which met the last period in the afternoon. The class was very large—thirty-eight students, and consisted mainly of boys. After I observed this class for a few days, my critic teacher told me I was ready to do some actual teaching.

The assignment for my first experience as a teacher was one that concerned the discussion of books. Each student had been told to read a book of his choice for the class discussion. My critic teacher suggested that the assignment should be handled in a way that was different from the ordinary individual book report type of participation. I therefore decided to prepare an outline—sometimes called an *agenda*— to guide me in leading the discussion on books. I planned a series of

[14] Reported by Mary Jane Mills, Class of 1953, College of Literature, Science, and the Arts, University of Michigan.

questions which ranged from how to pick a book to what makes a book interesting.

On the day I was to take charge of this class my critic teacher greeted me by saying that he had had some very interesting discussions on books in his morning classes and that he hoped my discussion would be a good one too. I felt that my class would do well also; in fact, I felt very confident because I had spent several hours in preparing my list of discussion questions. After my class arrived, we arranged the desks in a large discussion circle and I made a few introductory comments. Then I asked my first question. To my surprise, I could get only a few words of discussion from the class. I tried other questions and had the same result. It was soon clear that my ideas and questions were going over like a "lead balloon." The students knew this was my first experience in teaching and they apparently had decided that they were going to have some fun. I could hold the attention of some of the students as long as my material lasted, but there seemed to be just so many questions you can try to discuss about books. After fifteen minutes the discussion had turned into a monologue by me. At this point I began to get nervous—the thirty minutes ahead seemed endless. This was the cue the class had been expecting. Everyone picked up his pencil and began to tap on his desk so that any control over the class I had held previously was gone. I had to figure out something to do in a hurry.

Plan by Using the Vital Issues Pattern

When a series of questions are asked that touch upon the most important phases of a problem they can be called vital issues. These questions may be sufficiently comprehensive to cover the major steps of reflective thinking. When this is true, the vital issues pattern is not a departure from the reflective process.

Suppose, however, that you use short-cuts in problem-solving by omitting a number of questions that are usually regarded as important. This might or might not be a serious error. Much will depend upon the problem and the persons in your group as to whether or not you are inviting disaster by simplifying the process of problem-solving.

These three examples (on page 179) of short-cuts through the use of the vital issues pattern show how greatly the reflective process can be changed.

1. *Causes and Solutions As Vital Issues*
   (Problem: Lunch Period for Employees)
     (a) What are the causes of employee dissatisfaction with departmental lunch period assignments?
     (b) How can these causes be corrected?
2. *Effects and Solutions As Vital Issues*
   (Problem: Plan for the Election of the President)
     (a) What effects (positive and negative) arise from the use of the Electoral College System in presidential elections?
     (b) Are there more desirable plans that could be followed for presidential elections?
3. *Advantages and Disadvantages As Vital Issues*
   (Problem: Over-Time *versus* Part-Time Workers)
     (a) What are the advantages and disadvantages of the over-time work plan?
     (b) What are the advantages and disadvantages of the part-time worker plan?

You should follow these abbreviated forms of the vital issues plan only if you are sure that the members of your discussion group are especially well informed, and that nothing will be gained by spending time on a complete analysis of the problem. In the first example you must be able to assume that the effects of the present lunch period assignments are already fully known and agreed upon by the group; in the second, that everyone understands the electoral system; and in the third, that the appraisal of the two types of work plans is the correct place to begin the discussion. Normally, as we have said, you should not limit the structural pattern of the discussion to the selective issues we have listed. The issues given in the examples are certainly very important, but the danger is that other important issues might be entirely neglected.

Plan by Using the Divisions of the Problem Pattern

Another structural pattern that occasionally suits discussion problems can be called the divisions-approach. In this pattern the problem is divided into major areas and the discussion is centered in turn on each of the areas. A steel strike, for instance, may be discussed from the point of view of the workers, the management, and the public; a political issue, in terms of Democratic and

Republican positions; or a change in college policy, from the point of view of the college administration, the faculty, and the students. Areas of the problem such as these do of course receive attention in any effective discussion, but usually the specific divisions do not become the dominant form of organization of the discussion.

Plan by Using the Pattern Suggested by the Contributions of Members

Suppose that you are the leader of a discussion dealing with how superiors should discuss progress and performance reports with subordinates. Instead of opening the discussion with a question calling for definition, background, or causal factors, suppose that you say, "How do you feel about this problem?" or "What ideas do you have?" or "Who wants to start our discussion?" Questions like these invite participants to respond in any way they wish: they can talk about what the problem means, how it originated, reasons for its importance, or even how the problem should be solved. When you ask general questions like these the group members determine the starting-point in the discussion. They tend to begin talking about what is most interesting and important to themselves instead of responding to the question you think they should answer. This plan of leadership, as you probably suspect, is usually called non-directive or permissive leadership.

When you lead this type of discussion you should nevertheless give attention to logical structure. If you do not, the discussion may become a talk-fest. Thus, after listening to a number of the early remarks, you can pose questions or give statements that knit the discussion together. The structural pattern that emerges may be any of the four patterns we have described. But it will be a pattern that has been suggested, at least in part, by the undirected contributions of the members of the group. Your job in this situation is to detect the correct time to follow up on the remarks given, and thus achieve a degree of orderliness in the discussion pattern. Actually, this practice is probably more difficult to carry out than following a pre-determined pattern. If it is carried out skillfully, it can prove to be a highly successful plan of leadership.

What to Do When Progress Is Blocked

In a discussion there are quite a number of uncertainties. There is the human element. You cannot be sure that what is successful in one discussion will be successful in another. Structural patterns and lists of questions, even if they are carefully chosen, cannot fully protect you from the barriers that stop progress in a group.

Meet Problem Situations As They Arise

Usually you should try to correct problem situations in a discussion as soon as you detect them. In our previous chapter on leadership functions (Chapter 10) we mentioned some of the problem situations that you will face; still others are described in our three chapters on participation in discussion (Chapters 12, 13, and 14). In these chapters, and others, we have shown that there are hosts of roadblocks that arise in a discussion. We have also given many practical suggestions for overcoming these obstacles.

Suggest a Short Intermission Period

On December 12, 1941, Dwight D. Eisenhower was suddenly ordered to proceed to Washington to confer with General Marshall. When he appeared before Marshall on a Sunday morning, two days later, he naturally sensed the urgency of our military needs, but he did not know what tasks he might be expected to perform. The Declaration of War that followed the Japanese attack at Pearl Harbor and our losses in the Pacific would require many readjustments in our military plans. "General Marshall," says Eisenhower, "took perhaps twenty minutes to describe all this, and then abruptly asked, 'what should be our general line of action?'" In reporting his response, Eisenhower says, "I thought a second and, hoping I was showing a poker face, answered, 'Give me a few hours.'" In the interim before appearing at his conference with Marshall again, Eisenhower must have carefully appraised our military needs, for the plan of action he recommended brought an "I agree with you" response from General Marshall. "His tone," says Eisenhower, "implied that I had been given the problem as a check to an answer he had already reached." [15]

This interesting illustration of the "pause" in deliberations has important meanings to all persons who wish to make discussion as fruitful as possible. In the case of Eisenhower the intermission period was probably used in identifying significant facts and weighing alternative choices. There are surely occasions when discussion groups should encourage this practice, particularly if the problem is a very difficult one and yet does not demand a split-second decision. The "break" in the conference like the "period of silence" in Quaker meetings may have greater value than continuous talking. Conferees during an intermission are given an opportunity calmly and silently to restructure their thinking, and perhaps, to discover solutions that had not previously occurred to them. When the group convenes again, the intermission period may therefore have had a therapeutic effect that is related to successful decision-making.

The "pause" in deliberations by the group has been described by Walser as an occasion when members question facts, values, and attitudes.

As soon as the last speaker's voice is forgotten the individual mood of each conferee will return to him, and faith, critical scepticism or introspection will invade each according to his background. With some, the contrast of sudden quiet after much talking will drive them to question the honesty of their own contributions. Inconsistencies between their attitude and their belief, between their impulse and their reason, may appear then with sobering clarity.

*   *   *

Such a deliberate pause may last for only a matter of sixty or one hundred seconds but it can transform our whole outlook in a way that resembles the effect of listening to good music, looking at a fine picture, or seeing again an old friend.[16]

---

[15] From *Crusade in Europe*, by Dwight D. Eisenhower, p. 22. Copyright 1948 by Doubleday and Company Incorporated. Reprinted by permission.

[16] Frank Walser, *The Art of Conference*, pp. 19–20. New York: Harper and Brothers, 1948. Reprinted by permission.

A pause or intermission may be useful in at least four situations: (1) when conflict is particularly strong and promises to become centered upon personalities rather than upon issues, (2) when the discussion is characterized by apathy and indifference, (3) when participants need added information or when they find it particularly difficult to discover solutions, and (4) when the discussion is to be conducted for a time interval of more than one hour. The recess, except perhaps in the case of the two or three hour conference, must not be a mechanical procedure that is invariably followed. A purpose must be served by the pause in deliberations.

Before the group ceases its deliberations you and members of the group should determine the length of the recess, and perhaps, whether refreshments should be served during the intermission. As we have indicated, the recess period may be only a few minutes in length. Many times conferees do not even leave their seats in the conference room. The pause should not be looked upon as an extended vacation. For this reason a brief recess is probably preferable to a longer period.

Suggest Postponement to a Later Date

After an Athenian jury of more than five hundred persons found Socrates guilty of corrupting the youth, Socrates suggested that the trial should not have been concluded in a single day. In the *Apology* he says: "I am convinced that I never intentionally wronged anyone, although I cannot convince you of that—for we have had a short conversation only; but if there were a law at Athens, such as there is in other cities, that a capital cause should not be decided in one day, then I believe that I should have convinced you; but now the time is too short. I cannot in a moment refute great slanders." Socrates apparently wished greater time to present his views and periods of postponement during which the jurors might silently reflect. As the trial was conducted, however, his time for speaking was limited and the jurors had no opportunity "to sleep" on their decision.

There are many situations when postponement of a decision is desirable. When a problem is either comprehensive in scope or very complex, postponement permits conferees to discover additional data, to analyze these data, and to think of productive solutions. If this procedure is followed we will not be like the man who invariably thought of ideal solutions while driving home after conferences were over. Even though decisions in discussion should always be subject to re-examination and modification, they are often regarded as final. Therefore, when time permits and the situation calls for further deliberation, there are valid reasons for deferring action. It is very likely true, under the conditions we have suggested, that a series of short conferences will bring about decisions that are superior to those reached in a single group meeting. It is difficult to imagine a different result if the group members lack knowledge and understanding, or are unable in a single meeting to assess the relevant data and alternative solutions.

How to Close the Discussion

The conclusion that you give in a discussion meeting should be a relatively *brief* report, and it should be a *fair* report. A long and involved summary is usually inappropriate. People generally do not like summaries that restate in detail what they have already experienced in a discussion. In somewhat the same way they resent practices by leaders who fail to give a fair conclusion. Remember that a conclusion that summarizes the thinking of the group to the satisfaction of the group itself is much better than one that falls short of gaining acceptance. You may find that you should ask group members to make some suggestions about what should be included in the conclusion. At least you should be willing to have group members indicate whether they think the conclusion you have given is a satisfactory one.

Summarize the Main Parts of the Discussion

If you have not made frequent internal summaries in the discussion, it may be appropriate for you to review the main parts of the discussion. This step-by-step report demands discernment by you in identifying findings and in selecting what should be reported. Brevity as a criterion applies to this type of conclusion in the same way that it applies to all other types of conclusions.

Summarize Agreements and Differences

When full agreement is not reached in a discussion, you may summarize by reviewing points of agreement and points of difference. Malcolm P. Sharp illustrates this method of closing a discussion on the problem "Must Men Fight?"

We have seen that, so long as we are healthy animals, we shall continue to value our lives—and still more the life of our kind. Science leaves open the question whether the disposition to fight is part of so-called "human nature" or the result of changeable human arrangements.

Dr. Mead, as a scientist, takes the position that the impulses which lead to fighting can be molded by improving our society. I am more impressed by the persistence of fighting in other societies and in our own and more inclined to think that our official representatives will need to learn how to repress fighting in us and in themselves.

Dr. Mead looks for great new contributions in what we call "social sciences." Dr. Shapley has made a notable contribution here and elsewhere in his discussion of moral substitutes for war. Both of them have the faith of scientists, a faith in the capacity of reason to solve problems—a faith in which all of us who love life must have some share.[17]

Summarize by Giving a Progress Report

The progress report applies to discussions that are to be continued at a later meeting, or perhaps, to discussions that are inconclusive in their outcomes. Two ends are served: (1) The report shows the accomplishments of the group, and in the case of discussions to be held at a later date, shows the point in the discussion where deliberations should be resumed; and (2) the report tends to keep participants from feeling that they have fully failed in their efforts. A hopeful sign, even in the most difficult cases, is usually desirable.

---

[17] Malcolm P. Sharp, "Must Men Fight?" *University of Chicago Round Table* (September 22, 1946), 16–17.

Summarize by Restating the Decision Reached

A restatement of the decision of the group is a very common way to close a discussion. Sometimes your restatement will be very brief. Different problem-solution discussions will determine the degree of detail that is needed.

Summarize by Outlining the Plan of Action

When a specific plan of action is needed to make a decision meaningful, your summary may be limited to the plan itself. In this way you especially emphasize execution of the decision. Failure to do this sometimes means that participants remember the decision of the group, but they forget about the action that is required to put the decision into effect.

PART IV

Participation

12. Interpersonal Relations: Group Unity

Thus far in this book we have discussed many aspects of problem-solving and other intellectual activities that take place in discussions and conferences. In addition, we have explored many of the problems related to leading discussion groups. From time to time, however, we have seen that another very important factor enters into a complete consideration of the processes of group discussion. Let us turn our attention now to this factor: interpersonal relations within a group.

In general, we mean by interpersonal relations, the emotional and personal relationships that exist among the members of a group and that may be found in the atmosphere of the group as a whole. In our discussion of leadership, we have seen that one very important aspect of good discussion leadership is creating a "climate" for good discussion. And members of the group, as well, should be interested in setting up a good atmosphere for group discussion. Establishing good interpersonal relations in the group is important for two general reasons: (1) Good interpersonal relationships help in the problem-solving process, and (2) good interpersonal relationships make the group task more enjoyable.

By and large, when we speak of good interpersonal relations, we are speaking of making a group of *individuals* into a unified, cohesive *group*. In an interesting article Keltner makes a point of this fact.

In any group the individual members represent divergent skills, goals, social orientation, action concepts, and the like. Before a group can move forward it must become *welded* into a team unit.[1]

Our concern here is with ways of transforming a heterogenous group of individuals into a homogenous, cohesive group.

GROUP UNITY

Individuals come into a conference group from a great variety of backgrounds, with a great variety of interests, with a great variety of attitudes toward others in the group, toward the group's task, and toward the particular problem the group is discussing. As Haiman says:

The individuals in any group vary in the degree to which they are really a part of the organization and committed to achievement of the group's goals. Some are on the fringes—they are peripherally involved. Some devote the major part of their lives and thoughts to the group— they are centrally involved. The others range in between.[2]

The closer the members of the group come to the "centrally involved" type of group, the more cohesive, or unified, they are. Hence, the degree of cohesiveness of a group is determined by a feeling toward *group* involvement and depends largely upon (1) the attitudes of members toward other individuals in the group, (2) the attitudes of members toward the group as a whole, and (3) the attitudes of members toward the work and goals of the group.

Some of the terms used to describe this type of close working, harmonious interpersonal relations are: "group cohesiveness," "we-feeling," "group unity," and "group belongingness." We will use the term "group unity" to refer to the outcome of desirable interpersonal relations in the group. But it can be seen from all

---

[1] John Keltner, "Committee Dynamics: Basic Concepts," *The Gavel of Delta Sigma Rho*, XXXII (November, 1949), 10. Reprinted by permission.

[2] Franklyn S. Haiman, *Group Leadership and Democratic Action*, p. 82. Boston: Houghton Mifflin Company, 1951. Reprinted by permission.

these descriptive terms that the important thing in achieving a strong unity in the group is the subordination, for the duration of the life of a conference session, of an individual's goals to the goals of the group he's working with. Naturally, this does not mean that each member of the group must give up his individual goals in order to be a part of a well-functioning unified group. It simply means that for the time being he must make the group's goals his own goals.

IMPORTANCE OF GROUP UNITY

A conference group is somewhat like a football team. Even though individual players on a team may each be an expert, even All-Americans, unless the players cooperate, then they will be easily beaten by an opposing team made up of inferior individual players. So, in a conference, even if all members are individually quite expert, unless they take part in real teamwork, and strive together toward a common goal, the results are apt to be poor. As Keltner says:

A collection of undisciplined and uncooperative individuals will not be able to produce distinctively valuable results as compared to highly skilled and disciplined individuals. On the other hand a group of people seriously concerned with a given problem and endowed with the discipline and skills of group operation can consistently produce results superior to any individual operation.[3]

Not only is the group decision apt to be better if a group is cohesive, but also the member's satisfaction with what happens in the group and with the outcomes of the group will be increased. The degree of group unity is related to the following aspects of conference work:

Member Satisfaction with the Group

Where the cohesiveness is high, members tend to feel that their group is a pretty good group and that the members in the group

---

[3] Keltner, *op. cit.*, p. 5.

are pretty fine people.   Conversely, where there are many disruptive elements in the group's interpersonal relations, the members are almost certain to feel that there is little or no satisfaction in working with the group.

Member Satisfaction with the Group Decision

If the members of a group feel that the group is working well together, they also will feel that the decisions reached by the group are of a high caliber.   You probably have had the experience of serving on a committee where everything seemed to go very well, where the atmosphere was friendly, and where the only disagreements were on an impersonal basis.   The chances are that under those conditions you felt that the decisions reached by that committee were good decisions.   On the other hand, if there is a lot of strong personal animosity among the members of a group, there probably will be a lot of dissatisfaction not only with the group meeting itself but also with the group decisions.

Member Satisfaction with the Process of Conference

One reason why people often complain that "conferences are just a lot of talk," is that they have not identified themselves closely with the group; group unity is low.   In general, when the group feels unified, the members of the group will feel a very high degree of satisfaction with the group meeting as a whole.

Better Decisions

The more unified the group feels, the better the decisions the group will be able to produce.   A cohesive group works better and produces better decisions than a disjointed, non-unified collection of individuals.

Freer Participation

When a group is unified, members feel free to participate fully in the conference.   The more widespread the participation, the more ideas there will be for the group to utilize in reaching its conclusions.

Better Motivation to Carry Out Decisions

If members of a conference group feel that the decisions were reached by "us" rather than by "them" or "him," there is a much greater motivation to participate in the actual execution of the decisions.

FACTORS THAT MAKE A GROUP UNIFIED

Now let us see if we can isolate the various things that, added together, make a group cohesive. Obviously, the factors tending toward cohesiveness in a conference will depend to a large measure on the individual conference group. Since we are dealing with human beings, we cannot expect to be able to set down a formula which will always produce a tight, cohesive group. We can, however, consider some of the factors that operate to make individuals "centrally involved" in the group.

Personal Liking for Other Individuals in the Group

All of us function more effectively as part of a group when the other members of the group are people that we like. Since we select friends who have goals similar to our own, it becomes easier to be a part of a cohesive group when the people in the group have goals similar to our own.

Involvement with the Group

A group quickly becomes cohesive and unified when each individual becomes involved with the group's goals and purposes. If a football player feels that the most important thing is winning for his *alma mater,* his own individual goals become secondary and he functions as a true member of the team. Perhaps a more accurate description is to say that the football player *identifies* his own individual goals with the team goals. The same sort of thing happens in a conference. The extent to which indivdual goals become identified with or become the same as group goals determines to a large measure the extent to which the group is unified.

Previous Acquaintance with Other Members of the Group

If we know other members of the group, we are in a better position to evaluate their goals, attitudes, and feelings. We know how far we must go in order to become "centrally involved" with the other members of the group, where we must compromise, how much we can participate, how much cooperation is expected of us, and so on.

Equality of Status

Status or prestige is often closely tied up with the degree of cohesiveness of the group. Sometimes we find it difficult to identify ourselves closely with a group where there are members of a higher status or greater prestige than our own, and, on the other hand, we may also find it difficult to identify with a group where the status or prestige of other members is lower than our own. In general, greater unity is reached in a group where status is approximately the same, or, if that is not possible, where the inequalities of status are compensated for in some way.

Receptiveness by Other Members of the Group

The chances of a strongly unified group are greatly increased when we are easily and quickly received into the group, when our participation is asked for, and when our opinions are listened to carefully. How willing members of a group are to be receptive and permissive often determines how cohesive the group will be.

These five factors, then, may be looked upon as a set of criteria for helping to determine the degree of cohesiveness of the group.

BARRIERS TO UNITY

There are many things that can happen in a group to prevent the group's becoming unified and cohesive. In the next chapter some characteristics of participants that tend to disrupt a group will be considered in some detail. In addition to these specific participation "roles" which undoubtedly reduce the amount of cohesiveness in a group, there are some other barriers to good interpersonal relations.

Negative Attitudes

Members of a discussion group who take a negative attitude toward things that are said or that happen in the discussion, or toward other members of the discussion group are certainly disruptive influences. We should hasten to point out, however, that we do not mean that members of a discussion group must never disagree. Disagreements on principle, on evidence, on lines of argument, are healthy in a discussion.

Unwillingness to Cooperate

We have seen that discussion and conference rely heavily upon the cooperation of individual members of a group. Therefore, there can be no effective discussion if the unity of the group is disrupted by uncooperative members.

Lack of Consideration for Others

Any group process involves give-and-take. This means that members of the group should do more than simply cooperate, but that they should make it a point to be considerate of other members of the group. Unless this kind of personal, individual consideration for the rights and feelings of others does exist, a cohesive group cannot exist.

Excessive Formality

Most of us find it very hard to feel like an integral part of a group unless the atmosphere is somewhat permissive. An extremely formal atmosphere is often forbidding and tends to inhibit the members and make them withdraw from the group.

Excessive Control

We have seen that an autocratic type of leadership is usually a poor type of leadership. An autocratic leader, exercising strong,

iron-fisted control over a group, can often produce a surface re-
semblance of cohesiveness. What really exists, however, is un-
welcome, unwanted submissiveness. If the autocracy is removed,
the only binding factor holding the group together is removed.
Needless to say, this kind of cohesiveness is far from being the vol-
untary, self-imposed type of unity that we have been discussing.
Autocratic controls often prevent real unity from arising in the
group.

Lack of Clearly Defined Group Goals

Another barrier to good interpersonal relations in a group is the
lack of clearly defined, clearly understood group goals. We have
seen that group cohesiveness depends to a large extent on the individual's adopting the group's goals as his own. If the group
goals are so poorly defined that the member of the group does not
perceive them clearly, then it is clear that a real obstacle to group
unity exists. In order for the member to identify himself with the
goals of the group, it is necessary for him to know and understand
what the goals are.

Lack of Discipline

While we would not expect to find a high degree of cohesiveness in a group operating under strict controls, it is necessary for
the group to have a minimum amount of discipline and orderly
procedure. Ideally, this discipline should arise from the group
itself, with the expert guidance of a democratic leader. Discipline
imposed from without too often becomes a form of autocracy. But
a group without any discipline is apt to be disorganized, lack definite
goals, lack commonness of purpose, and certainly lack unity and
cohesiveness.

ACHIEVING UNITY

To begin with, groups should try to avoid the pitfalls discussed
above as barriers to cohesiveness. Members of a discussion group

should also try to avoid some of the poor participant functions discussed in the next chapter. In addition, there are several specific
measures that might be taken in a discussion group, both by the
leader, and by members of the group, to help insure a high degree
of cohesiveness. First let us consider methods that may be used
by the leader and then methods that may be used by participants
in a discussion.

The Conference Leader

1. *Whenever possible, assemble conference groups that contain
a minimum amount of personal hostility.* If possible, select for
your conference people who like each other personally. Of course,
this is not always possible, so when some hostilities exist, try to
minimize them. This can be done in several ways.

(a) *Serve as a compromiser of differences between people who
are unfriendly.* One of the important functions of a leader should
be that of a compromiser. Since he normally is not deeply involved with either side of an argument in a discussion, he is in an
ideal position to propose a compromise solution that might prove
satisfactory to both disputing parties. At any rate, he should attempt to arbitrate differences in a friendly fashion.

(b) *Allow equal opportunities to participate to all members of
the conference group.* Sometimes hostility can be overcome if the
hostile parties have an opportunity to talk it out. The leader
should never allow one of two disputing parties unlimited time to
talk and provide no time for the other side to present its case.

(c) *Avoid topic areas where hostility might appear.* This is not
always possible, but if the leader knows the members of his group
as well as he should, he probably also knows where disputes are
most apt to occur. If these matters can be avoided, then the
chances of hostility arising are reduced.

(d) *Use a seating arrangement that will separate potentially
hostile members.* If the leader knows where in the group hostility
is apt to arise, he can often prevent or at least minimize this hostility by the simple expedient of keeping unfriendly members physically apart from each other.

2. *Secure identification of individuals with the group.* Keep the talk geared toward the goals and purposes of the group. Discourage members who want to consider individual problems rather than the group's problems. State clearly what the group's goals are and how the group's goals involve the individual members of the group. Make it clear, in other words, that this group is a team, setting out on a common journey, to travel a common road, and to reach a common destination.

3. *Allow time for a warm-up, social session before beginning the conference.* Give members time to know each other if they do not already. If the members of the conference group already are acquainted, give them time to relax in each other's presence and to exchange idle, social conversation before settling down to the problem at hand. This procedure is a standard one for many conferences and discussion groups, particularly where the members do not know each other well before the discussion.

4. *Whenever possible, secure conference members of an equal status.* If you have free choice in the selection of members of your group, this is an important consideration. Other things such as knowledge of the subject, interest in the subject, and so forth being equal, the group will function with much more unity if the members have equal status. This kind of member selection is not always possible, particularly in many staff meeting situations. Where status or prestige tends to disrupt group cohesiveness, compensate for it in the following ways:

(a) *Find some common ground among members of the group.* This often can be done by a heavy emphasis on the individual's involvement with the problem the group is discussing.

(b) *Eliminate as far as possible any symbols of status.* Avoid using titles. Avoid any discussion of the position a member occupies. Encourage the use of first names. In short, find ways of giving, for the time being, an equality of status to the members of the group.

5. *Encourage an attitude among the group of open-mindedness, freedom to participate, and general group permissiveness.* These are, by and large, individual attitudes that well trained discussion

members will bring with them to the discussion. But these attitudes are so important that their presence should be encouraged by the leader. Many of the other obstacles to group cohesiveness can be overcome if the members feel a permissive attitude toward participation and expression of ideas.

6. *Play up the group's goals.* Make the group's goals important to all the members of the group. Emphasize from the beginning what the group's goals are and what their importance is to the members of the discussion. Try to get the members of the group to identify their own goals with these important group goals.

7. *Keep the group relatively small.* A recent experimental study showed that groups probably become less cohesive as they get larger and larger in size.[4] This study indicated that as a group gets larger in size, cliques and sub-groups begin to form. It is quite likely that a participant's involvement might then be with one of the cliques rather than with the group as a whole. In very large groups, the cliques might become more important to the members in them than the larger group. In small groups, cliques are less apt to form, and the attention of the members can be concentrated on the work at hand.

8. *Whenever possible, avoid changing the personnel of the group.* Here again, this may be a matter out of the control of the leader, but if the leader has free choice of group personnel, he should pick the same people to work together over a period of time. A group that has functioned well together in the past will be much more unified than a group where the membership changes from meeting to meeting.

The Conference Participant

1. *Use tact.* Remember that you are dealing not only with a problem, but with the feelings, emotions, and attitudes of other people. Be tactful and you will contribute to a healthy group attitude.

---

[4] N. Edd Miller, "Effect of Group Size on Policy Making Discussions," Unpublished Ph.D. Thesis, University of Michigan, 1951.

2. *Be enthusiastic.* Obviously, you need not "bubble over" with enthusiasm about everything that comes up in a discussion. At the same time, display sincere enthusiasm over your ideas. Sound as though you are interested in the things you say in a discussion. It is important, in terms of good interpersonal relations, that you also show enthusiasm toward the ideas of others. Display enthusiasm for the work of the group, for the importance of this work, and for the goals of the group.

3. *Use your sense of humor.* This is not an admonition to make light of the work of the group nor of the contributions of others in the group. Nor does this mean that you are to restrict your own contributions to jokes, anecdotes, and humorous material. What we mean here is that you keep a sense of perspective and balance about things that happen in the discussion. Don't allow yourself to become annoyed at minor things that happen, or at things that might be said in the discussion. Don't take yourself or your ideas so seriously that you become a disruptive force in the group.

4. *Be cooperative.* We have already seen that the leader should attempt to foster a climate of cooperativeness. Do your part in being cooperative with other members of the group. In particular, be willing to compromise with others with whom you might be in strongest disagreement. Remember that discussion is basically a cooperative, not a competitive activity.

5. *Minimize differences that might exist between you and others.* Differences will inevitably arise in a discussion, and these differences are valuable and useful. But if differences transcend disagreement over subject matter and become personal differences, the cohesiveness of the group can easily be destroyed. A member of a discussion group should always try to keep differences on the subject matter level, and even there, he should try to minimize differences as far as possible. Criticism of ideas should exist in discussion, but the criticism should be impersonal. Criticize the ideas, but not the person who expresses the ideas.

6. *Be friendly.* Establish a good, easy, friendly relationship between yourself and the other members of the group. If you do

not already know the other members of the group, become acquainted with them early and remain on friendly terms with them throughout the discussion.

7. *Accept the group goals as your own.* This point cannot be over-emphasized. We have pointed out several times that the cohesiveness of the group, and therefore to a large extent the success of the group rests upon how closely parallel individual goals are with the over-all group goals. As a member of the group, identify yourself and your goals as far as you possibly can with the aims and goals of the group.

13. Methods of Participation

We have seen that a participant can and does perform many different kinds of roles in a discussion. Whatever function he might be performing, however, it is often useful to have some specific methods and procedures to follow. It is the purpose of this chapter to consider some of the more practical aspects and specific methods of participation.

What Is Participation?

By participation we mean the activity of the group member in the discussion. This activity may be of two kinds: non-verbal participation and verbal participation.

Non-verbal Participation

A member of a group can take part in the group's deliberations in a non-verbal manner almost as actively as in a verbal way. In fact, sometimes non-verbal activity is more desirable than verbal activity. A group member who talks randomly without really contributing to the discussion might actually be participating more effectively if he were listening carefully to the verbal participations of the other members of the group.

Non-verbal participation may be described, generally, as reacting with and to the group in ways that do not call for talking. Such reacting may take many forms. A member who listens carefully to the verbal participations of others in the group might well

202

be considered a real participant, although a non-vocal one. It cannot be denied that effective listening for comprehension and understanding of others' points of view is an essential ingredient for successful group discussion. Since discussion is a process involving the pooling of ideas, information, and points of view, it is necessary that members of the group listen to each other in order for this pooling to take place.

In addition to listening, non-verbal participation might also involve such physical reactions to the process of discussion as nodding agreement, smiling, frowning, and so forth. While this kind of reaction does not involve vocalization, nevertheless it does indicate in many instances a very active participation. Support of ideas, rejection of points of view, agreement, disagreement, all might well be indicated by just such physical signs, without a single word being spoken. Indications of whether a member of the group is really "in," or whether he has "withdrawn from" and is outside the group, may often be seen by these non-verbal signs of participation.

Verbal Participation

While these kinds of activities are of great importance in a discussion group, we are primarily concerned with verbal participation. By verbal participation, we mean the "talking" that goes on in a group discussion, the vocal expression of information, ideas, points of view, and so forth.

FREQUENCY AND LENGTH OF PARTICIPATIONS

Frequency of Participation

How often should a person talk in a discussion? The answer to this may be determined by many factors. Obviously, the size of the group will be one determinant of frequency of participation. The larger the group grows, the fewer the opportunities there are for each member to talk. The amount of time available for the group is another factor to be considered in determining how often a person should talk. The greater the available amount of time, the more opportunities there will be for each individual to contribute. Some indication of approximate opportunities to talk might be given by considering some typical discussions. In four student discussions, each lasting one hour, the total number of contributions were: 270, 274, 307, 405. If we assume that there are nine participants and a leader for each group, the "quota," mathematically, of each of the members in these discussions would have been an even 10 per cent for each group, or 27, 27, 31, 40 respectively. As it happened, however, the range of participation, percentage-wise, by individuals in these groups was from 0 per cent to 37 per cent. In other words, at least one person contributed in one of the discussions more than one-third of the total participations. So, while it is important to consider such elements as the size of the group and the amount of time available to the group as determinants of how often to talk in a discussion, there are, obviously, other factors which influence frequency of participation.

One of these other factors is what we have to say. A cardinal rule for participating in discussion is to talk only when you have something to say. Otherwise listen, and give other members a chance to talk. A second factor relating to participation in a discussion is relevancy. Ewbank and Auer put this well in stating what they call "the rule of relevancy:"

First, he [the participant] should be sure that what he intends to say is on the phase of the general subject announced by the leader. Next, he should ask himself whether what he is planning to say is in accord with the announced purpose of the discussion. Finally, he should be sure that his remarks are relevant *at the moment*.[1]

It should be kept in mind that even though as members of the group we are eager for all to have an opportunity to talk, it is not necessary for each member of the group to use up his full "quota" of participations in a discussion. A common fallacy in many discussions is one that might be labeled the "fallacy of equal spread of participation." Equal *opportunities* to talk should be made available by the leader and by other members of the group, but

---

[1] H. L. Ewbank and J. Jeffery Auer, *Discussion and Debate: Tools of a Democracy*, p. 344. New York: F. S. Crofts and Company, 1941. Reprinted by permission.

nothing but a mechanically satisfying discussion will result with a forced equal spread of actual participations. Some members in a group simply have more to say on a subject or on a phase of a subject than others. They should be allowed to talk and develop their ideas; the members with less to say should not be forced to talk. It should be kept in mind, too, that a few participations, carefully thought out and well expressed may be more meaningful in terms of problem-solving than many poorly thought out and poorly expressed contributions. In short, we should undoubtedly consider such pure quantitative factors as size of the group and amount of time available for the discussion as determinants of frequency of participation, but other qualitative factors such as what we have to say and the relevancy of a contribution are perhaps more important as determinants of how often we talk in a discussion.

Length of Contributions

Many participants in a discussion are concerned not only with how often to talk, but also with how long a single contribution should be. Here again, we are faced with a great deal of difficulty in setting a rigid rule, since many factors might determine the length of a participation. Again, an examination of typical student discussions might be somewhat revealing. In the same four student discussions mentioned above, the average word length of individual contributions was: 24, 33, 34, and 45 words; in point of time, the average contributions were 9, 11, 13, and 16 seconds long. But we are dealing with averages, and the range of length was great, as it will be in most discussions. Naturally, a contribution should be kept as brief as possible, but the length probably depends at least on these three factors:

1. *The complexity of the contribution.* An idea that is complex will take much longer to present than a simple idea. Explanation for a complex idea often involves such time-consuming devices as specific instances, illustrations, and analogies. Simple ideas can often be expressed clearly and understandably in a few well chosen words.

2. *The newness of the idea in the contribution.* If the idea is

new to the group it will take more time to explain than if it is a familiar and well understood notion. The participant will have to move more slowly and carefully with a new idea and be very certain that other members understand it well. With a familiar idea, a brief reference by a participant is often enough.

3. *The atmosphere in the discussion group.* In general, we find it easier to make ourselves understood when the atmosphere in the group is friendly and permissive. When there are hostile elements in the group, or when there are marked divisions in the group, we sometimes find it necessary to talk longer and perhaps more persuasively just to get a good listening to an idea.

In summary, we might say that short contributions are desirable in a discussion, but that complex and new ideas often require long contributions. Also, an unfriendly atmosphere might well mean longer contributions.

ORGANIZING THE CONTRIBUTION

Since the individual contribution is the method whereby problem-solving is carried out in a discussion, it is important that members express themselves well in these contributions. In a group situation, just as in a public speaking-audience situation, it is important that others understand what the speaker is saying. One way of helping to secure this necessary understanding is by being sure that individual contributions are well put together. Therefore, let us turn our attention briefly to the matter of organizing contributions. Organization might be considered important, if for no other reason than because of some of the findings of the studies on listening. These studies have found that the ability of a listener to structuralize a speech influences his listening comprehension.[2] If, as participants in a discussion, we are able to assist our group in structuralizing by providing a well organized contribution, then we are helping other members of the group to comprehend what

---

[2] Ralph G. Nichols, "Factors in Listening Comprehension," *Speech Monographs,* XV (1948), 54–163.

we are saying. Another study found that listeners believe a well organized speech to be more effective than a poorly organized one.[3] Why not be as effective a contributor as possible, with a well organized contribution? Common sense tells us that, especially on longer contributions, we will simply be easier to follow and easier to understand, if the contribution is well organized.

Let us consider one possible plan for organizing a long contribution in a discussion. The plan of organization involves three steps:

Relate the Contribution to Something That Has Already Been Said

This helps place the contribution in a framework and helps make it a part of the continuing problem-solving process. Not only is continuity established, but it is easier for a listener to "flow" smoothly along from one idea to another, rather than coming to a complete stop on one idea, then starting fresh on a new one. Notice how this contribution, from a student discussion, starts by a reference to the preceding speaker and what he has said:

Roberson: Mr. Chairman, I think, as Mr. DiPaul says, we should provide arms for the troops of Western Germany. . . .[4]

Develop the Point of the Contribution

In this step, the participant would give his main idea, the gist of his contribution. The development of the idea may follow any one of several different specific methods, as we will see in the next section of this chapter. In general, however, development may be either anti-climactic presentation of the main point, followed by

[3] Raymond G. Smith, "An Experimental Study of the Effect of Speech Organization Upon Attitudes of College Students," Ph.D. Thesis, University of Wisconsin, 1950, abstracted in Speech Monographs, XVIII (1951), 198–199.

[4] This and all the other quotations from a student discussion in this chapter are purposely selected from a single discussion, to show that the elements discussed commonly appear in a discussion. This is a student panel discussion, but similar types of contributions appear in other types of discussion. This discussion was held by students at the University of Alabama and a transcript of it may be found in: Ruth Ulman (ed.), University Debaters Annual, 1950–1951, pp. 46–60. New York: The H. W. Wilson Company. This contribution is to be found on page 48. Quotations are reprinted by permission.

supporting material, or climactic presentation of supporting material followed by the main point. The following examples will show the difference in method of development:

   1. *Anti-climactic:*

Miller: The first thing that comes to my mind, in that light, is the fact that the Russians have equipped and trained a police force of 350,000 in Eastern Germany, and the satellite nations surrounding Eastern Germany are also well equipped. Albania has 60,000 troops; Bulgaria, 190,000; Czechoslovakia, 160,000; Hungary, 65,000; and Poland, one of the most strategic countries of the area, 200,000.[5]

   2. *Climactic:*

Miller: We must remember that the Eastern nations—that is, the Communist satellite countries—have been rearming for five years under Russia; whereas, the North Atlantic Treaty nations have just recently awakened to the fact that rearmament is necessary. I think that we, more or less, are three to five years, and in some cases six to seven years, behind the Russian-dominated countries as far as rearmament goes.[6]

Connect the Contribution with the Problem or with the Portion of the Problem Under Discussion

In other words, tie the contribution in with other contributions, much in the same fashion as we described relating a contribution to something that has already been said. In our sample discussion the group has been talking about advantages to NATO of rearming Western Germany. Notice how the last sentence of this contribution ties in with the general area of discussion.

Miller: A careful look at the map of Europe shows us that, in order to march across Europe, Russia and her satellites would certainly have to start in Germany; and we would like to have Germany as a buffer or deterrent to ward off aggression. Certainly her position in history has shown that he who controls Germany, more or less, controls Europe; and it is certainly to the advantage of the NATO to have her rearmed.[7]

---

[5] *Ibid.,* p. 48.
[6] *Ibid.,* p. 49.
[7] *Ibid.,* p. 51.

In summary, a good three step plan for organizing a long contribution is: First, relate to what has already been said, second, present the point of the contribution with supporting material, and, third, connect with the immediate problem or phase of the problem under discussion.

FORMS OF THE CONTRIBUTION

Earlier, we mentioned that contributions could be organized climactically or anti-climactically. We also said that contributions may be organized in many more specific ways. Let us consider some of the forms a contribution may take. You may notice some repetition between the "types of contributions" discussed in the next chapter and these "forms of the contribution" discussed here. Despite apparent similarities, however, we are concerned with two different things. In the next chapter our interest will be centered around the behavior of members of the group as revealed in their contributions; in this chapter our concern is with the presentation of suggestions for framing and organizing material for contributions in a discussion. Naturally, these suggestions apply only to the longer, more substantive, contributions, not to the short "yes" or "no" type of contribution. But bear in mind that our concern here is with the *structure* of the contribution, not with the function of the contribution or the contributer, as considered in the earlier chapter.

Contributions May Be Built Around a Definition

It is sometimes necessary and important to define words and terms in a discussion. In this situation, it is natural to build the contribution around a definition. Definitions also serve as good devices for straight exposition. Notice the following example:

DiPaul: Mr. Chairman, I believe that the term *rearm* should mean that the Atlantic Pact nations are to provide arms and equipment for German troops.[8]

---

[8] *Ibid.,* p. 48.

Contributions May Be Built Around
Facts and Statistics

Statistical material is often an important part of a discussion. Hence, we may find examples of entire contributions built around this kind of material:

Roberson: Mr. Chairman, by *potential,* I mean industrial capacity. We see that 75 per cent of Germany's resources were not even hampered by World War II. Today they are producing 82 per cent of their capacity. This 82 per cent is supplying their own needs with very few exports. Therefore, the potential advantage from Western Germany to NATO would be that other potential which she is capable of producing but is not producing at the present time.[9]

Contributions May Be Built Around an
Authoritative Statement

Just as it is necessary to bring statistical evidence into a discussion, so it is often important to get opinion evidence introduced. Many times contributions will center on and be built around a quotation from an authority:

DiPaul: I think another point of interest here which should be considered is the fact that not only are these troops of a sufficient number to cause trouble if they decided to aggress, but also that all of these satellite armies are being trained under conditions very favorable to the Soviet. According to a news story by M. S. Handler, Belgrade correspondent, *New York Times,* of August 22, 1950. . . .[10]

Contributions May Be Built Around Another
Participant's Statement

There are at least three ways in which another participant's contribution can be used as the foundation for building a contribution:

1. *To add something to another participation.* This example shows how material is added to a previous contribution:

---

[9] *Ibid.,* p. 51.
[10] *Ibid.,* pp. 49–50.

Miller: I would like to add that we certainly should rearm Western Germany to a point sufficient to ward off aggression either by Eastern Germany or by the Russian satellites.[11]

2. *To agree with another participation.*   A sample of this kind of contribution, built around agreement with a previous contribution, can be seen when one of the panel members agrees by saying, simply: "The point is very well taken." [12]   Such agreement is often very short, but may be elaborated into additional reasons for agreeing with a preceding speaker.

3. *To disagree with another participation.*   An example of disagreement as the base for building a contribution may be seen here:

Roberson: Mr. Chairman, I don't quite agree with Mr. DiPaul on that because we see that the Marshall Plan aid is the only means by which Western Germany is fed today.   Certainly she would not move an army against the nation that is supplying the food because it would naturally cut off the supply.[13]

Contributions May Be Built Around a Question

The question may be a rhetorical one to which no answer is really expected, but usually it is a question directed at the group or at some one member of the group and attempts to get more information or to raise new points for consideration about a topic. An example of the question type contribution may be seen in this sample participation:

Roberson: Well, may I ask you this question, then, Mr. DiPaul.   By turning against us, would that mean that Western Germany had decided to fight with Russia or to fight an individual war? [14]

Contributions May Be Built Around a
General Statement

We have already seen that a general statement, followed by supporting material, is one method of developing a main point in a

---

11 *Ibid.,* p. 48.
12 *Ibid.,* p. 53.
13 *Ibid.,* p. 53.
14 *Ibid.,* p. 53.

contribution. Another example of the general statement as a way of building a contribution may be seen here:

DiPaul: I believe that if we are to rearm Western Germany, we must accept her as an equal partner in the North Atlantic Organization. If we try this, we are going to get disagreement among the other Atlantic Pact nations because, in order to take another nation in the Atlantic Pact, it requires a unanimous vote, as stated in Article X of the North Atlantic Treaty. If we are to take Western Germany in, say as second-rate troops, they are not going to like that idea so much, because, as we have pointed out, Germany can be a first-class power, and as long as they have this bargaining power, which they now possess, they are not going to accept a second-class status.[15]

Contributions May Be Built Around Specific Instances

Often the participant builds his contribution around a series of specific instances. An example may be seen in this contribution:

DiPaul: Well, for instance, France, Belgium, the Netherlands, Great Britain, Norway, Italy, Greece, and especially Turkey, who is only three air hours away from Moscow, and not more than one air hour away from almost all of Russia's oil supply. Western Europe would be a very good place to spend some of that money as they are perfectly willing to cooperate with NATO. They are also perfectly willing to accept this aid. In fact, nearly every Atlantic Pact nation has requested military aid from the United States, and they are counting on us to provide them with adequate arms with which they might defend themselves. It was not more than a few weeks after the signing of the North Atlantic Treaty that the United States received arms aid requests from eight Atlantic Pact members—the United Kingdom, France, Denmark, Italy, Norway, Belgium, Luxemburg, and the Netherlands. As long as these nations are willing, it seems foolish to me to pour arms and equipment into a nation whose loyalty is uncertain. I maintain that whole-hearted cooperation is an asset in any undertaking. It seems to me that in an undertaking of this magnitude, whole-hearted cooperation is a must.[16]

---

[15] *Ibid.,* p. 55.
[16] *Ibid.,* p. 58.

SUMMARY

Our interest in this chapter has focused on participations. We have seen that participation may be either non-verbal or verbal in nature. The frequency and length of participations often depend on the nature of the things the speaker has to say as well as on such quantitative factors as equality of participation and brevity of participation. It is important that contributions be well organized and a three step method of organizing a participation was discussed. In addition, it was discovered that participations may be built around definitions, facts and statistics, authoritative statements, other participations, questions, general statements, and specific instances.

14. Contributions and Role Patterns

"The biggest trouble with industry," says John L. McCaffrey, President of International Harvester, "is that it is full of human beings." Thus, for example:

You will learn to your sorrow that while a drill press never sulks and a drop hammer never gets jealous of other drop hammers, the same cannot be said for people. You will learn that a turret lathe may run one part for ten years without affecting its ability or its willingness to be switched at any time to another part. But men are not that way. They develop habits and likes and dislikes.

*   *   *

You will discover that problems change rapidly, techniques change rapidly, products can be transformed in a period of months; but unfortunately people change slowly if at all.[1]

Some of these ideas (people change slowly, they develop likes and dislikes) prove to be true, in varying degrees at least, if you take the trouble to check the types of contributions that people habitually give in discussions.

YOU AND YOUR CONTRIBUTIONS

In our previous chapter we mentioned many of the forms that your contributions may take. We said that contributions may be

---

[1] From a speech delivered at the University of Chicago on June 10, 1953. See "What Corporation Presidents Think About at Night," *Fortune*, XLVIII (September, 1953), 128. Reprinted by permission.

centered around definitions, facts, authoritative statements, statements given by participants, questions, general statements, and specific instances. It is through these and other forms of contributions that you reveal many things about yourself. Your abilities, emotions, habits, and interests are exhibited. You show whether you habitually give only certain types of contributions, or whether you give many different types. You show whether your contributions are problem, procedure, or participant-centered by the proportion of your contributions that fall into these general classifications. All of this is an important way in which you reveal behavioral tendencies.

Problem-Centered Contributions

We are defining problem-centered contributions as statements that deal directly with the problem under discussion. Eight types of contributions will be mentioned. If you are a well-rounded participant, you will usually give some contributions that fall into many of the eight categories, excepting, perhaps, the category labeled "irrelevant." If, on the other hand, all of the statements you make are of one or two types, you probably should try to become a more versatile participant. Suppose, for example, that Participant A does nothing but ask questions in a discussion, or perhaps, he does no more than clarify or summarize. These are important types of contributions, but certainly the failure to give other types of contributions marks Participant A as a person who is unable to adjust to the needs of a discussion.

1. *Giving goals, aims, or conditions.* When you answer the question, "What are we trying to accomplish?" you are identifying goals you hope to achieve. Thus, you might say:

(Intercollegiate Football)
   (a) The aim is not to eliminate football, but to keep it on an amateur level.
   (b) Our solution should be one that does not discriminate against the smaller colleges.

2. *Giving information.* You should neither neglect facts nor make every contribution you give factual in nature.

(a) It costs many universities more than $275,000 annually to keep a good team in addition to the subsidies and other hidden expenses.

(b) Princeton does not permit subsidies for players, and yet they have good teams.

3. *Giving clarification or summary.* These types of contributions, as we have said, are often given by the discussion leader, but there is no valid reason to keep you from clarifying or summarizing.

(a) She means that the fact that big schools can sell TV rights keeps them in business and shuts out the smaller schools.

(b) Five solutions have been suggested: the maximum fund, faculty control, investigations by college presidents, equal treatment for all students, and the nationwide football scholarship plan.

4. *Giving suggestion or solution.* In very many cases suggestions or solutions are given by only a few of the participants in a group. But since contributions like these are a clear sign of initiative, we believe all persons should learn to develop skills in drawing inferences and conclusions.

(a) Football players should be treated like every other student in regard to scholarships, subsidies, jobs, room and board, and grades.

(b) The Pacific Coast Code on enlistment of players is the plan I suggest.

5. *Giving an evaluation of own contribution.*

(a) Here is why I think the football player should receive some rewards. He spends three or four hours, and sometimes more, each day in practice or games. During this time he might otherwise be engaged in work or study.

(b) I feel we should be skeptical about our ability to control actions of the alumni, because what they do is outside the jurisdiction of the colleges.

6. *Giving an evaluation of another person's contribution* (opposing or supporting). A good point to remember is that you may

agree or disagree with portions of what others say. You should not habitually accept or reject without qualification.

7. *Asking a question relating to the problem.* Questions in a discussion are often an indication that participants are honestly interested in understanding the ideas of one another. Other ends that are less desirable may be served by questions, but the communicative value of questions can be very helpful in achieving a worth-while discussion.

8. *Giving an irrelevant statement.* Sometimes a participant says, "My idea may not have much to do with our problem, but I think you will be interested in it." In other cases, you might give irrelevant material because of an unintentional error in reasoning, a lack of knowledge, or a lack of interest in the problem. If there are a large number of irrelevancies in a discussion, you should search for causes and try to correct them.

Our experience has shown that you can easily identify the problem-centered contributions we have mentioned. If you do a sentence by sentence analysis (subject-predicate statements), you can get agreements as high as ninety per cent from pairs of trained analysts using a typed script of a discussion in making identifications.[2] A less exacting, but reasonably effective method, is one that makes each contribution a unit to be categorized in one or more of the classifications. The more categories you have, the greater will be your difficulties. Thus, you might wish to combine some of the eight problem-centered categories when you make your first efforts in categorizing contributions.

Procedure-Centered Contributions

A successful discussion depends in part upon how the discussion is conducted, phases of the problem that are taken up, and the time

---

[2] In a study by Roger W. Heyns, two analysts showed a 90 per cent agreement in identifying twelve types of contributions: Goal setting, problem proposals, information seeking, information giving, solution proposals, development seeking, development giving, opposing, supporting, summarizing seeking, summarizing giving, and non-problem directed. See Roger W. Heyns, "The Effects of Variation in Leadership on Participant Behavior in Discussion Groups," Unpublished Ph.D. Dissertation, University of Michigan, Department of Psychology, 1948.

spent upon these phases. If you believe that you have a good suggestion about these procedural matters, you should usually report your ideas to the group. When you do you show that you are a good planner, or at least that you are interested in having the discussion conducted in the best possible way.

1. *Giving a procedural suggestion.*

(Intercollegiate Football)
   (a) Everything we have said so far concerns the large colleges. I think we should devote a portion of the discussion to conditions in smaller colleges.
   (b) I don't think we should try to reach a decision on these five solutions in the few minutes remaining in this hour.

2. *Asking a procedural question.*

   (a) Wouldn't it be appropriate to see if there are some good results arising from present-day football?
   (b) Could we talk about some of our aims before we make our final decision?

Participant-Centered Contributions

We may have given you the impression that problem and procedure-centered contributions are emotionally neutral and have no effect upon the feelings of persons in the group. Now, of course, this is not true. Anything you say in a discussion may affect interpersonal relations either positively or negatively. And certainly the way you speak, your voice and attitude, has a bearing upon how others feel about you. Thus, a participant-centered contribution, as distinguished from the other classes of contributions, is really an artificial distinction made in order to help you understand the importance of attitudes and emotions in a group.

1. *Promoting teamwork.* If your words suggest friendliness, understanding, fairness, praise, shared responsibility, and goodwill, your contribution (unless nullified by other factors) tends to promote teamwork. These examples are clear signs of cordiality and respect shown by one participant toward others in the group.

(Intercollegiate Football)

(Praise— *Agreement—* *"We" Spirit)*	(a) The ideas we have been having from the other end of the table—by George, Frank, and Sandra—are very important. They show that schools having good football teams want to control abuses.
(Shared *Responsibility)*	(b) I want to withdraw my suggestion that we should control the actions of alumni. The rest of you are probably right in what you have said.

2. *Discouraging teamwork.* If you are indifferent toward the feelings of others, you can create divisive actions within the group quite easily. These two contributions do a fairly good job in condemning others in the group, and, doubtless, in establishing the person who makes them as a "troublesome" participant.

(Dogmatism)	(a) No, it was my idea in the first place! It is the only good suggestion that has been given.
(Superior *Status)*	(b) Well, I know the players. I know how they feel, and therefore I don't think I have to read the articles you are talking about.

The participant-centered contributions we have given tell only part of the story about the building of teamwork in a group. What is missing here is knowledge about the participant's personality, attitude, and voice when expressing any of these contributions. Some participants might be able to make critical statements without creating feelings of resentment; and others, even when they say the kindest of words, might cause disunity. But within the limits we have mentioned, the participant-centered contributions as identified correctly depict the two extremes in promoting and discouraging teamwork.

RELATIONSHIP OF CONTRIBUTIONS TO ROLE PATTERNS

By "role pattern" we mean a form of behavior that distinguishes you from others. When you show relatively consistent attitudes in discussions and give a preponderance of certain types of contributions, it is not difficult to characterize your behavior.   You might demonstrate that you are a good thinker, a considerate and kindly person, or a person who is a careful planner.   On the other hand, you might be gloomy and fearful, or stern and relentless, or emotional and excitable.   But whatever your role in discussions, it is perceived by others, and sometimes by yourself, because you tend to be consistent in your attitudes and types of contributions.

The role you play in discussions is usually affected by a number of factors.   Your personal motives, experiences and learning, and your physiological and neurological makeup help to determine the role that you pursue.   In a real sense the role pattern that you follow is understood by you as a way of getting along in the world. It is your way of satisfying aspirations.   Thus, your attitudes, actions, and contributions are means leading to goal satisfaction. Therefore, you must change motives if you expect to change the role you ordinarily follow in discussions.

But situational factors may also affect your role in a conference. For example, a leader who monopolizes giving of solutions, evaluating of solutions, and clarifying and summarizing of contributions will restrict your opportunity to give contributions of these types. Similarly, others in the group will sometimes affect you in a way that causes you to change your customary pattern of behavior.   In other words, although your role from discussion to discussion is likely to be quite constant, it may also vary in accordance with the conditions operative in a particular discussion.

Desirable Role Patterns

Competent participants are adaptive.   They tend to give the types of contributions that are dictated by the requirements of the specific situation.   As a result, the able participant probably cannot be assigned to a single role unless it is a general one.   His role is usually a multi-purpose form of behavior.   Briefly stated, *the valued participant does not play one role both "in and out of season."*

In the eight desirable role patterns given here, the competent participant should usually excel in two or more of the roles.

Organizer Role

1. Identifies goals and objectives
2. Plans procedure
3. Initiates transitions to new phases of problem
4. Helps to determine how each person's talents can be used
5. May easily direct the discussion too much

Fact Finder Role

1. Prepares for discussions carefully
2. Knows many facts
3. Seeks facts from others
4. Sometimes fails to analyze and organize his facts

Creator of Ideas Role

1. Reveals imaginative abilities
2. Proposes solutions
3. Perceives many possible solutions
4. Usually can create a solution to resolve conflicts

Critical Tester Role

1. Clarifies facts and ideas
2. Appraises facts and ideas
3. Predicts consequences
4. Knows how solutions relate to causes and effects of problem
5. Knows conditions of a good solution

Questioner Role

1. Seeks to clarify
2. Tests through questioning
3. Reveals curiosity
4. Can easily become obnoxious to others

Energizer Role

1. Reveals enthusiasm
2. Believes the group problem is important
3. Anxious to attain goals
4. Stimulates others to aspire to high productivity

Helper of Others Role

1. Wishes success for others
2. Tries to assist in making success for others possible by providing opportunities for them to speak
3. Helps the disturbed and fearful to feel accepted by the group
4. Believes in the competence of others even when abilities and skills are not clearly apparent

Conciliator Role

1. Breaks deadlocks by finding acceptable solution
2. Minimizes personality clashes
3. Maintains an objective attitude
4. Shows good will toward all

To be perfect in all of these roles is an accomplishment that fits a superman. Your task, however, is not an impossible one. While you should strive for a high level of skill in regard to the eight roles, you can enjoy success as a participant without being especially recognized for each of the roles.

UNDESIRABLE ROLE PATTERNS

Extremes in behavior are usually undesirable roles. Thus, the frequent and the infrequent speaker, the well informed and the poorly informed, the confident and the fearful may easily become harmful to the success of a discussion. In fact, any of the eight desirable role patterns we have just mentioned can be harmful if carried to excess.

It would not be difficult to name fifty or more undesirable types of behavior that are revealed in discussions. We shall, however, be content with a description of fifteen undesirable role patterns. Some of these, you will recognize, overlap with one another.

Silent (See Chapter 10, Leadership Functions in Discussion)

Monopolist (See Chapter 10)

Beside-the-Point (See Chapter 10)

Attention Seeker

This type of participant makes a special attempt to be unusual. He tries to be different either in voice and action, or in the contributions that he gives, or in both of these respects.   Occasionally he tries to show cleverness and humor, but he may also be a serious contributor.

Suggestions:
1. Try to make him feel accepted and respected by others.
2. Help him to develop competence in fields that are valued by others.
3. Help him to discover that his attention-seeking exploits are unwise.
4. Help him to discover that being interested in the attainments of the group is more important than trying to be a "star."

Orator

This participant usually speaks with great vocal force, sweeping gestures, and table-pounding.   His remarks, generally long ones, seem to be addressed to an audience of hundreds of people.   Mr. Orator is likely to use many generalizations and emotional words in the contributions that he gives.

Suggestions:
1. Try to have him speak directly to you or to other group members.
2. Question him calmly and courteously.
3. Make him feel an interest in the group rather than in some imagined audience.
4. Interrupt him, offer a word of recognition and praise, and thus give him an opportunity to perceive the difference between oratory and conversation.

Fearful

Persons who are in this role feel insecure and are sensitive to actual or possible criticism.   Generally Mr. Fearful is an infrequent contributor; often when he does speak, he talks very rapidly.

Suggestions:
1. Give him recognition and praise.
2. Help him to center his attention upon the problem.
3. Give him a special responsibility that will permit him to excel.
4. Help him maintain his ego when others in the group criticize what he has said.

Isolate

The "outsider" is either rejected by the group or else the group members are rejected by this individual. Techniques for changing the behavior of Mr. Isolate are thus dependent upon whether the group or the individual is responsible for the role of isolation. The suggestions listed for Mr. Fearful, especially suggestion three, are worth trying.

"Yes-Yes"

This person agrees with everyone about almost anything. Possible reasons for his actions are: to avoid trouble, to please, or to keep from defending his own position.

Suggestions:
1. Help him to improve his ability to reason.
2. Encourage him to study the discussion problem well.
3. Help him to develop self-confidence by getting him to demonstrate skill in critical thinking.
4. Get his opinions early; ask him questions that require evaluation.
5. Help him to realize that no catastrophe will occur if he opposes, fully or in part, contributions given by others.

Executive Complex

This person enjoys directing persons, planning procedures and assigning tasks. In short, he wants to do the thinking for the group. His actions represent an extreme form of the "organizer role" that we have listed as a desirable role pattern.

Suggestions:
1. Spend a few minutes in deciding whether his suggestions are the best choices you can make. Do not be afraid to change or reject his plans.

2. Suggest that others in the group might have some helpful ideas.
3. Help him to realize that the planning that he does interferes with the opportunity of others to show initiative.

Know-It-All

An individual who claims to know everything has many traits in common with Mr. Monopolist, Mr. Attention Seeker, Mr. Orator, and Mr. Executive Complex.

Logic Machine

Usually, a person who follows this role pattern does not discriminate between ideas that must be tested carefully and those that must be accepted or rejected without absolute proof. He gives special attention to all possible errors in reasoning, and thus blocks progress by the group.

Suggestions:
1. Learn when to use the services of Mr. Logic Machine and when to disregard his counsel.
2. Suggest that unimportant points should not be evaluated in great detail.

Emotional Antagonist

We are all capable of becoming angry when our ideas are refuted or when we sense a loss of status. But apart from these situations, some participants reveal antagonism quite consistently. Mr. Emotional Antagonist centers his attention upon personalities; he is not an objective thinker. Whenever he speaks, he appears to be fighting an enemy.

Suggestions:
1. Make him feel accepted as a group member.
2. Restate his emotional remarks objectively, and thus show that it is the problem rather than personalities that is at stake.
3. Suggest a brief recess or relieve tension in some way following an emotional outburst.
4. Praise and rewards are usually more helpful than a direct attack against Mr. Emotional Antagonist.

Contrary

This type of participant is sometimes not active early in a discussion. But when a decision is about to be made, Mr. Contrary invariably has a host of objections to it. Unless other persons in the group recommend that the discussion continue without unanimous agreement on a particular point, you may make very little progress.

> Suggestions:
> 1. Make him feel "at home" and valued by others.
> 2. Give him recognition and perhaps praise.
> 3. Try to get his recommendations early in the discussion.
> 4. Request that his objection be considered at a later time.
> 5. If disruption is serious, limit his remarks.
> 6. Ask him to accept the group solution on a trial basis.

Clown

The person who is clever as a humorist, and who does not repeatedly try to evoke laughter, may be a wholesome influence in a discussion. But if his clownish remarks are given too often, you should seek to bring about changes.

Dictator

What we have said about the authoritarian conference leader in Chapter 9 applies here. Group members should insist upon self-direction. To do this you may have to expose the dictator openly for what he is.

The suggestions we have given for these fifteen undesirable roles concern (a) what the members of the group can do, and (b) what the individual can do himself. We have shown that group members can often help to change behavioral patterns of others, or they can in some measure control the harmful effects that arise from undesirable roles. But for permanent changes in roles, the individual must also be involved in the process. Ideally, he should force himself to *perceive* his role as objectively as possible, and then take deliberate steps to change his behavior. To do this, as we have said earlier, the individual must substitute new motives for those that he has habitually accepted.

Your Program for Improvement

If you discover that you either fail to give certain important types of contributions, or give too many of other types, you should plan a remedial program. You should do this deliberately and carefully. In other words, we do not think you can become a competent participant by a stroke of magic. Efforts in the direction of deliberate intent are likely to bring better results and quicker results. This applies both to the contributions you give and to the role patterns that are revealed by your contributions and attitudes.

This short outline should be helpful in suggesting some of the points you should remember.

A. *Train Yourself to Offer Contributions That You Give Infrequently.*
  1. Practice giving the problem-centered contributions you tend to neglect.
    (a) By giving goals, aims, or conditions of a good solution
    (b) By giving information
    (c) By clarifying or summarizing
    (d) By giving suggestions or solutions
    (e) By giving evaluative statements
    (f) By asking questions
  2. Practice giving procedure-centered contributions you tend to neglect.
  3. Practice giving participant-centered (teamwork) contributions you tend to neglect.
B. *Train Yourself to Refrain from Over-Dependence upon Certain Types of Contributions or Classes of Contributions* (problem, procedure, and participant-centered).
C. *Train Yourself to Give Types or Classes of Contributions Called for by the Situation.*
D. *Train Yourself to Achieve Several of the Eight Desirable Role Patterns as Called for by the Situation.*
E. *Train Yourself to Control the Tendencies You Might Have Toward the Undesirable Role Patterns.*
F. *Train Yourself to Control Roadblocks Caused by Others Who Reveal Undesirable Role Patterns.*
G. *Train Yourself to Help in Modifying the Behavior of Persons Who Reveal Undesirable Role Patterns.*

PART V

Speech and Language

15. Speech in Discussion

What happens in a conference is essentially communication of ideas. The manner in which ideas are transmitted may have a great deal of bearing on the success or failure of a discussion group. In this chapter and the next we will be primarily interested in problems related to the communication processes in a discussion— problems centered around speech behavior and around language behavior of members of conference groups.

THE NATURE OF CONFERENCE SPEAKING

What kind of speaking should take place, ideally, in a conference situation? Quite often, we have had occasion to observe a great variety of speaking styles, from the person who talks so quietly that he is hardly audible to the other members of the group, to the domineering speaker, who feels every word must be shouted, even though the group and the room are small and a normal conversational voice would carry well. We may have observed speakers, too, who did such a successful job of speaking that we recall only the ideas they communicated, and not the defects in the delivery of those ideas. That type of speaking, unobtrusive, yet really communicative, should be our goal in conference speaking.

Good conference speaking, having for its aim the communication of ideas, probably falls somewhere between good conversational speaking and good public speaking. It certainly has the elements of informality and directness characteristic of the best in conversational speaking. At the same time, it has the forcefulness, energy,

231

and care which characterize good public speaking. Good conference speaking should avoid the pitfalls of some conversational
speech—a tendency toward carelessness, lack of variety, and even
monotony. Likewise, good conference speaking should not show
some of the frequent weaknesses of poor public speaking—bombast,
indirectness, and, sometimes, excessive formality.

A necessary prerequisite for good conference speaking is a clear
realization that the primary objective of the speaker is not show or
exhibition, but the careful communication of ideas to others. All
advice about how to speak in a conference should be based on the
single criterion of making a participant a better communicator.
Let us consider some of the faults in speaking which often interefere
with this communication process, and then examine some of the
traits of conference speaking which might increase the communica-
tiveness of the participant.

Common Faults in Conference Speaking

We might well ask ourselves at this point, "What are the factors
in speaking that most often interfere with the communication process?" In other words, what are some of the more common faults
to be found in conference speaking? If these specific failings in
conference speaking can be eliminated, we will be on the road to
better communicative speaking in conference situations. Here
are eight of the most common faults to be found among participants
in conferences.

Insufficient Volume in Speaking

We might call this person the "mumbler." He's a familiar type,
one who speaks so softly as to be hardly audible, even to those nearest him, and plainly inaudible to any one at any distance from
him. It is the first duty of any speaker, in any speech situation,
from conversation to formal platform speaking, to make himself
heard easily. And the word "easily" deserves a stress. No auditor
should be asked or expected to strain in order to hear a speaker. If

it involves a great deal of effort to hear someone talk, most of us just do not make the necessary effort.

Too Much Volume in Speaking

At the other end of the scale are the speakers who do not adjust the volume of their voices to small rooms or small group situations. These are the "shouters," who feel they must talk extremely loud at all times. Most listeners are irritated or repelled by speakers who do not adjust the volume of the voice to meet the sensible requirements of the group to which they are talking. In most conference situations, a normal conversational volume is most appropriate. Large audience, public speaking volume should be avoided.

A Belligerent or Contentious Speaking Style

Remember that conferences call for cooperative effort on the part of all participants. The speaker whose voice quality indicates a kind of "Oh, yeah!" belligerency is making it difficult for cooperation or for good communication to take place in the conference group. Naturally, we should strive for a pleasant voice quality in all speech situations, but this is particularly true in a group situation, where the emphasis is placed on cooperation. A friendly and pleasant approach to the group's task should reveal itself in the voice.

A Too Rapid Rate of Speaking

Our individual speaking rates vary considerably. One study showed a range in speaking rate among twenty-four college speakers from 125 words per minute to 328 words per minute.[1] Many of us with a very fast speaking rate can still be easily understood. But when the rate becomes so fast that syllables and words seem to pile on top of each other and the whole effect is a cluttered one, then the rate is too rapid and is interfering with communication. While it is not necessary for the fast speaker to slow down his rate, it is

---

[1] H. C. Kelly and M. D. Steer, "Revised Concept of Rate," *The Journal of Speech and Hearing Disorders,* XIV (1949), 222–226.

important for the speaker whose rate is so fast that it interferes with his communication to slow down so others will have no trouble understanding him.

A Too Slow Rate of Speaking

Just as a rapid rate, so can a slow, hesitant, dragging rate of speaking get in the way of effective communication. We are apt to lose patience with a speaker whose rate is considerably slower than the average, or who seems to take forever to get his ideas expressed. Long pauses, hesitations, and extremely slow pacing should be avoided wherever possible. Naturally, some pauses are inevitable, and some are effective devices of communication in themselves—pauses used for emphasis, for example—but a characteristic slow rate is often irritating to others in the group.

A Monotonous Pattern of Speech

Really worse than a very fast or very slow rate is a pattern of speech that repeats itself over and over and becomes monotonous. Many conference groups, as well as public speaking audiences, have been lulled to sleep by speakers who lacked vitality, energy, and variety in the pattern of speech. Variety in rate, pitch, volume, and quality of the voice are very important.

An Expressionless Voice

Perhaps this is another way of saying that the voice lacks variety. The voice that speaks on and on with little or no emphasis and placing little or no meaning on key ideas is not only monotonous, but is not communicating effectively. The speaker should be able to help the listener in sorting out which ideas are more important, which are supporting or subordinate ideas, and so forth. An expressionless voice offers no such help to listeners and consequently is not communicating very effectively.

The Unenthusiastic Speaking Style

Some speakers seem to avoid monotony, but nevertheless lack enthusiasm in their voices. They do not seem to be really concerned or interested in the ideas they are discussing. Little vitality or energy displays itself. Enthusiasm is contagious, and lack of enthusiasm is also contagious. A speaker will have difficulty arousing much interest in his ideas if he does not sound interested himself.

Desirable Traits in Conference Speaking

It is clear that avoiding the faults just discussed will lead to better and more communicative conference speaking. Let us now discuss some of these positive approaches to good speech in discussion.

Audibility

As has been indicated, the first responsibility of any speaker in any speech situation is to make himself heard by his auditors. A conference speaker should always speak loudly enough to be heard by all other members of the group. As a participant in a conference, watch the other members of the group and look for any indications that you may not be speaking loudly enough. You can usually tell whether or not the group is able to hear you by their reactions while you are talking. If you are not being heard, increase the volume of your voice until the group can hear you with no effort. Naturally, you should also avoid talking too loudly. So the key to success as far as volume of the voice is concerned is adaptability—an increase or decrease of volume as necessitated by the size of the room, the size of the group, or external noise factors.

Variety

Many of us are not very expressive in the use of our voices. We sometimes talk in a monotonous manner and meanings which could be and should be conveyed by vocal inflection are not communicated. As speakers in a conference, we should strive for variations in our voice for the sake of emphasis and meaning. Variety can be achieved in rate of speaking, in pitch of the voice, in volume, and in the quality of the voice.   Shades of meaning not conveyed by the language itself can very often be put across with variety in one or more of these essential aspects of voice.

Energy and Enthusiasm

Variety in speech often takes care of itself and comes naturally when the speaker uses a good deal of energy in his speech.   Enthusiasm for one's subject will nearly always show itself in an energetic and forceful delivery.   If there is any single key to effective conference speaking, it is *enthusiasm*.   Conferences are many times dull, not because the subject matter is dull or unimportant, but because the participants in the conference speak about it in a dull, unenthusiastic manner.   Real enthusiasm in speaking is contagious.   Listeners will understand better and react better to speakers who sound sincere and enthusiastic about their subject. As a member of a conference group, be enthusiastic, and many of the other faults in speaking will disappear.

Clarity

Obviously, no premium should be placed on over-exactness or over-preciseness in diction.   At the same time, we owe it to other members of the group to speak distinctly enough to be easily understood.   Just as it is important that a conference participant talk loudly enough to be heard, so it is important that a participant talk distinctly enough to be easily understood.   Articulate clearly, so that stressed and important syllables and words will not be lost.

Fluency

In a prepared public speech, we expect the speaker to be able to talk without noticeable, lengthy pauses and without stumbling around in his speech as he grasps desperately for the right word or words.   Our level of expectation cannot be reasonably as high in conference speaking, but we should attempt generally to achieve an easy flow of words, without too much stumbling and pausing. As a conference speaker, try to avoid the all too typical vocalized pauses "uh," "er," "and uh," and other such meaningless sounds, used solely as gap-fillers. Organize your thoughts in advance, before making a contribution, and express yourself as far as possible in an enthusiastic, fluent way. Naturally, we cannot expect a perfect flow of words, but we should try to make our talking in conference as fluent and easy as we can. Other members of the group will listen more easily and understand better when the thoughts are expressed with fluency, and without hesitation.

Adaptability

Many speakers are able to achieve most of these desirable traits in conference speaking and yet are not doing an adequate job, speechwise, because they are not adaptable in their speaking. We mean by that, that the speaker must not only be audible, use variety, be enthusiastic, clear in his speech, and fluent, but that he must adapt these qualities to the particular speech situation in which he finds himself. Some of the factors to which he must adapt are the size of the room, the acoustics of the room, extraneous noises, the size of the group to which he is talking, the seating arrangement used in the conference, the interest of the group in the problem being discussed. In order to adapt well, a speaker must analyze his situation and his audience both before the conference and during the conference. Before the conference he should try to find out as much as he can about the factors listed above, and during the conference he should be able to adjust easily to whatever changes might take place in these factors. Thus, the loudness of the speaker's voice will be determined by such factors as the size of the room, the acoustics of the room, and the presence or absence of extraneous noises. The amount of energy and enthusiasm the speaker uses might well be determined by the interest of the group in the topic being discussed, the size of the group, and so forth. These things, or many of them, may change in the course of the conference. As they do, the speaker should adapt himself to the changing conditions. Hence it is important to realize the speaker should be adaptable not only from conference to conference, but also during a single conference.

Summary

We have examined the basic nature and characteristics of conference speaking. Good conference speaking is basically good communication of ideas. Some of the common faults in conference speaking are: insufficient volume, too much volume, a belligerent or contentious speaking manner, too rapid rate, too slow rate, monotonous pattern of speech, expressionless voice, and unenthusiastic manner of speaking. The desirable traits to be aimed at in good conference speaking are: audibility, variety, energy and enthusiasm, clarity, fluency, and adaptability.

16. Language in Discussion

The kind of language we use and the way we put words together make a lot of difference in how effective we are in a discussion. The person who is able to express himself well and say precisely what he wants to say makes a much better conference participant than the person who fumbles his language. What is the nature of ideal language usage in a discussion situation? First, as in any situation where language is used, *effective communication* of ideas should be the primary goal. We should be concerned with elements of language usage that will help to attain this goal. Second, language usage in discussion is frequently characterized by *informality*. By that we mean that participants in a discussion ideally recognize the essential informality inherent in the face-to-face situation and adapt the use of language to this informality. Contractions, frequent use of proper names, even occasional use of slang are fairly common in discussion groups. A third element which should always be present is a level of *understandability* adequate for the group. That is, care should be taken by participants to talk in such a way that other members of the group can easily grasp the ideas being expressed. In a recent study of the readability or understandability of union-management agreements, it was found that the "reading ease score" of the grievance clauses in these agreements was at a level considerably above the average educational level of the workers involved.[1] This kind of difficulty in understandability will inevitably lead to disputes and misunder-

---

[1] Joseph Tiffin and Francis X. Walsh, "Readability of Union-Management Agreements," *Personnel Psychology*, IV (1951), 327–337.

standings. The same kind of thing can happen in a discussion group where language with a high "understanding ease score" is used. Finally, good language usage in a discussion should be characterized by *expressiveness*—saying exactly what one wishes to say. Too often discussion participants are unable to say precisely what they mean, and, again, disputes and misunderstandings arise unnecessarily.

Requisites for Good Language Usage

What are the conditions which must exist in a discussion group to bring about good language usage? Some of them we have mentioned or implied already Let us examine them a little more fully, since they are important in creating the atmosphere for good use of language.

Informality

In an informal atmosphere we tend to be more relaxed, and feel easier about expressing ourselves.

Freedom of Expression

Sometimes we get in group situations where informality exists, yet we feel that there is little real freedom of expression possible. It may be that the leader is an authoritarian who denies us the right to say the kinds of things we want to say, or it may be that other members of the group inhibit our free expression of ideas. At any rate, good language usage can best be obtained in groups where everyone feels he has the right to say what he wants to say and that his opinions will be respected, although perhaps not always accepted.

Knowledge of Subject

Frequently we find difficulty in expressing ourselves well—finding the right words to express our ideas, or even finding the right ideas to express—simply because we do not know enough about the subject under discussion. It's always easier to talk understandably and intelligibly about a subject which we know well than it is about a subject about which our knowledge is limited. Knowing your subject is a necessary requisite for good understandable speaking in discussion.

Knowledge of Listeners

It is easier to adapt what we say to our listeners if we know something about them. If we have information about their educational background, interests, attitudes, beliefs, and knowledge of the subject under discussion, we can better aim what we have to say to them. The nature of the language we use to express our ideas will thus be affected by the amount of information we have about those who listen to us.

Atmosphere of Cordiality and Friendliness

The nature of the language we use will be influenced not only by the informality of the group, but also by the general atmosphere of friendliness which might exist. We can feel freer to talk among friends and in situations where the atmosphere is one of cordiality than in situations where feelings of hostility and antagonism might exist.

Face-to-face Situation

A different kind of expression of ideas exists in a face-to-face group than in a typical speaker-audience situation. The speaker usually finds it easier to talk, and can be more informal and more natural in the use of language in a face-to-face situation.

MAKING YOURSELF UNDERSTANDABLE IN DISCUSSION

We have examined some of the conditions that exist outside the speaker himself that make it easier for him to use language effectively in expressing his ideas. Now let us turn our attention to the participant himself and how he may most effectively use language to make himself understood by others in the group.

Be Interesting

As listeners, we pay more attention to ideas expressed interestingly than we do to ideas expressed in a dull manner. To be understandable, therefore, a speaker in a discussion should attempt to use devices of language and expression to clothe his ideas in as interesting a fashion as possible. Humor, suspense, concreteness, animation, and conflict are some of the devices that a speaker can use to make his ideas attractive.[2]

Organize Your Communication

As we have pointed out earlier, a communication which is well organized is remembered better by a listener than one which is disorganized, or one where the organization is not apparent to the listener. The important thing to remember here is that a speaker in a discussion can make what he has to say more understandable if he organizes his contributions.

Connect the Unfamiliar with the Familiar

When new ideas are being introduced into the discussion one sure way of securing understanding from your listeners is to tie in the new ideas with ideas and things already familiar and well known to them. Relating the unknown to the known is a good principle to follow in making what you say understandable to your auditors.

Employ an Understandable Style

In addition to the elements we have just considered, there are many stylistic elements the good speaker may employ to make his contributions more understandable. Many of those to be discussed here are style elements considered important by the readability ex-

---

[2] For a detailed discussion of these and other factors of interestingness in speaking, see James H. McBurney and Ernest J. Wrage, *The Art of Good Speech*, Chapter IX. New York: Prentice-Hall, 1953.

perts, the people who have experimented with ways of making written communications more understandable.[3] Let us now consider some of the specific style suggestions that are applicable to the conference situation, style suggestions which should make discussion participations more easily understood.

1. *Use short sentences.* Short sentences usually mean the speaker is handling a single idea at a time. The fewer the complicating factors (grammatically, such things as modifying phrases and clauses), the more easily the idea is understood. It is easier to comprehend a little at a time, than a long, complex idea expressed in a single unit.

2. *Use short words.* The short words in our language are, by and large, the more common words, and are, therefore, better known to everyone. Short words usually mean that the speaker is talking a language in which vocabulary presents no serious problem. Naturally, there are times when precision and exactness demand that longer, more obscure words be used, but generally speaking short words are more easily understood and therefore more desirable in a conference situation.

3. *Use personal references.* A contribution with a good many personal pronouns and proper names generally is more easily understood than a contribution with indirect, impersonal references. Notice how much easier it is to follow a communication when the speaker uses the pronoun "you" rather than the impersonal "one." It is more effective and more understandable to say: "You should use personal references when you talk in a conference," than it is to say, "One should use personal references when one talks in a conference."

4. *Be concrete.* Avoid abstractions wherever possible. If abstract ideas are being discussed, bring them down to the concrete by the use of specific examples and illustrations. Abstract ideas present many difficulties to most listeners, and can best be trans-

---

[3] See Rudolf Flesch, *The Art of Plain Talk.* New York: Harper & Brothers, 1946. This is the most popular presentation of the work of one of the more prominent readability experts. The first three style elements discussed here are three that are used in the *Flesch formula* presented in *The Art of Plain Talk.* Many of the other elements presented here are discussed in his book.

lated or interpreted by relating them to concrete, specific things. Democracy is made much more understandable as a concept by describing a specific instance of democracy in action, than by defining the term with other abstractions.

5. *Use verbs.* Verbs indicate movement, action, being. Consequently, of all parts of speech they are best in making a communication alive and understandable. Notice that in normal conversation you and your friends use a great many verbs and relatively few modifiers. The ease in understanding normal conversation may well be attributed, in part, at least, to the frequent use of verbs.

6. *Use a minimum of adjectives and other modifiers.* Just as verbs make the style and language move and have high interest value, so modifiers tend to slow down the pace and add more elements to interfere with the direct understandable communication of ideas. Sometimes, of course, modifiers are essential to the meaning of the communication and really assist in making it more understandable. Most of us, however, probably use more modifiers in discussion than we need.

7. *Avoid empty words and phrases.* Some words and phrases have been used over and over again until they have lost all or nearly all their meaning. These clichés should usually be avoided, since they do not help in expressing anything. Phrases like, "a scholar and a gentleman," "now and forever," "a friend in need," "far be it from me to . . . ," or even two of the phrases used just above, "over and over again," and "all or nearly all," are generally meaningless to an auditor because they say nothing. Sometimes such clichés have value because they are well known and may serve as familiar points of reference for an audience. They may have real merit when expertly used, but little merit when, as often happens, they are clumsily used.[4]

8. *Avoid fancy language.* Rudolf Flesch gives good advice about the use of "mere rhetoric" or fancy language, used for esthetic rather than communicative purposes. He recommends the following list of "do nots" to communicators:

---

[4] Edd Miller and Jesse J. Villarreal, "The Use of Clichés by Four Contemporary Speakers," *The Quarterly Journal of Speech*, XXXI (April, 1945), 154–155.

Do not use rhythm. (Maybe your reader won't catch on.)
Do not use periodic sentences.
Do not use rhetorical questions.
Do not use metaphors without an explanation.
Do not use contrasts without an explanation.
Do not use irony. (Half the people won't get it.) [5]

These suggestions apply as well to spoken communication in a conference as they do to written communications. Conference participants would do well to follow them.

9. *Adapt your vocabulary to your audience.* Use words that your listeners will understand. There is nothing to be gained by impressing others with your large and excellent vocabulary, if the meaning of what you are saying is lost. When your listeners can understand technical language, it may be wise to use a technical vocabulary since you will be able to say what you wish with greater precision. But you must be sure they understand this technical jargon, or the meaning of what you are talking about will be lost.

10. *Avoid loaded words.* Words that require an evaluation for understanding are frequently called "loaded" words. Such words as "Democrat," "Republican," "liberal," "conservative," "reactionary," "communist," "fascist," are loaded words. In each case, an interpretation or evaluation is called for by the speaker of the word. In a discussion of industrial relations, William Exton has pointed out that differences in evaluation of words, propaganda techniques in the use of words, talking in absolutes, and the use of subjective labels, are some of the semantic sins that lead to misunderstandings in management-labor communications.[6] Avoiding the use of "loaded" words can mean better understanding, fewer misunderstandings between people in a conference situation.

11. *Make brief contributions.* Just as short sentences are usually easier to understand, so short participations in a conference are usually easier to comprehend than long ones. The longer the contribution, the greater the number of different ideas there are apt to be in it. This increase in idea density in a contribution is

---

[5] Rudolf Flesch, *op. cit.*, p. 105. Reprinted by permission.
[6] William Exton, Jr., "Language and 'Reality'; Semantics of Industrial Relations: II," *Personnel*, XXVII (1950), 194–201.

well apt to make the contribution more difficult to understand. As
Utterback points out:

> Typically discussion takes the form of conversation rather than of an
> exchange of long statements. Seldom should a contribution be more
> than a few sentences in length, and often a few words are sufficient.
> The long contributions that slow up progress are sometimes due to
> sheer verbosity; many words are used to say what could have been said
> more clearly in a few words. Terseness is a virtue, for unnecessary
> words usually cloud the point.[7]

12. *Be precise—say what you want to say.* Try to avoid ambiguities and circumlocutions. Get right to the point of what
you have to say. Many misunderstandings arise in discussion because a speaker will not or cannot say with precision what he wants
to say. This is important, and if the other suggestions made here
may sometimes interfere with precision of statement, then you
should make precision most important. Violate any of the other
rules, but always say what you want to say.

13. *Be vivid.* Use colorful language and colorful expressions.
These help hold attention, and attention is essential to good listening. Unless it becomes an end, rather than a means, vivid language can help tremendously in securing understanding.

14. *Use emphasis.* Use words that will help emphasize key
ideas. In addition, repetition and restatement have been found
to be effective devices for emphasizing important ideas. Understanding will be increased when emphasis is used, because the
speaker is helping the listener to select the really important words
and ideas.

Summary

In this chapter we have discussed the nature of the use of language in discussion. Some of the requisites for good language
usage to be found in a conference group are informality, freedom

---

[7] William E. Utterback, *Group Thinking and Conference Leadership: Techniques of Discussion,* p. 55. New York: Rinehart & Company, Inc., 1950. Reprinted by permission.

of expression, knowledge of the subject, knowledge of the listeners, an atmosphere of cordiality and friendliness, and a face-to-face situation. Some of the ways of making yourself understandable in conference speaking are: being interesting, organizing your communication, connecting the unfamiliar with the familiar, and using an understandable style. We have discussed many style elements which lead to better understanding: short sentences, short words, many personal references, concreteness, many verbs, few modifiers, avoidance of empty words, avoidance of fancy language, adapting vocabulary to others in the group, avoidance of loaded words, brief contributions, precision, vividness, and emphasis.

PART VI

Public Meetings

17. Radio and Television Discussion

So far, our attention has been directed primarily to non-audience conference situations, chiefly those designed for problem-solving. We now turn to some types of discussion aimed at audiences, discussions having as a purpose, as Utterback says, "not to resolve differences of opinion in the panel, but to interest and inform the listener and to clarify his thinking." [1] These discussions are best seen in operation in the typical radio and television discussions.

TYPES OF RADIO AND TELEVISION DISCUSSIONS

While most public discussions have as their goals the three elements of informing an audience, interesting an audience, and crystallizing the opinions of an audience, the forms of these discussions are varied. Let us consider now some of the more common types of radio and television discussions.

The Round Table

This is probably the most usual type of radio and television discussion. It is typified by a group ranging in size from three to six,

---

[1] William E. Utterback, *Group Thinking and Conference Leadership: Techniques of Discussion*, p. 127. New York: Rinehart & Company, Inc., 1950.

with a moderator or leader. Most such round table discussions employ four panelists and a moderator. The discussion is unrehearsed, as a usual thing, with a relatively free give-and-take in participation. The moderator has the job of introducing the discussion, maintaining order, seeking to assure fairly equal participation among the members of the panel, raising pertinent questions about the subject under discussion, and closing the discussion. The atmosphere usually is one of informality. Panel members are selected not only on the basis of their information about the subject under discussion, but also because they represent divergent points of view. The typical round table program is thirty minutes in length. It should be borne in mind, however, that of these thirty minutes usually three are taken up by opening and closing announcements, particularly in television. In a commercially sponsored half-hour program, there may be as little as twenty-four minutes air time available for the actual discussion.

Debate

Although one may object, on the basis of our definition of discussion, to considering the debate form as a type of discussion, many so-called discussions on radio and television are, in reality, debates. These "discussions" are typified by a balanced presentation of the pros and cons of a subject. Usually, there are two speakers for the proposition under discussion, and two against, with a moderator, although occasionally there may be a single speaker for and a single speaker against the proposition. This type of program tends to be a little more formal than the round table, since the speakers normally are allowed to make short prepared speeches as well as to engage in the give-and-take of the more informal round table. A typical format would call for a short (perhaps three minutes) speech from each of the panel members, followed by a period of cross-questioning or informal round table type discussion. The moderator introduces the question, introduces the speakers, and leads the informal discussion. This type of program is usually scheduled for thirty minutes.

Inquiry

Congressional investigations on radio and television have high-lighted still another type of radio and television discussion: the inquiry. One variety may be seen on such a program as "Meet the Press." The procedure in this type of program is for an expert witness to be interrogated by a group of three or four people. The purpose of this type of discussion is to bring out information from the witness. There usually is a moderator who maintains order in the discussion and sees to it that only one panelist at a time asks questions and that the witness is given an opportunity to answer the questions asked him. The program, too, is usually a thirty-minute one.

Interview

Still in the general category of radio and television discussions is the interview. The interview may be either an interview of one person or of several at a time. Chiefly, the purpose of the inter-view is to bring out information from the "interviewee." In this type of program, one person has the role of interviewer or questioner and the other person or persons responds to his questions. In many respects, this type of program resembles the inquiry, although it is frequently characterized by a slightly more polite and defer-ential attitude toward the person being questioned. This type of program normally is a fifteen-minute program, although occasionally it may be a thirty-minute program.

PHYSICAL ARRANGEMENTS FOR RADIO AND TELEVISION DISCUSSION

This is not a technical book on radio and television direction and production, and our purpose here is to indicate very briefly only some of the more common physical arrangements necessary in radio and television discussion. The station originating the program will, in nearly all cases, provide a trained member of its staff to take care of the technical aspects of production.

Size of the Group

As we have already indicated, the number of people involved in a radio or television discussion is usually quite small. There are physical limitations in the media which make this necessary. In a radio discussion, the difficulty for the audience in making identifications by voice only and in keeping the personnel of the discussion panel fixed in mind, dictate that a small group be used. In a television discussion, the limitation of the size of the picture is a real one that argues against a large number of people. With expert direction and camera work, however, larger groups can be handled on television. In general, it is safe to say that for either radio or television, a good size is four people plus a leader or moderator.

Arrangements for Radio Discussion

The physical set-up for a typical radio round table discussion (by far, the most common type used) involves simply a table large enough to accommodate the members of the panel and the leader, plus enough microphones to pick up the voices of the people involved. One difficulty frequently encountered in a radio round table is the natural tendency of members of the group to talk to each other rather than to the microphone. Hence, the more microphones the better. Certainly a minimum of two microphones for a group of four panel members and a leader is a must. Ideally, there should be a microphone for every two members of the panel and one for the leader.

Arrangements for Television Discussion

Here again, the director or producer will be able to suggest the best physical arrangements. It has been found, however, that the traditional round table arrangement used in radio broadcasts is not suitable for television. One obvious reason for this, of course, is that in a typical radio round table set up, at least one person would have his back to the camera.   Consequently, it is better to have a kind of L shaped or V shaped table arrangement so that the camera can get a face view of all members of the panel.   This kind of physical arrangement has the advantage not only of giving a better camera shot, but also of preserving some of the elements of the face-to-face discussion.   Such an arrangement is diagrammed here:

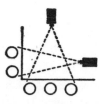

If a boom microphone is used members of the panel have a little more freedom of action with regard to microphones in a television discussion than in a radio discussion, but the problem remains of talking always so the voice is directed toward the microphone.

Leading the Radio and Television Discussion

The Moderator

We usually refer to a leader of a debate or an inquiry discussion as a moderator.

1. *The debate moderator.*   Some of the functions of this type of leader have already been mentioned.   They might be summarized by saying he performs the following duties:

(a) He opens the debate by presenting the statement of the topic being debated.   This statement is usually best presented in the form of a question, for example, "Should the European nations unite into a single nation?"   "Should the president of the United States be elected by a direct vote of the people?"   You will notice that the proposal under debate is given in both these questions.

(b) The moderator introduces the panel.   He does this not only by giving names and other biographical information, but also by telling which side of the proposition each member will uphold.

(c) The moderator introduces the first speaker.

(d) The moderator introduces the other members of the panel in order. The speakers in most instances will talk in an alternating order, first, one speaker for the proposition, then one against, and so on.

(e) The moderator begins the informal, round table discussion, or if there is a cross-question period in its place, the moderator conducts this. His leadership in the round table phase of the debate is essentially like that which will be described later for the leadership of the round table type of discussion.

(f) The moderator closes the discussion. The close quite often involves a brief (perhaps 30 seconds) statement from each of the panel participants. If this is not done, the moderator attempts to summarize the opinions and points of view brought out by the panel.

2. *The inquiry moderator.* The duties of the moderator in the inquiry type of discussion may be summarized as:

(a) Introduction by the moderator of the panel of questioners and of the person to be questioned. In this introduction, some mention should be made of the general subject area of the investigation. This can be best done in the introduction of the expert who is being quizzed by the panel. A statement or two about his job or the reason why he has been asked to appear on this program will usually make the subject area of the investigation clear.

(b) The moderator maintains order during the inquiry. Generally speaking, this is not a difficult job, although occasionally tempers will flare and the discussion will get somewhat out of hand. Usually, the moderator tries to see to it that questions are asked in an orderly fashion, and that all members of the investigating panel have opportunities to ask questions. In addition, he should see to it that the expert is given sufficient opportunity to answer questions put to him by the group.

(c) The moderator closes the discussion. The close is usually a simple recapitulation of who the expert was, who the panel members were, and what the topic under discussion was.

The Interviewer

The interviewer's chief task is asking questions. This may sound simple, but sometimes it is very difficult. In order to ask intelligent questions, the person preparing to be an interviewer needs to know a good deal both about the subject or subjects to be discussed in the interview and about the person or persons to be interviewed. A thorough preparation of this sort is in order, then. In the course of making this kind of preparation, the interviewer should jot down a series of questions to ask the interviewee. Much of this preparation can be done in a pre-broadcast conversation with the person being interviewed. As an interviewer, never trust to the spur of the moment to provide you with questions to ask, you may find yourself with nothing to say. Naturally, a good interviewer does not restrict himself to the prepared list of questions, but asks other questions that may arise out of answers given. The interviewer should begin the interview by introducing the interviewee, and he should indicate in the introduction the reason for the interview and the subject matter to be covered. As he conducts the interview, he should remember that his is strictly a secondary position, and that the interviewee should be given ample time in which to answer questions. As an interviewer, let the expert being interviewed do most of the talking. The interviewer should ask questions that he feels will have interest to the listening audience. He should look upon himself as a kind of representative of the audience, asking the questions the audience would like to have an opportunity to ask. He should close the interview by a restatement of the name and qualifications of the person or persons being interviewed and by a restatement of the subject matter of the interview.

The Round Table Leader

In most respects, the radio and television round table leader operates like the leader of other informal discussion groups. There are some special considerations, however, that this kind of leader should keep in mind.

1. *Pre-discussion meeting.* Many leaders of radio and television round table discussion have found it to be a valuable experience to get the group assembled twenty or thirty minutes before broadcast time for a planning session. This serves not only to prepare the leader on the general approach to the topic to be taken by the panel members, but also serves as a warm-up period for the panel members. The discussion is apt to get off to a better start if the ice is broken before broadcast time rather than after the group is on the air.

2. *Opening and closing.* Most discussion leaders are aware of their responsibilities to the group in stating the problem at the beginning of the discussion and of attempting a summary of the group's work at the end. This should be done in radio and television discussions. But the leader should keep in mind that he performs these functions not only for the group participating in the discussion, but for the radio and television audience as well. Consequently, his opening, in particular, should be fuller, and, perhaps, more stimulating from the standpoint of attracting attention to the subject than it would be in a non-audience situation.

3. *Encouraging participation.* While the discussion leader should not force a participant to talk when he has nothing to say, it is more important in radio and television discussion than in other types that there be something like an equal spread of participation. Therefore, the leader should be more active here than in other discussion situations in encouraging members to participate.

4. *Raising points of view and questions.* The leader can perform a useful function also by raising questions and points of view that are not adequately treated by the members of the group. He should keep in mind that one of the purposes of radio and television discussion is to interest an audience. For this reason, as well as to increase the amount of information coming from the group, the leader should not hesitate to raise points of view or questions that he knows will lead to argument and the presentation of different opinions. Conflict is one of the best ways of keeping a round table discussion interesting to an audience. A limited amount of conflict over ideas will serve a useful purpose in a discussion.

5. *Organizing the discussion.* The leader of a radio or television discussion, just like the leader of any discussion group, should try to maintain a sense of organization and order about the subject under discussion. This should be done both by attempting to outline the problem for discussion before the discussion begins, and by trying to keep the discussion somewhat organized as it progresses. If irrelevancies can be reduced to a minimum and a general pattern of organization followed in the discussion, listeners will gain much more than if the discussion is pointless, goes off on tangents, and is completely disorganized.

6. *Maintaining order.* Since the radio or television discussion is a public appearance, a reasonable degree of order is necessary. This is not to say that differences of opinion are to be discouraged. If anything, they should be encouraged. But the fact is that the leader should see to it that the members of the group do not get out of hand. No one profits when several members talk at the same time, or when there are little sub-discussions going on at the same time that a member is participating. For the sake of the listening or viewing audience, the leader should maintain order in the group.

PARTICIPATING IN RADIO AND TELEVISION DISCUSSION

Again, good participation in any of the discussion situations we have considered in earlier sections of this book will constitute general good discussion behavior for radio and television discussion. Let us re-emphasize some of the more important points, however, for effective participation in a radio or television round table discussion.

Be Prepared

This is an essential of good discussion of any kind. The need for adequate preparation is, if anything, greater in a radio or television round table where the group has the responsibility of supplying the listening or viewing audience with information they do not already possess.

Be Interesting

To keep the interest of the audience high, the need for interesting presentation of material is greater in these public kinds of discussion than in any other.   The participant should talk in a lively, animate, vital manner about his subject, and he should express his ideas in a style that will keep interest and attention focused on the problem under discussion.

Be Brief

One way of keeping audience interest in a round table type of discussion is to have a frequent interchange of ideas among the members of the group.   The audience expects each member to be relatively brief in his presentation and not to present an elaborate public speech.   Give others in the group an opportunity to talk.   Keep your comments as brief as you can.

Be Relevant

We have already stressed the importance of good over-all organization of the subject in a round table discussion.   As a participant, you can assist the leader in keeping the discussion organized and to the point by trying to keep all your contributions relevant to the point under discussion.   Avoid the temptation to get off on tangents, however appealing they might be.

Be Courteous

Although conflict is one of the ways of keeping a round table discussion interesting, this does not mean that members should be rude or discourteous.   You can disagree and argue with other members of the panel, and still be courteous.   Your audience expects it of you, and good taste demands it.

Be Clear

Say precisely what you want to say and say it in a manner that will be clear not only to the other members of the panel (who may know a good deal about the subject you are talking about) but also to the audience. Remember that many members of your listening or viewing audience may know little about your subject and you should, therefore, make a special effort to be clear to them.

Don't Be Afraid to Disagree

We have mentioned several times the interest value of disagreements and conflict over ideas in a discussion. To make the discussion interesting, as well as to express your own ideas and points of view, never be afraid to argue and disagree with other members of the panel. Obviously, though, you should never carry such disagreements to the point of disrupting the entire discussion.

Be Specific and Concrete

Remember, again, that your audience does not bring into the discussion the same background of information you and the other members of the panel may have. As a result, you should always be careful to be concrete and specific and to avoid vague abstractions as much as possible.

Organize What You Say

Earlier in this book we have talked about the value of organizing individual contributions and about some methods of organizing them. The need for organization of contributions is greater in radio and television discussions than in any others, since you have the responsibility not only of making yourself clear and easily followed by the other members of the panel, but by an audience also. Remember, too, that material that is organized is remembered better and longer than the same material presented in an unorganized fashion.

SUMMARY

In this chapter we have discussed the three purposes of radio and television discussion: to inform an audience, to interest an audience, and to assist an audience in crystallizing opinions. We have discussed the four types of radio and television discussion: the round table, the debate, the inquiry discussion, and the interview. We have considered some of the basic physical arrangements necessary for radio discussion and for television discussion. We have presented some of the functions and duties of the leader or moderator for the various types of radio and television discussions. And, finally, we have emphasized that the participant in a radio or television round table discussion should: be prepared, be interesting, be brief, be relevant, be courteous, be clear, not be afraid to disagree, be specific and concrete, and organize his contributions.

18. Large Group Meetings

Throughout this book our discussion has centered around small group meetings. Yet, there are many occasions when matters must be discussed by large groups—groups of 75, 100, or more. Many times important decisions are reached or important information is presented in these large group meetings. Consequently, a group leader should know something about chairing large meetings as well as small ones. He should be able to plan and secure participation from members in large groups.

Types of Large Group Meetings

The types of large group meetings may conveniently be classified according to the purpose of the meeting.

Learning Meetings

This is the kind of meeting where a speaker, or speakers, presents information to an audience. A single speaker may simply lecture to an audience, or he may employ motion pictures or other visual aids as part of his presentation of material. In other situations, a group of speakers may present material to an audience. In fact, almost any of the standard types of conference and discussion considered earlier in this book may be adapted for audience presentation. Whatever the nature of the program, its aim is to enlighten the audience, and increase its information about the subject being discussed.

Policy-making Meetings

Often the purpose of a large group meeting is to determine policy. The typical business meeting of any organization is an example of the policy-making type of meeting. Generally, rather formal rules of procedure are followed and business is presented in the form of motions or resolutions.

Entertainment Meetings

Sometimes the whole reason for a large group of people assembling is entertainment. No informational or business outcomes are expected from such a meeting.

PREPARING FOR LARGE GROUP MEETINGS

Regardless of the type of meeting, the essential steps in preparing to lead or chair a large group meeting are the same.

Program Arrangements

Aside from his own personal preparation for a large group meeting, the chairman has certain responsibilities in planning for other aspects of the meeting.

1. *Securing a program.* This kind of preparation applies, of course, only to learning meetings and entertainment meetings, but since business sessions are sometimes combined with one of the other two types of meetings, every chairman should know something about this aspect of making program arrangements. In securing a program, the first decision to make relates to the type of program needed. Whether the program is to be serious or entertaining should be decided early. The exact type of program wanted should be considered. The chairman should keep in mind adaptation to the audience, to the occasion, to the kinds of programs the group has been accustomed to having. Once these basic decisions are made, the mechanics of making arrangements with the speaker or speakers should be undertaken. If a speaker is to be invited to

appear before the group, he should be contacted early—weeks or even months before the occasion. The prospective speaker should be told exactly what will be expected of him: the kind of topic he is to talk about, how long he has in which to present his speech, other items on the program, the exact time and place of the meeting, the kind and size of audience he will speak before, whether or not he will be expected to answer questions from the audience, and, not the least important item, the size of the fee or honorarium.

2. *Planning an agenda.* We have already implied that the chairman should have a clear notion of the events on a program at the time he extends an invitation to a guest speaker. For learning meetings and entertainment meetings this kind of planning should be done far in advance not only to supply needed information to visiting speakers, but also to assist the chairman in keeping the meeting running on time, and to provide copy for publicity, programs, and other materials to be used in connection with the meeting. In the case of a business meeting, it is equally important for the chairman to plan his agenda far in advance and with some care. In many organizations, the proposed agenda for a policy-making meeting is sent to members in advance of the meeting. Even if this practice is not followed, a carefully planned agenda will assist the chairman in conducting an orderly meeting. The standard agenda for a business meeting is an amplification (by filling in specific items and details of business) of the following order of business:

1. Call to order
2. Reading of minutes
3. Reports of officers and committees
4. Unfinished business
5. New business
6. Announcements
7. Adjournment

3. *Physical arrangements.* Care should be taken in providing adequate physical arrangements for a meeting. Some of the factors which should be considered are:

(a) *Size of the meeting room.* The room should be sufficiently large enough to accommodate the expected attendance, yet not so large that the group will feel lost or swallowed up in the room. The chairman must rely on his best judgment and on his knowledge of previous meetings of the group to estimate the size of the expected audience. In many situations a regular meeting room is used. But if it appears that a particular program will have a larger audience than the regular room will accommodate, arrangements should be made for another room and notice sent to members that the meeting place has been changed. The place of meeting should be determined as early as possible.

(b) *Furnishing of the meeting room.* Shortly before the meeting, the chairman should see that the platform is adequately furnished—that enough chairs have been provided, that a lectern has been provided, and, when needed, that a public address system is available. The chairman should see to it that the rest of the auditorium has been adequately furnished; that there are enough chairs, for example, for the expected audience. A few minutes spent in this kind of preparation can save much time and embarrassment at the time of the meeting.

(c) *Lighting and ventilation of the meeting room.* The chairman should also be sure that the lighting is adequate, particularly that there is good light directed toward the platform. He should also be sure that the meeting room is properly ventilated. Many audiences have gone to sleep not only because of the quality of the meeting but also because of the poor quality of the ventilation of the meeting room.

The Chairman's Preparation

The chairman should prepare himself for the job of presiding over a meeting. Good, confident chairmen are those who know what they are doing, who know what to expect in a meeting, and who have planned on ways of dealing with matters that will arise in the meeting.

1. *Know the program.* A chairman should know the items or events on his program or agenda so well that he need not refer to

notes. He should know the exact order in which events will take place, how long each event will probably last. Although, as we have said, this should be very well known by the chairman, many chairmen make it a practice to have their agenda carefully written out, as a safeguard in guaranteeing that the events on the program proceed in the order in which they have been planned.

2. *Know the speaker.* If a speaker or a group of speakers are to appear on the program, it is important that the chairman know enough about them to be able to do a creditable job of introducing them to the audience. In his earlier correspondence with a prospective speaker, the chairman should not hesitate to ask the speaker for information about himself. This information can often be supplemented by other sources—friends of the speaker, references to *Who's Who in America* or other biographical sources.

3. *Know the rules of procedure.* This applies primarily, of course, to preparation for policy-making or business meetings. We will consider these rules of procedure in more detail later in this chapter.

4. *Know the audience.* Most chairmen do know their audiences well, but if you are to chair a new group or if your regular group is to be supplemented with new members, try to find out as much as you can about the new people in the meeting. Having this information will assist the chairman in meeting events that may not be expected—or, at least he will be in a better position to predict the kinds of reactions he is apt to get from his group.

Conducting a Large Group Meeting

Opening the Meeting

A meeting should begin on time. As simple as this rule sounds, it is probably the most frequently violated rule of any in the conduct of meetings. It is not fair to participants in a program nor to members of the audience to keep them waiting idly for fifteen, thirty, forty-five minutes, or sometimes longer before starting a meeting. A delay at the beginning of a meeting usually means a delay in ending the meeting. Both a late start and a late finish are inexcusable.

Adhere to the Prepared Timing of the Program

Not only should the program begin on time, but each segment of the program should stick closely to its time limits. The first responsibility for seeing that a speaker, for example, confines himself to his allotted time is probably the speaker's. But the chairman has the ultimate responsibility of seeing that a speaker does not exceed his time limits. Even at the expense of seeming rude to the speaker, he should inform the speaker by signal or orally when his time is up. In most cases, a clear understanding with a speaker before the meeting will prevent the necessity of stopping him at the time of the meeting. Timing becomes especially important when more than one speaker appears on a program. Most of us have had the experience of attending a meeting where several speakers are to talk, and watching while the first speaker uses all or nearly all the time allotted to the entire panel of speakers. Once again, the chairman must take firm measures to see that time limits are observed. When the chairman stops a long-winded speaker, the possibility of seeming rude to the speaker is more than offset by the courtesy and kindness to the audience.

Be Fair in the Conduct of the Meeting

This rule applies primarily in business meetings, where fairness and impartiality are usually considered to be important characteristics of good leadership. In any meeting, however, the chairman should be fair, impartial, helpful, and tactful in running the meeting.

Speak Loudly Enough to be Heard

Many chairmen of large group meetings speak as though they were conducting a small, informal conference. An easy conversational method of speaking is to be desired, but the chairman should be sure, above all else in his speaking, that he can easily be heard by everyone in the room. It is often a good practice for the chairman to ask, right at the beginning of the meeting, whether or not everyone can hear him clearly.

Opportunities for Participation Should Be Allowed

Methods for securing participation or allowing participation in business meetings are carefully prescribed by standard rules of order. However, in many learning situations, problems may arise about how best to allow the audience freedom to participate. Some methods for securing audience participation will be considered here.

1. *Prepared questions.* Often the difficulty in getting adequate audience participation centers around the difficulty of getting the first one or two questions asked. That is, an audience often is more willing to participate after the first couple of questions have been asked, after the ice has been broken. For that reason, many chairmen prepare a few questions in advance and either ask these questions themselves, or, in advance, make plans to have some one or two members of the audience ask these questions.

2. *Submitted questions.* Another method of securing audience participation in large group meetings is to have individual members of the audience submit questions to the chairman before the meeting begins. Relevant questions that have not been answered in the course of the speaker's talk may then be read at the conclusion of the speech and answered by the speaker. If the questions are submitted far enough in advance, they may be given to the speaker for his use as a guide in preparing his talk.

3. *Buzz groups.* Many situations lend themselves to the use of small sub-groups within the audience as a means of securing audience participation in the program. After the speaker or speakers have concluded the prepared portion of the program, the chairman may then ask the audience to break up into small groups of six to ten people. These small groups confer then for five or ten minutes and decide on one or two questions to be asked the speaker. A spokesman for the group is selected. When the general meeting is re-convened, the chairman then calls for the questions from the buzz groups. Each spokesman is given an opportunity to present his group's question to the speaker. The chief advantage to this

procedure lies in the opportunity given for each member of the audience to have some kind of participation in the meeting. It should be pointed out, however, that sometimes physical conditions or the lack of time make this kind of procedure unusable.

4. *Questions from the floor.* The final method of securing participation from the audience is the method of simply asking for questions from the members of the audience. Any one is allowed to ask questions at the conclusion of the speech. The chairman recognizes individual members of the audience, the member states his question, the question is answered, and another questioner is recognized. While this method allows the audience considerable freedom in questioning, it is a very uncertain method. Sometimes questions simply are not asked, or sometimes questions may not be relevant to the matter being discussed, or sometimes members of the audience take advantage of the question period by making long speeches. Consequently, considerable skill is demanded of the chairman in stimulating questions from the audience, in dealing with members whose questions may not be relevant, or in tactfully discouraging members who wish to make speeches of great length.

Leading the Question Period

When questions are asked from the floor to a speaker, the chairman should preside. He should be sure the question can be heard and is clear not only to the speaker, but to other members of the audience as well. Often he will need to repeat or sometimes rephrase a question for the sake of clarity or audibility.

Courtesy Functions of the Chairman

In addition to presiding over a question-answer period and over a business session, the chairman often has certain courtesy functions to perform. Normally, he is the master of ceremonies, with the job of introducing speakers, presenting gifts or awards, receiving gifts or awards, and other such matters not directly connected with the business of running a meeting. In general, these matters should be handled with brevity, courtesy, tact, and enthusiasm.

Closing the Meeting

Many groups have an announced beginning and ending time and these should be observed; other groups, however, have no specified time for closing. In this situation, the chairman should see to it that the meeting lasts sufficiently long for the announced purpose of the meeting to be accomplished, yet not so long that members lose interest in the proceedings and become restless. In business meetings, of course, adjournment rests with the discretion of the membership by a majority vote or with the conclusion of the announced business of the group. In other situations, the chairman should be the judge about closing the meeting.

CONDUCTING THE BUSINESS MEETING

In general, our discussion so far has dealt with the learning type of large public meeting. Business meetings are conducted in a slightly more formal manner and under a set of pre-determined rules of procedure. These rules of parliamentary procedure have been codified and are so frequently followed because they serve some very useful functions: (1) they guarantee that the majority will triumph, (2) they protect the rights of the minority, (3) they provide order in a situation that otherwise could become chaotic, and (4) they allow for a careful consideration of matters of policy.

Chairing the Business Meeting

The key figure in a business meeting run according to established rules of parliamentary procedure is the chairman. His interpretation and application of the rules of procedure can determine the fairness and success of a business session. A good chairman of a business group should be fair and impartial. He should not allow his own feelings and attitudes toward a matter under discussion to influence his conduct of the meeting. He should make a real effort to recognize speakers on both sides of a resolution, and he should see to it that the rules of procedure are clear to all. A good chairman should be confident, quick, and firm in reaching decisions. He should, of course, make every effort to reach correct decisions and he should be willing (even eager) to have incorrect decisions corrected by members of the group. At the same time, the tempo and the business-like quality of a meeting can be slowed considerably by a chairman who is uncertain or vacillating in his decisions. Implicit in all this is the absolute requirement that the chairman should know the rules of procedure governing his group extremely well. The constitution, by-laws, traditions of the group should be known thoroughly by him, as well as the rules of procedure in a standard reference work on parliamentary law.

Rules of Procedure

It should be clear that we do not propose the use of formal rules of procedure for all groups and all occasions. Small, informal policy-making groups should follow the procedures discussed in other chapters of this book. However, when the size of the group reaches fifty, sixty, seventy, or more, then established, pre-determined, codified rules of procedure become necessary. Let us consider some of the more commonly used motions, incorporated in standard rules of parliamentary law.[1] These motions will be considered first from the standpoint of the general purpose of the motion, and second from the standpoint of the order in which action is taken on the motions (precedence of the motions).

1. *According to the purpose of the motion.*

(a) *Motions for the conduct of business.* As indicated earlier in this chapter, business in a policy-making session is carried on through the use of motions or resolutions. These normally begin with the words, "I move that . . ." In each case, of course, the speaker must be recognized by the chairman before he offers his resolution. All the motions used for the conduct of business in a group require a second. After the motion has been properly made and seconded, it is stated by the chair, is debated, and at

---

[1] This section of this book does not purport to be a complete manual on parliamentary procedure. Probably the most widely used source of authority on these matters is, Henry M. Robert, *Robert's Rules of Order,* Revised, New York: Scott, Foresman and Company, 1951.

the conclusion of the debate, a vote is taken on the motion.

(b) *Motions for disposing of other motions.* Certain motions have as their aim the disposing of other motions or items of business. In addition to a final vote on a matter of business, motions may be referred to committees, postponed, withdrawn, or disposed of permanently or temporarily in other ways.

(c) *Motions concerning debate on business.* Sometimes the members of a group wish to curtail or extend the time allowed for debating a motion, or they may wish to cut-off debate completely. To accomplish these objectives motions may be made to limit debate, suspend the rules, etc.

(d) *Motions concerning the members of the group.* Certain motions are designed to protect individual members of the group or extend privileges to them. These motions may be used to secure information for members concerning rules of order, or they may be used to appeal from decisions of the chair, or they may be used for a great variety of personal privileges.

(e) *Motions concerning the conduct of the meeting.* Certain motions have to do with the conduct of the meeting itself—such things as adjourning the meeting, calling a recess, etc.

Specific information about motions falling in these five categories may be found in the following table.

TABLE OF IMPORTANT, FREQUENTLY USED MOTIONS

Motion	Second?	Amendable?	Debatable?	Vote?	Interrupt?
A. Conducting business					
1. Main motion	Yes	Yes	Yes	Maj.	No
2. Amend	Yes	Yes	Yes	Maj.	No
3. Take from table	Yes	No	No	Maj.	No
4. Reconsider	Yes	No	Yes*	Maj.	Yes
5. Rescind	Yes	Yes	Yes	2/3	No
6. Make special order	Yes	Yes	Yes	2/3	No
B. Disposing of motions					
1. Lay on table	Yes	No	No	Maj.	No
2. Postpone to a certain time	Yes	Yes	Yes	Maj.	No
3. Refer	Yes	Yes	Yes	Maj.	No
4. Postpone indefinitely	Yes	No	Yes	Maj.	No
5. Object to consideration	No	No	No	2/3	Yes
6. Withdraw a motion	No	No	No	Maj.	No

* Generally true, but with exceptions.

C. Concerning debate

1. Previous question	Yes	No	No	2/3	No
2. Close nominations	Yes	No	No	2/3	No
3. Limit debate	Yes	Yes	No	2/3	No
4. Suspend rules	Yes	No	No	2/3	No

D. Concerning members

1. Question of privilege	No	No	No	Ch.	Yes
2. Question of order	No	No	No	Ch.	Yes
3. Appeal from decision of chair	Yes	No	No*	Maj.	Yes
4. Parliamentary inquiry	No	No	No	Ch.	Yes
5. Request for information	No	No	No	Ch.	Yes

E. Concerning the meeting

1. Fix time for next meeting	Yes	Yes	No	Maj.	No
2. Adjourn	Yes	No	No	Maj.	No
3. Recess	Yes	Yes	No	Maj.	No
4. Committee of the whole	Yes	Yes	Yes	Maj.	No

* Generally true, but with exceptions.

2. *According to the precedence of motions.* These same motions may be re-classified according to the priority of action which each has. While only one main motion for business may be considered at a time, there may be several motions introduced properly by members of the group. When two or more motions are introduced and before the group, there is a set order in which they are acted on. The following list of motions is arranged in the order of precedence, with the motion carrying the highest priority of action at the top of the list:

Privileged motions:
    Fix time of next meeting
    Adjourn
    Recess
    Question of privilege
Subsidiary motions:
    Lay on the table
    Previous question
    Limit debate
    Postpone to a certain time
    Refer to a committee

Committee of the whole
Amend
Postpone indefinitely
Main motions (these have no set order of precedence):
Main motion for general business
Take from the table
Reconsider
Rescind
Make special order of business
Incidental motions (these have no set order of precedence):
Question of order
Appeal from decision of chair
Suspend the rules
Object to consideration
Parliamentary inquiry
Request for information
Withdraw a motion.

A final word of caution should be added: A good chairman does not necessarily adhere rigidly and exclusively to the letter of the law; it should be remembered that the traditions of an organization about rules of procedure should carry more weight than the rules to be found in a reference work on parliamentary law. Traditional methods of operation have somewhat the same standing as common law does in our legal system.

Appendixes

Appendixes

Appendix A. Case Problems

CASE No. 1: *Acceptance of Decisions* (Reported by Frank A. Thorn, Supervisor of Employment, Carboloy Department, General Electric Company, Detroit, Michigan)

Situation. Eye accidents in the production area of a metal fabricating company continued to be a serious safety problem. There were certain machines and operations where safety glasses were required in order to protect the eyes of operators from flying chips.

Everything was being done to encourage employees to wear their glasses. Articles on the subject of safety glasses appeared in the house organ and a poster campaign was also initiated. These methods of communication were aimed at persuading employees to wear their safety glasses.

In spite of these attempts at persuasion there were occasions when employees neglected to wear their safety glasses. This was proven by the fact that eye accident cases continued to mount. The foremen did not seem to be accepting their responsibility for enforcing the safety rule regarding the wearing of protective glasses. On the other hand, it was felt by the company that safety is a foreman's responsibility, just as meeting production schedules, maintaining quality, and avoiding waste are the responsibilities of foremen.

Solution. The problem was discussed at a regular weekly supervisory training session. The foremen discussed the frequency of eye accidents, their causes, their effects and what could be done to curtail these accidents.

They determined that something must be done about this safety problem and that it was up to them to see that their employees wore safety glasses.

Results. A concentrated program was begun by the foremen in January 1953. At the end of the year it was discovered that there had been a 40% decrease in the number of eye accident cases over the preceding year.

Questions for Discussion. Why did methods other than the group decision method fail in this case? How do you account for the successful results of the group decision solution?

CASE No. 2: *Promoting Problem-Solving Behavior* (Reported by Charles H. Goebel, Assistant Cashier, The Wayne Oakland Bank, Royal Oak, Michigan)

Situation. Bill Brown was a young unmarried veteran who decided to complete his college degree program while working as a trainee in a suburban bank. His work consisted of learning to be a teller, doing credit investigation, and assisting the manager in the operation of the bank. Bill was very industrious and impressed all persons with whom he worked because of his unusual ability to grasp the new jobs that were assigned to him. He completed his initial training in about half the time considered standard. The added work of completing his education did not interfere with the work he did at the bank.

After Bill had been on the job about a year another young man with considerably more experience and seniority received a promotion. Bill thought he had been by-passed and he immediately made an appointment with the personnel manager to find out what was what. Bill was not reluctant in the least to voice his disappointment.

Solution. Recognizing that Bill's ego had been dealt a severe blow, the personnel manager spent considerable time in discussing Bill's own record with the organization. No attempt was made to justify the promotion of the other man as it was stressed that the personnel department was concerned with Bill's own problem. Limitations of Bill's ability at the present time were next discussed. It was emphasized that Bill could increase his ability by continuing his studies and by keeping the same attitude about new assignments and responsibilities that he had had since the beginning of his employment. In other words, it was pointed out that as long as Bill kept bettering himself, his goals would be realized and as this was accomplished new ones could be established. Opportunities for advancement for Bill in the organization were discussed last and this completed the discussion.

Results. Since the interview Bill has renewed interest in his job. In fact his enthusiasm is going to make the job of selecting the next young man for a promotion a simple one.

Questions for Discussion. Why was it better for the personnel manager to get Bill to think about his own future rather than about the case of the person who had been promoted? Could the approach used by the personnel manager be used successfully in all situations of this kind?

CASE No. 3: *Failure to Consult Others* (Reported by Tom Murray, Class of 1953, College of Literature, Science, and the Arts, University of Michigan)

Situation. The one hundred and eighty residents of a campus housing unit split on the issue of House dues. War drums began beating when the House Council approved a measure to assess $2.25 from each resident. Many of the boys in the housing unit were very disturbed because the measure had been passed without an expression of opinion from the members as a whole. No explanation had been given of why the dues were needed.

The Council members and those who supported the Council countered by saying: "Residents do not have to be consulted on this matter. Any person who objects to paying the dues is an obstructionist and does not have the group's interest at heart." But when pressed further the Council reported, "We need the money for social events."

The issue actually became very serious. The residents divided into hostile factions with one corridor pondering secession. Another group burned the Council members in effigy and signs popped up in the halls warning anti-dues men to stay out of pro-dues corridors. The members of the Council threatened to resign and residents were intimidated as personal attacks and old gripes were thrown into the fray.

Solution. The Council agreed to put the matter to a house vote and the $2.25 dues were defeated by a slim margin. Later, after publicizing a tentative budget, the Council submitted a measure for $1.00 dues. This proposal was passed unanimously.

Results. Peace and unity reigned again.

Questions for Discussion. How could this problem have been avoided? What specific suggestions would you give the House Council?

CASE No. 4: *Failure to Respect Goals of Others* (Reported by Wendell J. Cocking, Class of 1953, College of Literature, Science, and the Arts, University of Michigan)

Situation. The Michigan House Plan for University Residence Halls makes provision for junior administrative "educational officers" known as staff-assistants. In the men's dormitories these representatives of the University are upperclassmen with likable personalities, a good academic record, and the ability to get along well with people. Their job consists of:

(a) Creating and maintaining an atmosphere in which the study required of college students can be accomplished

(b) Exemplifying respectable conduct, reputable manners, and reg-
    ular study habits to the residents
(c) Enforcing quiet hours and quelling nocturnal disturbances
(d) Educating the younger and less experienced residents to the
    necessity for diligent and regular attention to their studies
(e) Aiding any resident in a friendly, interested, and honest way
    with problems, academic or personal, for which he is seeking
    or needs help
(f) Maintaining a respect for himself and the respect of the residents
    for him coupled with an attitude toward diligent study and
    decent behavior precluding the necessity for strong-arm methods
    in preserving the peace

I am a staff-assistant. Until three or four weeks ago I had been
getting along comparatively well with all the residents assigned to my
section and I felt (and still do) that I was fulfilling these obligations
quite acceptably. Many of the section members I had known previously and when they came into the section I treated them and
acknowledged them as close friends, maintaining an open, frank relationship with them.

Recent developments, however, have led me to be apprehensive of
this relationship. The fellows are making a practice of coming into
my room to carry on all their discussions and debates without consideration for my room-mate or me. It even seems that when they
have nothing to do and have the "wanderlust" they come in to see me,
. . . . This semester has swamped us (room-mate and me) with a
great deal of academic work and neither of us appreciate these thought-
less and inconsiderate interruptions.

Solution. We instituted a policy of visiting hours at mealtime only
with, usually, an half-hour coffee break at ten-thirty. At all other
times we keep the door locked and use the room solely for study
purposes.

Results. This pronouncement met with a great many guffaws and
intentional beating on our locked door. Now, when I try to execute
a duty imposed on me by my job the fellows are more than just dis-
respectful. They create disturbances specifically to irritate me though
I do a pretty good job of ignoring them.

It seems to me that in maintaining a student-to-student equality with
the residents instead of an attitude of reserved aloofness (which is
suggested for staff-assistants) I have lost the cooperation, respect, and
consideration needed from the men in the section for their good and
for my own. This problem has been increased in proportions, too,
because of the lack of a helpful attitude on the part of the staff-assistant
in the adjoining section.

Questions for Discussion. Should I have been more reserved and aloof in my relationships? How should I have solved the problem in a better way than using the locked-door approach? What is the best immediate solution to correct the solution that back-fired?

Appendix B. "The Humanities and Higher Education" *

Participants:
Lawrence A. Kimpton, Chancellor, University of Chicago
Norman F. Maclean, Associate Professor of English, University of Chicago
Richard McKeon, Distinguished Service Professor of Greek and Philosophy, University of Chicago

MR KIMPTON: I have just completed a long tour about the country, talking with everyone who would talk to me. Everywhere I have found a deep and growing concern about the place of humanistic values in our civilization. Parents are disturbed that their children do not know how to read; that their ethical and artistic standards come from the comic books and television; and that the primary and secondary educational programs no longer emphasize, if they even include, a study of ancient and modern foreign languages, history, and the masterpieces of art and literature. I find businessmen complaining bitterly that they can hire competent technicians at a dime a dozen but that their employees cannot communicate. They lack the flexibility and breadth of mind to solve or even understand new problems. They waste their newly acquired leisure time on trivial or actually harmful activities.

As I talk with other university presidents, I hear the same sad story that I tell myself at the University of Chicago—that the Humanities Division is undernourished, underpriviledged, and desolate, a blighted area surrounded by the mansions of science.

---

* N. B. C. Radio Discussion, *University of Chicago Round Table,* March 16, 1952. Reprinted by permission.

284

In spite of this almost universal concern, nobody seems able or willing to do anything about it. When I seek support for a humanistic area like Latin or philosophy, I am looked at with a shocked surprise. Latin may be of great importance in understanding our own language and civilization, and philosophy may be of tremendous value in teaching people to think and to make value judgments. The study of these disciplines may be useful in meeting precisely the problems about which everyone is most concerned, but nobody thinks them worthy of support. Am I fooling myself, or is there a real paradox here?

MR. McKEON: The problem of the humanities is one which the educators have discussed for over thirty years—ever since the end of World War I, in fact. Many of their statements of what is wrong with our attitude toward the humanities have been reported in the press. In the 1920's the teachers of Greek and Latin pointed out that Greek and Latin had all but disappeared from the central place of importance in secondary education which they once had. In the later part of the 1920's the teachers of modern languages and modern literature, including English literature, pointed out that English literature and the languages were not receiving the attention in the high schools which they deserved.

One of the great presses, the *New York Times*, pointed out in the thirties that the graduates of our high schools did not know history, even American history. More recently, the philosophers have tried to determine what could be done to make philosophy more effective in college. UNESCO is starting a study of the teaching of philosophy in the different countries which are members of UNESCO.

MR. KIMPTON: What do you think of this paradox which I have tried to phrase, Maclean?

MR. MACLEAN: You two sound too sad to me. I look at it differently. Here, in the first place, for the first time in history everyone has a chance at the humanities through the radio, through certain movies, through increased facilities of printing, and through the phonograph. Furthermore, I think that the twentieth century has contributed its fair share, if not a superabundant share, of great writers, great thinkers, and great historians. More than that, I think that, especially in the last fifteen or twenty years, there have been some very important advancements and developments which have gone on in humanistic training in the colleges and in the universities. And when I turn to the political world and the world of practical affairs and pick the two greatest leaders, one on the left and one on the right, I find that they were both trained in the humanities. Churchill and Roosevelt are not only a part of our civilization, but they played very important roles in saving it.

MR. McKEON: But Churchill and Roosevelt were educated more than fifty years ago. That is a long time; and, furthermore, if you look at the political aspects of the humanities, I think that you ought to consider also the picture which most of the world has of the United States. I have run into it at meetings of UNESCO and of the United Nations. We are a cultureless people, according to most of our critics. We have a culture of the level of comic books, the radio, the film. At the same time we are accused of trying to impose this culture upon the rest of the world in what is now called "cultural imperialism." The British in the nineteenth century were called the "tradespeople of the world." We are the technicians or the "plumbers" of the world, according to our critics.

MR. MACLEAN: That is an old song and I do not think necessarily a true one. The first blues singers were the European travelers to America in the nineteenth century—people like Mrs. Trollop and Harriet Martineau, and Madge Marlowe . . .

MR. McKEON: And Dickens.

MR. MACLEAN: . . . and Dickens. They found no culture here, nothing which was interesting. This is all right, I suppose, so far as they are concerned. But what worries me is that I think that they convinced Europe and, worst of all, convinced America that we really do not have culture. I really do not think that that is the case.

MR. KIMPTON: My friend Maclean is a congenital optimist. You will notice this all through the program. I think if he were treed by a bear, he would enjoy the view.

MR. MACLEAN: What would you do? Enjoy the bear?

MR. KIMPTON: I have no answer to that, for the moment. It is the case, of course, that I have to agree with Maclean that the humanistic values are eternal. It is true that they have always been and, I suspect, that they always will be. But what we are talking about now is the sad case of the humanities at the moment; or at least that is the point which I am trying to make. Before we go any further, could we be quite sure that we know what we are talking about in talking about the humanities? What are the humanities? What do they include?

MR. McKEON: That is a large question. I think that it really divides into two parts: first, the question of what the humanities are in the traditional list of studies; and, second, the humanistic attitude. The first includes the study of the arts—literature, music, sculpture, painting, the graphic arts—and their history; the study of the languages; the study of history; and, finally, the study of men's ideas in philosophy and in related intellectual studies. But I think that the attitude which is humanistic is even more important. And, in this sense, Newton and Adam Smith, economists and physicists, were as much humanists as were historians like Gibbon or poets like Milton.

MR. MACLEAN: I am glad that you make humanities consist of more than just certain achievements of human beings but also a way of looking at any great achievements of human beings in order to appreciate the human qualities behind them. If you did not make that second point, I do not know how I would justify, for instance, my teaching occasionally such works as Darwin's *Origin of Species*.

MR. KIMPTON: I suppose scientifically that it is a great book only in so far as it approximates the truth; but it seems to me that it is also the work of a very great human being. This man is a biologist, remember, but you are still saying that he is a humanist.

MR. MACLEAN: I say that he has great human qualities. He has, in addition to incredible powers of observation playing over problems which are very important to humanity, this tremendous character which permeates every page which he writes—dispassionate character dedicated to the truth. He is, in addition, something that many scientists are not—he is a very great writer. Now, those are humanistic values.

MR. KIMPTON: Could I interrupt at this point to ask you gentlemen a question which is so commonly asked me as I go about the country seeking support for this University and particularly the humanities: What is the good of the humanities? They bake no bread. It has been suggested that they consist of history, philosophy, art, and languages. But what good are they? What value do they have?

MR. McKEON: That sounded like one question when you started, but I think that it is two now. One is the question of what the humanities are in one's own activities, in one's own life. But the second one which you tacked on when you explained the question is what the values of the humanities are in doing one's job, in being more efficient—what their value is in relation to other things.

MR. KIMPTON: Could you call that the intrinsic value of the humanities and the extrinsic?

MR. McKEON: That will do as tags.

MR. MACLEAN: I would like to make the point, though, that if you do not get the first value, that of appreciating the humanistic achievement—achievement of humanity as a great achievement of a human being—then nothing follows.

MR. McKEON: That goes without saying. You do not have the humanistic value, and therefore you do not get the additional utility out of it.

MR. KIMPTON: Could you describe that further, Maclean?

MR. MACLEAN: I take naturally as my example the case of when one comes to the death of Hamlet. What you feel at that moment, it seems to me, is intrinsic in its value. Hamlet says, "The rest is silence," and his good friend Horatio says, "Good night, sweet prince; and flights of angels sing thee to thy rest!" Now I say that what you say to yourself at that moment is not "This play is going to make me a better man— or a better citizen, or help me to adjust my neurosis, or make me a better writer." Some or all of these things may turn out to be true— and I hope some of them will—but I say that, when you read *Hamlet*, that moment in itself is sufficient reason for being.

MR. KIMPTON: I must confess that I have found exactly that same thing to be true of philosophy, which is my own primary interest in the field of the humanities. If you take a man even so esoteric and difficult as Immanuel Kant, I must say that the greatest personal satisfaction— and even happiness, if I may call it that—which I have ever had was in finally being able to understand the very difficult argument in the *Deduction of the Categories*.

MR. McKEON: I think that we can go on and point out that the intrinsic values about which you are talking are found not only in literature and philosophy but in other parts of the humanities—in the languages and in history. Perhaps in the United States today, at the present time, one is apt to forget the importance of the study of the ancient languages—a language like Greek, with its subtlety and poetic possibilities, which, to my mind, exceeds any of those of the modern languages in its precision of association and detail. These are values that, coming from one's own native speech, one senses in the reading of Greek.

Much the same is true of history. One reconstructs the conditions of men; their achievements in the past; the problems which they faced; their solution. And one can, therefore, project one's self out of one's life in a moment which is, to use your tag, an intrinsic value.

Mr. Kimpton: On this subject of intrinsic values I freely admit that they do contribute to one's happiness and one's satisfaction in life; and in that sense they are ultimate.   But would you be willing to say anything about the possibility of a study of the humanities' contributing in some real sense to the formation of character, or of personality, or the development of tastes and standards?   What about that kind of thing?

Mr. Maclean: I do not think that that can be doubted.   Who would wish to doubt it even if it could be doubted?   Constant exposure to the greatest thoughts, the greatest actions, the greatest expressions of men, are bound to influence our own thoughts, our own actions, our own feelings.

Mr. McKeon: You have to push it even further than that.   You do not get the humanistic value without the repetition.   The first exposure to a painting or the first exposure to a poem frequently leaves the mind bewildered; but, as the repeated experiences build up, you see the value which you failed to see before.   With that repetition, attitude, sensitivity, perspective, insight, ability to communicate, appreciation of a point of view—all of these—are part of what follows.

Mr. Kimpton: You, McKeon, divided this thing into intrinsic and extrinsic in terms of the question: What good are the humanities?   We have been talking presumably about the intrinsic values up to this point. I would like to hear some discussion on the practical values of humanities.   After all, that is the question which is most customarily tossed at me as I move about the country.

Mr. Maclean: Maybe you are the one who ought to answer it. That is, both you and McKeon were trained in philosophy and evidently at least read a few pages of Plato—pages in which he recommends to young philosophers that in early middle age they go out into the world of practical affairs.

Mr. Kimpton: He spoke of that as a cave, did he not?

Mr. Maclean: What is it being Chancellor of the University?   And I would not think merely of your being chancellor of a university; but I am thinking also about you when I first knew you, as you were then administrative head of the atomic-bomb project.   What about humanities and the atomic bomb?

Mr. Kimpton: That is a dirty trick, throwing this back at me.   You know, philosophy is sometimes defined as the art of bewildering one's self methodically; and offhand, at least, it would seem rather difficult to make a case for philosophy as a training for practical affairs.

MR. McKEON: There is some indication that administrators are occasionally confused without the help of philosophy.

MR. KIMPTON: True. It is also indicated that administrators need all their philosophy, I can assure you. If I may be immodest for a moment, I shall now turn to trying to answer your question, Maclean. If I had any success in the early days on the atomic-bomb project, I do believe that it was in terms of establishing communication between three very recalcitrant groups. One was the United States Army, in the form of the Manhattan District; the second was a group of very distinguished and able professors who knew nothing about the Army and cared less; and the third was the University, of course, as the contracting agent in the situation.

MR. McKEON: You did not talk philosophy to them, did you?

MR. KIMPTON: Yes, I did. As a matter of fact, getting them to talk together, to try to take these groups and understand their viewpoints, each one sympathetically, and to get them talking together was an exercise in pure philosophy.

MR. McKEON: I do not think that I can match anything in the way of philosophic discussion such as you have indicated on the Manhattan project. But in the early years of the war the University contracted with the Army to help train its G.I.'s, and I remember discussing in Washington with an Army officer the problems which the University should try to solve. He said to me, "We don't want your program to train technicians. We want you to train in particular fields; and in particular what we want are people who can give commands, understand commands, and understand each other."
' And I said, "What kind of men do you think those would be?"
And he said, "Give me someone who has read Thucydides and Shakespeare."
Another colonel surprised me by saying that the two most useful men on his staff were two men who had Ph.D.'s in philosophy and in English, because he could send them to a meeting; they could argue with the other members of the group; they could understand arguments; they could put them together; they could eventually report what had gone on. And he looked upon this ability to communicate, to understand, and to present a position as being a result of humanistic training.

MR. KIMPTON: I cannot help but believe—and would you not agree, McKeon?—that a real case can be made for the humanities in terms of their very practical application as a background in administrative work. You and I both have been administrative officers in this university. I think that both of us have had some degree of success, at least. And would you not say that the ability to see things in organizational terms, to communicate, and to help other people communicate; to see problems in new aspects—all these things philosophy and, indeed, all the humanistic disciplines genuinely contribute to?

MR. McKEON: I think that the curious thing is—maybe this is the original paradox that you stated—that even men in government and industrialists will grant this. But the trouble is that it is never written into the job specifications which they send out.

Before we get off this field of practical applications, I think that a word must be said about the international aspects. In UNESCO, an organization which is a specialized agency in the United Nations and which is dedicated to the proposition that "since wars begin in the minds of men, the defenses of peace must be built in the minds of men," a good part of the program is precisely a program in the development of international understanding. But what is international understanding? How do we understand one another? How does one people project itself into the problems of another people? It is not merely a question of literacy. UNESCO is engaging on that. It is a question of understanding the values of other people, appreciating them, and cooperating.

MR. KIMPTON: We tried to start out at the beginning of our ROUND TABLE discussion by saying that the humanities were, at least from my point of view, in rather bad case. We tried to say what the humanities are and what they included. And we have just discussed the values of the humanities, both intrinsic and practical. What can be done about the humanities at the present time? Or, to put it the other way around, what is being done at the present time?

MR. MACLEAN: I assume that you are limiting that question now to higher education.

MR. KIMPTON: Let us operate for the moment on that premise.

MR. MACLEAN: I can make an even further limitation. I will confine it, for the moment, to my own field, the study of literature. There, during the first forty years, I should say, of this century, our study of literature was very much influenced by German scholarship of the nineteenth century. Literature was studied as a language or a philology and as history, but it was seldom studied as literature.

MR. KIMPTON: Some of that stuff was pretty precious and pedantic, too, was it not?

MR. MACLEAN: Some of it was. But they are both great studies in themselves; and, more than that, when properly oriented to literature, they form the total dimension, when joined with curiosities and insight into the literature, which any critic or scholar ought to have. There ought to be an end, it seems to me, to this very cold war between the scholar, on the one hand, who ought to be curious about literature and the critic who ought to know and to respect his facts about literature.

MR. McKEON: One can add to the accomplishments in the development of the study of literature and of literary history things which have happened in universities in the other fields of humanities. The study of language is one such field. In the last few years, particularly under the impulse of the war, we have learned to teach the languages much more effectively than before. We teach language so that it can be spoken; and, on the basis of the understanding of the sounds, the speech, we then proceed to the cultural aspect, including the literature. We have improved our teaching of history over the period of some three or four decades. History is not merely political history. It deals with all the cultural and intellectual aspects of the development of man. And it is now being taught at most colleges in this generalized form, showing how men have come together from small groups until the present world has emerged in what is effectively a community. In philosophy the example—and this is perhaps most striking—is that one of the things which UNESCO has tried to do has been to examine the philosophic bases of the confusion of the world today about such things as democracy, human rights, freedom. These are the changes such as you asked for, Kimpton.

MR. KIMPTON: They are genuine and significant changes. Neither of you, though, has mentioned general education, which seems to me to have had a tremendously important reemphasis in the United States, which is fundamentally humanistically oriented, would you not agree?

MR. McKEON: General education, I think, whether or not it is fundamentally oriented in terms of the humanities (I would like to leave something for the sciences and the social sciences) is, I think, one of the important ways in which these changes have taken place. That is, the humanities—language, literature and the arts, philosophy, and history—have taken a form now in which instead of studying scattered bits—getting a little language but not being able to read or talk, learning a little history but not getting a broad perspective—they are now organized so as to build a total education.

MR. KIMPTON: I am prepared to admit, I think, that there is a real renaissance in the field of the humanities which is occurring in our American universities today. But we need to remind ourselves that our universities, for better or for worse, are pretty much covered with ivy. The real problem is to what extent this renaissance, this reawakening of interest in the humanities, is getting out to the general public. Is it in any way? And how can it get out better to the general public?

Mr. MACLEAN: As a teacher I would have to say, first of all, that the most important direction to me is backward to younger students. We talked, for a moment, about general education in a college; but I also have to think about secondary education and elementary education in the preparation of teachers who will bring humanities in taste and morality to our children.

Mr. McKEON: It seems to me that what is happening, then, is that the general education to which Kimpton referred is now in a place in which it can be taken from the college and put into the high schools. This is actually happening. There are secondary-school institutions which are taking over what the colleges have now been doing and which high schools ought to do.

In the second place, the training of teachers in these new curriculums—teachers who are able, therefore, to translate general education into terms which would fit the high school—is important.

But it is two questions; it is not only the education of the youth but also of the adult.

Mr. KIMPTON: Yes, this is the point of the public at large, which is the way I framed the question at first.

Mr. McKEON: The public at large is in part the children of the public at large.

Mr. KIMPTON: Of course.

Mr. McKEON: I want to be optimistic at this point about the problem of adult education not because we are doing it well but because, on the one hand, we do have new instruments—instruments in television, radio, film, press—which could be used as never before to reach the general public. And, in the second place, I sense an interest, a desire, on the part of the people to appreciate the values which we have here classified as humanistic—the humanistic attitude—which is an interest in the works of the mind.

Mr. KIMPTON: You really do? That is, you think that there is a demand on the part of the public for a reawakening and a new interest in this very field? Can you give us some examples of that?

MR. McKEON: There are many evidences of it. The interest in the Great Books courses is an indication of such a desire. The interest in good art exhibits such as that of Cézanne is another example. The trouble is, however, that we have not educated the public to demand or the producers to produce.

MR. KIMPTON: We began, you will recall, with an apparent paradox —the great public interest in and concern for the humanities and the unwillingness of anybody to do anything about it. This is not quite the paradox which we thought it was. Somebody is doing something about it in the universities. There is a real renaissance going on in our universities today in the field of the humanities, but there still remain very real problems. How do we in the universities make known to the public this new enthusiasm and this new content? How do we better use these new media of communication—the press, radio, and television—to satisfy the public's interest and concern about the humanities? This is a problem for all of us. How do we get into the lives of our children, particularly through the primary and secondary schools, an awareness of the sensitivities, the standards, the tastes, and the content which an early study of the humanities uniquely provides?

Appendix C. "Human Relations" *

A New Art Brings a Revolution to Industry

"If it were desired to reduce a man to nothing," wrote Fyodor Dostoevesky in *The House of the Dead*, ". . . it would be necessary only to give his work a character of uselessness." In the 20th century, such a character of uselessness was, in fact, imposed on much of the work done in American factories and offices. It was not a sudden occurrence; it was the result of a long historical process, sped by typical American haste and thoughtlessness.

The Industrial Revolution, which replaced the tools of the independent workmen with machines owned by lenders of capital, had transformed handicraftsmen who were their own bosses into hired hands subject to the orders of managers. Gradually, men felt themselves swallowed by a vast, impersonal machine, which rubbed away their self-respect and, in a way, their identities. In anger against this betrayal of the human spirit by the Industrial Revolution, millions of workers listened to the false promises of Marx's counterrevolution which, as Russia has proved, offered only greater loss of self respect and, in the end, slavery.

Now a second Industrial Revolution, quieter but more profound, is sweeping through U. S. industry. Its name: Human Relations in Industry. Its purpose: to give the American worker a sense of usefulness and importance (and thus improve his work). Its goal (stated in one sentence): to make life more fun by making work more meaningful.

---

* Courtesy of *Time*, Copyright Time Inc., LIX (April 14, 1952), 96–97.

The Shovelers and the Spinners

The seeds of this change were sown by two great pioneers whose names are scarcely known—Frederic Winslow Taylor, a one-time day laborer, and Elton Mayo, an Australian immigrant turned Harvard sociologist. Their work did not seem related, but it was. Taylor, who died in 1915, was the father of scientific management; he increased industrial production by rationalizing it. Mayo, who died in 1949, was the father of industrial human relations; he increased production by humanizing it.

While working at the Midvale (Pa.) Steel Works in the 1880s, young Taylor made a discovery: it was the workers, not the bosses, who determined the production rate. The workers could go only so fast because, having learned their jobs by rule of thumb, they wasted steps, motion and time. Using a stop-watch, Taylor found that he could determine the most efficient speed for every operation by breaking it into its component parts.

Later, for Bethlehem Steel, he studied employees shoveling ore, coal, etc. He found that because they used different sized shovels, output varied widely. Taylor tried the workers with a shovel holding 34 lbs. of ore, then shifted to a shorter shovel holding 30 lbs. For every reduction in the load, each man's daily tonnage rose—until a 21-lb. load was reached. Below that, output fell. Taylor set 21½ lbs. as the ideal shovel load. Result: the yard force was cut by two-thirds, yet daily loadings rose from 25 tons per man to 45.

Taylor's pioneering in time and motion studies helped bring the mass-production era which enabled workers to raise not only their output but their wages as well. Taylor's own ruling motive, as Justice Brandeis observed at a memorial for Taylor, was to help his fellow men. Yet he also created a monster. By gearing human operations to the precision of machines, Taylor's system caused management to think of workers as little more than machines that had to eat. Since the only measure of efficiency was the utmost utilization of time, men were subjected to the intolerable nervous strain of the "speed-up," where assemblies moved always a little faster than men's natural work pace.

A point came where greater "efficiency" no longer yielded greater output. Example: at a Pennsylvania textile plant where the labor turnover in one of the spinning departments was 41 times higher than elsewhere in the plant, efficiency experts in 1923 set up various wage incentives, yet production remained low and spinners kept quitting. When Elton Mayo was called in, he discovered the men were poor producers for a reason which had not occurred to anyone: they were unhappy. The machines had been set up so as to deprive the men of virtually all human contact with one another; lonely, they fell into melancholy and hypochondria. Mayo prescribed four daily rest periods when the workers could relax, brought in a nurse to whom they could complain. The change wrought by these two relatively minor steps was startling. Turnover immediately diminished; production for the first time reached the established quotas.

Four years later, something even more startling happened. At its Hawthorne Works near Chicago, Western Electric tried to determine the effects of lighting on the worker and his output. As a test, it moved a group of girls into a special room with variable lighting, another group into a room where lighting remained as before. To its amazement, production shot up in both rooms. When the lighting was reduced in the first room, production continued to rise. But it also kept rising in the second room. Not until Mayo was called in to make tests of his own did the company discover what had happened. The simple answer: both groups were producing more because they had been singled out for special attention. The excitement of the experiments made them feel that they were no longer mere cogs.

Mayo's Hawthorne experiments were widely hailed as a landmark in social science. Actually, they revealed nothing which could not have been learned from any factory hand: every human being likes to feel that his work is important, that the boss is interested in him, and appreciates what he does. In a sense, the importance attached to Mayo's findings is a measure of the indifference to people into which management had fallen in its singleminded pursuit of Taylor's efficiency. Because of this indifference, the deep-rooted mutual interests of workers and management, as partners in production, were lost in shallow attitudes of suspicion and hostility. The folklore of each nourished a class warfare disturbingly like that which Marx had predicted.

The Myths of Labor and Capital

In the accepted myths of hardheaded, hardfisted management, tenderness was weakness; workers could not be "coddled" lest they loaf; the only drives to which they responded were greed (more money) or fear (of dismissal). To praise them was simply to invite increasing demands. Workers, for their part, nursed long memories of hired spies who betrayed their unions and of uniformed thugs (e.g., the "coal & iron police") who smashed them. In labor's mythology, management was a silk-hatted capitalist who automatically opposed anything good for the workingman; by reflex, the worker opposed anything management favored.

For Mayo's new science to make headway in this charged atmosphere, there had to be a great change in basic attitudes. The change began with the U. S. Supreme Court's 1937 decision upholding the Wagner Act; it made management realize it had to learn to live with unions. The change was sped by World War II, which not only brought the patriotic necessity for the U. S. industrial machine to achieve maximum output, but flooded the labor force with millions of housewives and other new recruits relatively free of the old suspicions and hostilities.

Management began to learn that the once-feared unions themselves held potentials of higher production. In Pittsburgh, the United Steel Workers challenged one management to name its most productive department. Then the union boosted production there by 210% in a month. In the Toronto plant of Lever Bros., union and management, working together, trimmed the payroll from 693 to 512, the wage bill by 17%, yet achieved greater output in a 40-hour week than in 48 before.

Moreover, housewives coming into war plants were amazed to discover that they could far exceed the normal output of old hands. At a big Cleveland war plant, one housewife found that she could easily produce 800 grenade pins daily, v. the plant quota of 500. When fellow workers warned her to slow down, she discovered another thing: old hands deliberately limited their output from fear that Taylor's time-and-motion-study disciples would cut their pay rates by raising production quotas. More and more managers realized that maximum output could be realized only by finding ways to remove these old fears.

In dozens of plants, surveys of employees exploded the prize cliché of management's folklore—that workers wanted only more money. Actually, higher pay rated far down the list of workers' desires. For example, 100 shopworkers who were polled by Psychologist S. N. F. Chant on twelve alternatives rated "high pay" as sixth. The Twentieth Century Fund found that wage disputes, the ostensible cause of 80% of all industrial conflicts, are only secondary causes: "Some of the industries most plagued by strikes . . . are among those where the highest wages are being paid." After ten years of polling workers, Elmo Roper concluded that their four chief desires are 1) security ("the right to work continuously at reasonably good wages"), 2) a chance to advance, 3) treatment as human beings, 4) dignity.

Yet the alarming fact, as agreed by all investigators, was that modern industry largely frustrates these desires. Detroit Edison, in a poll of its 11,000 employees, found that 43% did not believe that the company was "really interested" in their ideas. After a study of the auto industry, author Peter Drucker, management consultant, concluded that the average worker regards his status as frozen, with little hope of advancement, and hopes to keep his sons from doing the same work.

There was equal agreement on the causes of such widespread discontent and emotional frustration. Business had grown to such a size that the average worker lost all sense of personal contact with his employers. The constant increase in mechanization took away his sense of personal pride and self-identification with the final product; frequently he did not even know the use of the part he made. The robot nature of many tasks thwarted the craving for prestige; the hope of advancement was lost in the growing tendency to choose management material not from men up from the bench, but from young, college-trained technicians.

The New Managers

These discoveries came to a head at a time when U. S. management was best equipped to do something about them: management itself had undergone a revolution. Death and taxes had all but eclipsed the great owner-management dynasties epitomized by Carnegie, Ford and Rockefeller. In their place had come the professional managers, the engineer-trained technicians, e.g., Du Pont's Crawford Greenewalt, General Electric's Philip Reed, General Motors' C. E. Wilson, Standard Oil's (N. J.) Frank Abrams. They took over industrial societies grown so huge that the average owner (i.e., stockholder) seldom exercised more than theoretical control. Profits were still the test of efficiency, and a fair return to the stockholder a prime duty of management. But the tremendous diffusion of ownership enabled the professional manager to give first concern to the economic health of the whole corporate body, in which the welfare of workers was as vital as that of stockholders. Since increased welfare promised greater efficiency, the new managers welcomed experiments.

In Marion, Va., the Harwood Manufacturing Co., which had 600 employees, mostly women, making pajamas, discovered that whenever it changed the work, only one-third of the workers ever got back to their old output rate. Many others quit, and most union grievances followed such changes. The company tried an experiment: one group was simply told of the change, another was told of the necessity for it and permitted to work out for itself the necessary revisions in quotas and rates. Result: its production quickly passed the old average of 60 hourly units per worker, and reached more than 80. The first group barely exceeded 50 units, and 17% of its members shortly quit. It also filed a complaint with the union that the new rate was "unjust," although investigations proved it generous. Yet when the survivors of this group were trained in the new way, they went up to a score of 73 within eight days.

At Detroit's Bundy Tubing Co., which had a history of ill will against the speed-up and fear of cuts in output rates, every attempt to boost production by special incentives had failed. The company offered the union a novel proposal: set a certain standard for labor costs, and let workers and management share all the savings when increased output drove costs below that figure. Not only did production beat all records, but the workers themselves began prodding slackers and berating absentees.

These lessons have borne fruit. In most big U.S. corporations, the new field of human relations is regarded as important, and equally as promising, as industrial research. Ford Motor Co. is spending millions to explore the untapped potentials of man. General Motors, the world's biggest industrial corporation, is drawing useful lessons from its World War II experiences.

At one G.M. aircraft parts plant, the manager almost turned down the offer of a visit by a combat-scarred B-17 and crew; he feared it would disrupt production. Instead, output shot up, not because the workers were thrilled by the bomber, but because the maintenance crew told them for the first time what the parts they made were used for. Another G.M. plant, which had to train workers to make carbines, had each new employee shoot the actual carbine, take it apart to see the significance of the part he would make. Despite their lack of skill their output was high.

Other companies are tackling the problem of size and resulting loss of individual identity. Robert Wood Johnson, whose family's famed Johnson & Johnson had grown up as a huge plant at New Brunswick, N. J., decentralized much of it into small, new, ultramodern factories, each making a single product line and small enough so that the president can usually call every worker by name. Not only has Johnson & Johnson been free of strikes, but the C.I.O. Textile Workers union is the first to praise its enlightened methods.

Many plants are encouraging their workers at self-government through broadening their corporate responsibilities. Parker Pen replaced the hated time-clock with an honor system, found that tardiness virtually vanished. The Commerce Trust Co. of Kansas City met the time loss from the morning "coffee rush" by providing free coffee.

A new concept of the role of employers and employees in the corporation is being formed. Some examples: Pittsburgh's Wiegand Co. lends money, interest free, to employees who need it to buy homes, etc.; Allegheny Ludlum Steel holds "open houses" to let families see what their breadwinner does, and production goes up on visiting days;

Weirton Steel now tags almost everything moving through the plant to let workers know what it will make.

The New Philosophy

Actually, far from being an occult science, human relations is nothing more than good will—and applied common sense. Much of it depends on simple things, such as making a plant more comfortable, and a friendlier place to work. Virtually every big company now sponsors plant bowling, baseball, dances, etc.; Westinghouse abets employee operettas, orchestras, picnics, even shows movies in its plants during lunch hours.

Yet that does not mean that every employer has seen the practical value of the new concept, or has accepted it. Some bitter-enders still regard any concession to the workers as a threat to their own authority. Others sometimes do more harm than good by doling out favors with an air of paternalism. Said one Kansas City industrialist: "We give our employees a Christmas party and that keeps 'em happy until we throw 'em a summer picnic." Still others have made the mistake of trying to create good human relations by mere words.

But by and large, the intent of this swiftly growing trend is not only genuine, but represents a movement toward an entirely new philosophy of management.

Nowhere has this new philosophy been better expressed than by General Foods' Chairman Clarence Francis at a postwar convention of the National Association of Manufacturers. Said Francis: "You can buy a man's time, you can buy a man's physical presence at a given place; you can even buy a measured number of skilled muscular motions per hour or day. But you cannot buy enthusiasm; you cannot buy initiative; you cannot buy loyalty; you cannot buy the devotion of hearts, minds and souls. You have to earn these things. . . . It is ironic that Americans—the most advanced people technically, mechanically and industrially—should have waited until a comparatively recent period to inquire into the most promising single source of productivity: namely, the human will to work. It is hopeful, on the other hand, that the search is now under way."

In that search, at mid-century, lies the finest hope and promise of the Capitalist Revolution.

Appendix D. "The Art of Speech in Collective Bargaining" *

The topic of this meeting "Speech in Conciliation" is an important subject. But even more important, I believe, is the broader topic of Speech in Collective Bargaining.

It is the lack of adequate communication in collective bargaining which calls for the remedial services of the conciliator.

And the same training in vocal communication which can render the conciliator more effective as a peacemaker, can make the representatives of both labor and management more efficient practitioners of the art of collective bargaining.

One of the serious defects in collective bargaining in recent years has been a tendency of labor and management to show more concern with selling their respective positions to the public than with honestly trying to reach an understanding on the points at issue.

In every phase of collective bargaining, from the application of contract provisions in settling grievances, to the actual negotiation of the contract itself, there is always a ground upon which reasonable men can meet.

And reasonable men should be able to discuss any problem in the realm of collective bargaining in an atmosphere free of fear, suspicion, anger or recrimination.

Where such a procedure is followed it is probable that a workable settlement will result.

The psychology of debate is out of order in collective bargaining when it concerns negotiations between workers and management or any type of conciliation.

The purpose of a good debater is to convince an audience that his side of the argument is more worthy of support than his opponent's.

---

* Eric Peterson, *Machinists Monthly Journal*, February, 1949, page 44. Reprinted by permission.

It matters not whether he succeeds in changing his opponent's viewpoint on the subject.

In fact, the debater, to accomplish his purpose, often tries to anger, belittle, or ridicule the opposition if by so doing he can upset the opponent's powers of reasoning and thereby undermine his case.

When the negotiations have deteriorated into a debate, or a race for public favor, the main purpose of the negotiations has been sidetracked.

When this has happened, when labor and management have lost their ability to reason with each other, it is the function of the conciliator to assist them in reestablishing the channels of rational communication, to the end that they may seek again the ground of agreement.

The conciliator, and in the long run the bargaining representatives of labor and management, must be adept, not in the cold science of debate and recrimination, but in the intricate and elusive art of persuasion and diplomacy.

I believe that the teachers of speech can assist them in becoming more proficient in that art.

And, I believe too that the conciliators can be of great assistance to the teachers in bringing a more practical knowledge of the subject matter to the representatives of labor and management.

To the teachers of speech the need for better lines of communication between labor and management, and between the conciliator and disputing parties is a distinct challenge.

For basically, the failure of these two groups to iron out their disputes without ill-will or violence is part and parcel of the broader problem of discord which plagues the world today in its quest for peace.

Perhaps the starting point for the teachers is to pay a little less attention to Demosthenes, the ancient Greek, who became a great orator by practicing shouting until he could be heard above the roaring of the waves, and a little more to developing men whose voices may not be loud, but whose skillful persuasion can be heard above the misunderstanding in men's hearts.

Specifically, the teachers of speech can foster the development, both in their formal classes and among adult groups, of discussion sessions whose primary purpose is the development of a reasonable and concerted approach to a problem on which the group members may find themselves at odds.

The purpose of such discussions should be the attainment of a ground upon which all reasonable members of the group may reach agreement.

The teachers may carry the program growing out of such discussion groups to labor and management.

It may be advisable to start with separate labor and management groups, and then, as they learn the know-how of communication and become accustomed to the method of reasoning, to bring the two groups together for joint discussion.

In this way labor and management can become acquainted both with the techniques of peaceful discussion, and with each other.

Then, when they meet at the collective bargaining table, they will have the background of friendly discussion, that may better lead them to an understanding.

The conciliators may assist in the work of the teachers.

First, by taking full advantage of each situation into which they are called, to point out to each group, separately, the basic defect in the original approach which led to the breakdown of negotiations.

Secondly, by working with speech teachers, in setting up discussion groups in which labor and management may learn to reason together.

By helping the conciliators in performing their own functions better and by assisting them in training labor and management in practical communication techniques, the teachers can profitably contribute to the development of a more constructive and efficient pattern in the great and vitally important field of human and industrial relations.

Appendix E. "The Quaker Way Wins New Adherents"*

*This old technique for working out differences
is increasingly used in affairs of high policy.*

To persons who are not initiated in politics, a decision reached by
the processes of debate and majority vote acquires an aspect of sanctity
as the ultimate expression of democracy. But those in Washington
who deal with the complex problems of statecraft inevitably come to
see grave shortcomings in the honored old way of settling issues. Increasingly these men and women are resorting to a subtle and effective
method long used by the Quakers to arrive at essential unanimity in
their business sessions—the process known as taking "the sense of the
meeting."

The technique is being adopted by numerous directors of public and
private organizations in various parts of the country. It has in recent
years helped to settle policy on several national issues of great con-
sequence. Already one can detect the small but significant beginnings
of this approach in some actions of the United Nations. Doubtless
quite a few of those who are starting to employ the technique are not
even aware of its Quaker origin, but they are all too familiar with un-
fortunate results developing from the great reliance on the reaching of
decisions by majority rule.

The faults of the conventional parliamentary procedure arise from
its basic assumption—that there exists a divergence of interests rather
than a common purpose. The introduction of a resolution for a yea-
and-nay vote is conceived as a kind of contest between opposing forces,
each going into battle armed with fully formed conclusions which it

* Morris Llewellyn Cooke, *New York Times Magazine,* June 17, 1951, pages
21 and 40. Reprinted by permission.

then attempts to put over on the other side. If a group cannot force acceptance of the whole program, then it proceeds, by a process of barter, to swap point for point—often without regard to the right or wrong of the individual points.

The outcome of the vote, then, is a victory for one side and a defeat for the other, which leads to grudges. It is likely to represent no group decision based on the intrinsic merits of the case but a sort of ledger sheet showing the result of bargaining negotiations. And it imposes on the minority a course of action in which they do not concur and which they may positively resent. At its most extreme the tenor of this method may be described in the words of a prominent business man in the Twenties, who told a stockholders' meeting: "We will vote first and discuss later."

The Quaker practice of "taking the sense of the meeting," on the other hand, is a combination of free discussion and quiet thinking. "The Quaker form of church government," says Howard H. Brinton, director of Pendle Hill, Friends' Graduate School at Wallingford, Pa., "is the most complete democracy ever devised. Not only do the Quakers refuse to admit the imposed authority of any individual. They do not even admit the authority of a majority. All decisions must be made on the basis of unanimity, reached by a process that considers the opinion of every person, both expert and inexpert. Therefore, a Quaker committee sometimes appears to be amateurish and time-consuming."

It is well worth this time, in the Quaker view, to develop in a group the willingness to accept unanimously what appears to be the balanced judgment of the majority or the best informed.

First, according to this procedure, a subject is introduced not by presenting a resolution but by "reading a query." This is usually done by the chairman—or "Clerk of the meeting," as he is known in Quaker groups. Such a departure from parliamentary order is by no means a petty one, for by this simple device, the issue seems to come from the group as a whole instead of being sponsored by one faction within it.

Various points of view on the subject are expressed by individual members—whoever wishes to contribute. But strong words, provocative language and repetitive discourse are taboo; members are encouraged to speak just once on a given point, and only after careful thought. And, most significant of all, the individual speaks not simply as a man expressing his own conscience but as the voice of the group addressing itself to the issue at hand. If a contrary viewpoint is raised, it is considered as if it were one's own for the purpose of treating it objectively. "Getting under the weight" of the other man's doubts is the term the Quakers sometimes use to describe this attitude of respect for a minority view-point.

If conflict at any point becomes so heated as to make an agreement doubtful, the Clerk may halt discussion and ask the members to consider the subject for a while in thoughtful silence. The value of such a deliberative period was shown during World War II, when a group meeting in a mid-city Philadelphia office attempted to settle a troublesome strike. All interests were represented. The president of the concern was high in the councils of the Episcopal Church. The discussion having become bitterly deadlocked, he said: "My partner is a Quaker from Delaware County and I propose that after the manner of Friends we settle down to a period of silence and see if we cannot get some light on these troublesome differences."

After five minutes of a profound silence the meeting was called to order and the discussion resumed in a different atmosphere. In a very short time an agreement satisfactory to all was reached.

There is never any voting. When a positive program of action appears to have been indicated by the evidence brought to bear on the subject, the Clerk sums it up by "presenting a minute," expressing what he takes to be "the sense of the meeting"—the consensus, the course of action which would take into account the most significant pieces of evidence contributed by all the members. At that certain point "you can almost hear the meeting 'click,'" as one experienced Clerk describes this phase of the proceedings, "and that's the clue for the Clerk to present his minute."

The "sense of the meeting" stands as the group's decision unless some challenge is made by an unsatisfied individual. In this case the Clerk may suspend the subject for the time being—true unanimity obviously being out of the question—to permit more careful consideration and perhaps to gather more facts. A committee may be appointed for research and to prepare a report for the next meeting, when a new attempt is made to attain unity.

Much of the success of this technique depends on the skill and the character of the Clerk. He must not only be acute, intelligent, sensitive to the meanings expressed by the members, but he must take care to refrain from being domineering; in fact, must frequently suppress his own attitudes. From the membership as a whole the system requires thorough frankness, sincerity and a cooperative spirit.

Beyond these there are two principal elements in the practice. There must be a belief on the part of all or most of the participants in the meeting that agreement is desirable. Secondly, the belief must be entertained that in any decisions taken the way should be left open for the unconvinced, or for the skeptics, eventually to join in the view reached by the main body of the group.

If these two convictions are held by a substantial number of those present in the meeting, the Quaker practice has been known to surmount very great initial differences of opinion.

How successful is this temperate method when serious differences exist? The best answer lies in a recital of some important cases where agreement is, or has been, attained by the Quaker principles of unanimity.

(1) The President's Water Resources Policy Commission, recently published under its report under the title, "A Water Policy for the American People." The findings were concurred in unanimously by the seven commissioners. The commission, of which I was chairman, never took a vote and no record was kept of its proceedings. The report itself is its record. Even though its assignment from President Truman involved reaching decisions on many highly controversial questions affecting water and land, everything was talked out in conference until a meeting of minds was arrived at.

(2) The Acheson-Lillienthal atomic energy report was drafted by a group which tried to operate after the Quaker fashion. A helpful factor in creating the necessary deliberative quiet was that meetings were held in a storage warehouse on the outskirts of Washington, and no one but the participants knew of the project until the work was completed.

(3) The Joint Committee on the Organization of the Congress in 1948–49, commonly known as the La Follette-Monroney committee, drafted—without taking a vote—the voluminous report on the basis of which Congress was fundamentally reorganized.

(4) The present Senate Republican Conference, of which Senator Millikin is chairman, and to which all Republican members belong, takes no votes and such conclusions as are reached are stated by the chairman to be his interpretation of the committee's joint thought.

(5) The International Monetary Fund operates in accordance with this by-law: "The chairman will ordinarily ascertain the sense of the meeting in lieu of a formal vote" unless a vote is specifically called for. Frank Coe, the secretary of the fund, tells me that during the four or five years since it was organized decisions have been reached on over a thousand issues and that on only twelve or thirteen of them have votes been taken.

(6) The Committee on Economic Development, one of the major organizations studying public finance, carries on its discussions and frames its findings Quaker-fashion. At the conclusion members of its committees are recorded as voting for or against, with the opportunity accorded for explanatory footnotes.

(7) Finally, because it is frequently said that the Quaker method can be used only where relatively small groups are concerned, it is worth while to note that the First National Conference on Aging held in Washington during August, 1950, under the auspices of the Federal Security Agency, with an attendance of 816, used the group process of discussion and decision. Clark Tibbetts, who acted as chairman of one of the principal committees, thinks that the success of the several sections was "almost in direct proportion to the use made of the group method."

For all these striking examples, it would be false optimism to conclude that the "sense of the meeting" technique could be applied successfully to the deliberations of major political bodies, such as a Congress in full session. Here the limitations of the method must be acknowledged. For by its very definition it requires not only utter frankness, sincerity and mutual trust but also a suppression of any personal, factional, partisan or sectional interests.

There is no room in the Quaker practice for unreasoned obstinacy in the face of sound evidence, nor for resistance to unity on a particular issue based merely on traditional antagonism. Some Friends themselves go as far as to say that the practice cannot be applied with much hope of success in any group composed of elected representatives who must report back directly to a constituency, for often the constituency holds some minute but unshakable special interests that are contrary to the interests of the group as a whole.

This also raises the question whether anything can be gained from the Quaker method in the way of peaceful and effective deliberations among the United Nations. It must be recognized that the necessary frankness and trust between Eastern and Western nations are unfortunately lacking at present. We could not feel sure, for example, that "evidence" presented by the Soviet Union and her satellites would be anything more than a disguise for her real purposes or a calculated move undertaken for propaganda value.

Still there is a direct relationships between the Quaker practice and methods of securing agreements on disputes before the U. N. Assembly, once these disputes have been handed over to conciliation commissions or to mediators. Because it is possible for these commissions to operate in private, without the glare of press and radio publicity and without the necessity for individual members of the commissions to record their points of view, the way seems open for utilization of the Quaker practice.

In the case of the U. N.'s subsidiary agencies, those smaller non-political organs in which a group of nations represents the total membership, there is also good opportunity for using the "sense of the meeting," for in these cases the members are not expected to reflect only their own national interests. The Economic and Social Council, the Trusteeship Council and their subcommissions are examples in point. There have been occasions in each of these bodies when the chairman has been able, because of the thorough discussion that has taken place, to make voting a perfunctory step.

Do these instances of successful use of the Quaker method, and examples of public bodies which might try it, indicate a wider usefulness for the "sense-of-the-meeting" technique in the future? That they do. If the executives of organizations dealing with public affairs, from the municipal level up through the councils of the United Nations, will test this technique they will find that important decisions can be arrived at with less partisanship, more harmony and with greater faith in the results achieved. That much, in these irascible times would be a great deal.

Appendix *I.* *Selected*
Bibliography

I. Books

A. Books on Discussion and Conference

Auer, J. J., and Henry L. Ewbank, *Handbook for Discussion Leaders*. New York: Harper and Brothers, 1947.

Baird, A. Craig, *Argumentation, Discussion, and Debate*. New York: McGraw-Hill Book Company, Inc., 1950.

Baird, A. Craig, *Discussion: Principles and Types*. New York: McGraw-Hill Book Company, Inc., 1943.

Bradford, Leland P., and Stephen M. Corey, *Leadership and Participation in Large Group Meetings*, Bulletin No. 4. Washington, D. C.: National Education Association, 1951.

Busch, Henry M., *Conference Methods in Industry*. New York: Harper and Brothers, 1949.

Cantor, Nathaniel, *Learning Through Discussion*. Buffalo: Human Relations for Industry, 1951.

Clapp, John Mantle, *Effective Talking in Conference*. New York: The Ronald Press, 1948.

Cooper, Alfred M., *How to Conduct Conferences*. New York: McGraw-Hill Book Company, Inc., 1946.

Elliott, Harrison S., *The Process of Group Thinking*. New York: Association Press, 1932.

Ewbank, Henry L., and J. J. Auer, *Discussion and Debate: Tools of a Democracy*. New York: F. S. Crofts and Co., 1941.

Fansler, Thomas, *Creative Power Through Discussion*. New York: Harper and Brothers, 1950.

Haiman, Franklyn S., *Group Leadership and Democratic Action*. Boston: Houghton Mifflin Company, 1951.

Hannaford, Earle S., *Conference Leadership in Business and Industry*. New York: McGraw-Hill Book Company, Inc., 1945.

McBurney, James H., and Kenneth G. Hance, *Discussion in Human Affairs*. New York: Harper and Brothers, 1950.

Nichols, Alan, *Discussion and Debate*. New York: Harcourt, Brace and Company, 1941.

Stigers, M. F., *Making Conference Programs Work*. New York: McGraw-Hill Book Company, Inc., 1949.

Timmons, William M., *Decisions and Attitudes as Outcomes of the Discussion of a Social Problem*. New York: Teachers College, Columbia University, 1949.

Utterback, William E., *Group Thinking and Conference Leadership: Techniques of Discussion*. New York: Rinehart and Company, Inc., 1950.

Wagner, Russell H., and Carroll C. Arnold, *Handbook of Group Discussion*. Boston: Houghton Mifflin Company, 1950.

Walser, Frank, *The Art of Conference*, Revised Edition. New York: Harper and Brothers, 1948.

B. Books Related to Discussion and Conference

Adler, Mortimer J., *How to Read a Book*. New York: Simon and Schuster, Inc., 1940.

Bales, Robert F., *Interaction Process Analysis*. Cambridge: Addison-Wesley Press, Inc., 1950.

Beard, Charles A., *The Discussion of Human Affairs*. New York: The Macmillan Company, 1936.

Beardsley, Monroe C., *Practical Logic*. New York: Prentice-Hall, Inc., 1950.

Berelson, Bernard, *Content Analysis*. Glencoe, Illinois: The Free Press, 1952.

Berrien, F. K., *Comments and Cases on Human Relations*. New York: Harper and Brothers, 1951.

Black, Max, *Critical Thinking*, Second Edition. New York: Prentice-Hall, Inc., 1952.

Chase, Stuart, *Roads to Agreement*. New York: Harper and Brothers, 1951.

Festinger, Leon, and Daniel Katz, *Research Methods in the Behavioral Sciences*. New York: Dryden Press, 1953.

Flesch, Rudolf, *The Art of Plain Talk*. New York: Harper and Brothers, 1946.

Given, William B., Jr., *Bottom-Up Management*. New York: Harper and Brothers, 1949.

Gouldner, Alvin D. (ed.), *Studies in Leadership.* New York: Harper and Brothers, 1950.

Guetzkow, Harold (ed.), *Groups, Leadership and Men.* Pittsburgh: Carnegie Institute of Technology Press, 1951.

Haas, Kenneth B., and Claude M. Ewing, *Tested Training Techniques.* New York: Prentice-Hall, Inc., 1950.

Hummel, William, and Keith Huntress, *The Analysis of Propaganda.* New York: William Sloane Associates, Inc., 1949.

Lee, Irving J., *How to Talk with People.* New York: Harper and Brothers, 1952.

Lewin, Kurt, *Resolving Social Conflicts.* New York: Harper and Brothers, 1948.

Maier, Norman R. F., *Principles of Human Relations.* New York: Wiley and Sons, 1952.

Metcalf, Henry C., and L. Urwick (eds.), *Dynamic Administration: The Collected Papers of Mary Parker Follett.* New York: Harper and Brothers, 1942.

Newcomb, Theodore M., *Social Psychology.* New York: Dryden Press, 1950.

Peters, Raymond W., *Communication Within Industry.* New York: Harper and Brothers, 1950.

Rogers, Carl R., *Client-Centered Therapy.* Boston: Houghton Mifflin Company, 1951.

Swanson, Guy E., Theodore M. Newcomb, and Eugene L. Hartley (eds.), *Readings in Social Psychology.* New York: Henry Holt and Company, 1952.

Tead, Ordway, *The Art of Administration.* New York: McGraw-Hill Book Company, Inc., 1951.

Thomason, Calvin C., *Human Relations in Action.* New York: Prentice-Hall, Inc., 1947.

Wertheimer, Max, *Productive Thinking.* New York: Harper and Brothers, 1945.

Whyte, William H., *Is Anybody Listening?* New York: Simon and Schuster, 1952.

Wiener, Norbert, *The Human Use of Human Beings.* Boston: Houghton Mifflin Company, 1950.

II. PERIODICALS

A. *Purposes and Types*

Alexander, Fred G., "Let's Have a Student United Nations," *The Debater's Magazine,* III (September, 1947), 139–143.

Anderson, Martin P., "Discussion in Agriculture," *The Quarterly Journal of Speech*, XXXVII (December, 1951), 463–468.

Bavelas, Alex, "Some Problems of Organizational Change," *Journal of Social Issues*, IV (Summer, 1948), 48–52.

Behl, William A., "The United Nations Security Council," *Quarterly Journal of Speech*, XXIV (1948), 41–49.

Berwitz, Clement J., "The Work Committee—An Administrative Technique," *Harvard Business Review*, XXX (1952), 110–124.

Brandenburg, Earnest, "Public Discussion As A 'Propaganda' Technique," *Central States Speech Journal*, I (March, 1950), 29–32.

Brandes, Paul D., "The Mississippi Youth Congress," *The Southern Speech Journal*, XVI (September, 1950), 40–49.

Bryson, Lyman, "The Rhetoric of Conciliation," *Quarterly Journal of Speech*, XXXIX (December, 1953), 437–443.

Chapin, Leland T., "The Discussion Techniques of the Brookings Institution," *Quarterly Journal of Speech*, XXXII (1948), 34–39.

Coch, Lester, and John R. P. French, "Overcoming Resistance to Change," *Human Relations*, I (1948), 512–532.

Dickens, Milton, "Discussion Method in War Industry," *Quarterly Journal of Speech*, XXXI (1945), 144–150.

Dickens, Milton, and Marguerite Heffernan, "Experimental Research in Group Discussion," *Quarterly Journal of Speech*, XXXV (February, 1949), 23–29.

Ehninger, Douglas, and Mary Graham, "The Student Congress Movement Comes of Age," *The Gavel of Delta Sigma Rho*, XXX (November, 1947), 5–6, 11.

Gable, Martha, "Youth Discussion Programs on Television," *Civic Training*, XIX (April 16–20, 1951), 57–58.

Guetzkow, Harold, and Martin Kriesberg, "Executive Use of the Administrative Conference," *Personnel*, XXVI (March, 1950), 318–323.

Gulley, Halbert E., "Conference Discussion at Shrivenham," *Quarterly Journal of Speech*, XXXII (October, 1946), 316–318.

Gunderson, Robert Gray, "Group Dynamics—Hope or Hoax," *Quarterly Journal of Speech*, XXXVI (February, 1950), 34–38.

Guthrie, Warren A., "The Reserve Plan for Intercollegiate Discussion," *Quarterly Journal of Speech*, XXV (1939), 392–396.

Howell, William S., and Donald K. Smith, "Discussion Re-examined," *The Central States Speech Journal*, V (Fall, 1953), 3–7.

Isaacson, Carl L., "The Broadcaster Evaluates the Discussion Type Program," *Speech Activities*, VII (Summer, 1951), 46, 48, 50.

Johnson, Chester L., "The West Point Conference on United States

Affairs," *The Quarterly Journal of Speech*, XXXVI (April, 1950), 226–231.

Levine, Jacob, "Lecture Versus Group Decision in Changing Behavior," *Journal of Applied Psychology*, XXXVI (February, 1952), 29–33.

Oliver, Robert T., "The Speech of Diplomacy As a Field for Research," *Central States Speech Journal*, I (March, 1950), 24–28.

Phillips, Donald J., "Report on Discussion 66," *Adult Education Journal*, VII (1948), 181–182.

Probst, George E., "Liberal Education and Social Science Class Discussion," *School Review*, LVII (March, 1949), 158–164.

B. *Leadership*

Ansbacher, H. L., "The History of the Leaderless Group Discussion Technique," *Psychological Bulletin*, XXXVIII (September, 1951), 383–391.

Bass, B. M., "An Analysis of the Leaderless Group Discussion," *Journal of Applied Psychology*, XXXIII (December, 1949), 527–533.

Bass, B. M., "Situational Tests: II. Leaderless Group Discussion Variables," *Educational Psychology Measurement*, XI (1951), 196–207.

Bradford, Leland P., "Leading the Large Meeting," *Adult Education Bulletin*, XIV (December, 1949), 38–50.

Gibb, Cecil A., "The Principles and Traits of Leadership," *Journal of Abnormal and Social Psychology*, XXXXII (July, 1947), 267–284.

Jenkins, William O., "A Review of Leadership Studies With Particular Reference to Military Problems," *Psychological Bulletin*, XXXXIV (January, 1947), 54–79.

Knickerbocker, Irving, "Leadership: A Conception and Some Implications," *Journal of Social Issues*, IV (Summer, 1948), 23–40.

Lasswell, Harold D., "The Clarifier of Public Discussion," *Quarterly Journal of Speech*, XXXIV (December, 1948), 153.

Maier, Norman R. F., "The Contribution of a Discussion Leader to the Quality of Group Thinking: The Effective Use of Minority Opinions," *Human Relations*, V (1952), 277–288.

Pelz, Donald C., "Leadership Within a Hierarchical Organization," *Journal of Social Issues*, VII (1951), 49–53.

"Spotlight on Leadership," *Adult Leadership*, I (June, 1952).

Stogdill, Ralph M., "Personal Factors Associated with Leadership: A Survey of the Literature," *Journal of Psychology*, XXV (January, 1948), 35–71.

Utterback, William E., "The Moderator's Function in Group Thinking," *Quarterly Journal of Speech*, XXXIV (1948), 455–458.

Van Dusen, A. C., "Measuring Leadership Ability," *Personnel Psychology*, I (1948), 67–79.

C. *Participation*

Back, Kurt, "Interpersonal Relations in a Discussion Group," *Journal of Social Issues*, IV (Spring, 1948), 61–65.

Bales, Robert F., and Henry Gerbands, "The Interaction Recorder," *Human Relations*, I (1948), 456–463.

Beighley, K. C., "An Experimental Study of the Effect of Four Speech Variables on Listener Comprehension," *Speech Monographs*, XIX (November, 1952), 249–258.

Benne, Kenneth D., and Paul Sheats, "Functional Roles of Group Members," *Journal of Social Issues*, IV (Spring, 1948), 41–49.

Dale, Edgar, and Jeanne S. Chall, "A Formula for Predicting Readability," *Education Research Bulletin*, XXVII (1948), 11–20, 37–54.

Deutsch, Morton, "An Experimental Study of the Effects of Co-operation and Competition upon Group Process," *Human Relations*, II (July, 1949), 199–231.

Findley, Warren G., "A Statistical Index of Participation in Discussion," *Journal of Educational Psychology*, XXXIX (January, 1948), 47.

Flesch, Rudolf, "A New Readability Yardstick," *Journal of Applied Psychology*, XXXII (June, 1948), 221–33.

Fouriezos, Nicholas T., Max L. Hutt, and Harold Guetzkow, "Measurement of Self-Oriented Needs in Discussion Groups," *Journal of Abnormal and Social Psychology*, XXXXV (October, 1950), 682–690.

Giffin, Kim, "The Selection and Preparation of University of Chicago Round Table Participants," *Central States Speech Journal*, I (November, 1949), 30–34.

Green, Norman E., "Verbal Intelligence and Effectiveness of Participation in Group Discussion," *Journal of Educational Psychology*, XLI (1950), 440–445.

Hager, Cyril F., "Speech and Effective Communication: Re-Examination of Basic Assumptions," *The Quarterly Journal of Speech*, XXXII (February, 1946), 26–30.

Harnack, R. Victor, "Competition and Cooperation," *The Central States Speech Journal*, III (December, 1951), 15–20.

Jenkins, David H., "Feedback and Group Self-Evaluation," *Journal of Social Issues,* IV (Spring, 1948), 50–60.

Keltner, John, "Committee Dynamics: Basic Concepts," *The Gavel of Delta Sigma Rho,* XXXII (November, 1949), 4–5, 10.

Lewin, Kurt, R. Lippitt, and R. K. White, "Patterns of Aggressive Behavior in Experimentally Created 'Social Climates,'" *Journal of Social Psychology,* X (1939), 271–299.

Nichols, Ralph G., "Factors in Listening Comprehension," *Speech Monographs,* XV (1948), 154–163.

Phillips, David C., "Factors of Effective and Ineffective Conversation," *Speech Monographs,* XVI (September, 1949), 203–213.

Rogers, Carl R., and F. J. Roethlisberger, "Barriers and Gateways to Communication," *Harvard Business Review,* XXX (July–August, 1952), 46–52.

"Spotlight on Member Roles," *Adult Leadership,* I (January, 1953).

Young, Bruce F., and Morris Rosenberg, "Role Playing As a Participation Technique," *Journal of Social Issues,* V (Winter, 1949), 42–45.

D. *Problem-Solving*

Broadrick, King, "The Relationship of Argument to Syllogistic and Experimental Logic," *The Quarterly Journal of Speech,* XXXVI (December, 1950), 476–482.

Brown, Charles Thomas, "An Experimental Diagnosis of Thinking on Controversial Issues," *Speech Monographs,* XVII (November, 1950), 370–377.

Ehninger, Douglas E., "A Logic of Discussion Method," *Quarterly Journal of Speech,* XXIX (1943), 163–167.

Kettner, John W., "Goals, Obstacles, and Problem Formulation in Group Discussion," *Quarterly Journal of Speech,* XXXIII (December, 1947), 468–473.

Luchins, Abraham S., "Mechanization in Problem-Solving: The Effect of Einstellung," *Psychological Monographs,* LIV (1942), vii + 95.

Maier, Norman R. F., "An Aspect of Human Reasoning," *The British Journal of Psychology,* XXIV (October, 1933), 144–155.

Maier, Norman R. F., "Reasoning in Humans, I. On Direction," *The Journal of Comparative Psychology,* X (April, 1930), 115–143.

Maier, Norman R. F., "Reasoning in Humans, II. The Solution of a Problem and Its Appearance in Consciousness," *The Journal of Comparative Psychology,* XII (August, 1931), 181–194.

Maier, Norman R. F., "The Quality of Group Decisions As Influenced by the Discussion Leader," *Human Relations*, III (1950), 155–174.

Morgan, John J. B., and James T. Morton, "Distortions of Syllogistic Reasoning Produced by Personal Convictions," *Journal of Social Psychology*, XX (1944), 39–59.

Sattler, William M., "Socratic Dialectic and Modern Group Discussion," *Quarterly Journal of Speech*, XXIX (1943), 152–157.

Shaw, Marjorie E., "A Comparison of Individuals and Small Groups in the Rational Solution of Complex Problems," *American Journal of Psychology*, XXXXIV (1932), 491–504.

Wiener, Philip P., "Scientific Method and Group Discussion," *Journal of Adult Education*, IX (1937), 135–140.

III. Unpublished Studies

Barnlund, Dean Colquitt, "Experiments in Leadership Training for Decision-Making Discussion Groups," Ph.D. Dissertation. School of Speech, Northwestern University, 1951.

Douglas, Jack E., "An Experimental Study of Training in Verbal Problem-Solving Methods," Ph.D. Dissertation. School of Speech, Northwestern University, 1951.

Heyns, Roger W., "The Effects of Variation in Leadership on Participant Behavior in Discussion Groups," Ph.D. Dissertation. Department of Psychology, University of Michigan, 1948.

Miller, N. Edd, "The Effect of Group Size on Decision-Making Discussions," Ph.D. Dissertation. Department of Speech, University of Michigan, 1951.

Phillips, David C., "Some Factors That Make for Effective and Ineffective Conversation," Ph.D. Dissertation. University of Wisconsin, 1947.

Rickard, Paul B., "An Experimental Study of the Effectiveness of Group Discussion in the Teaching of Factual Content," Ph.D. Dissertation. School of Speech, Northwestern University, 1946.

Smith, Raymond G., "An Experimental Study of the Effects of Speech Organization Upon Attitudes of College Students," Ph.D. Dissertation. University of Wisconsin, 1950.

Sperling, Philip I., "Attitude Dispersion and Its Perception As Related to Satisfaction with A Group Product," Ph.D. Dissertation. Department of Psychology, University of Michigan, 1949.

Storey, Alfred W., "A Study of Member Satisfaction and Types of Contributions in Discussion Groups with Responsibility-Sharing Leadership," Ph.D. Dissertation. Department of Speech, University of Michigan, 1954.

Appendix G. Exercises

CHAPTER 1

1. Read the following excerpt from the *Fortune* survey of management personnel practices in businesses and organizations.

Question: While most people use all three, which of the following methods do you find most satisfactory for gathering information about your business?

Reading reports from your subordinates	23.0%
Calling in your subordinates for oral reports	55.6
Making inspection tours	37.0
Holding scheduled staff meetings	18.0

Here . . . many executives were unable to select any one method. Nevertheless it is clear that the printed page runs a poor third to direct conversation and personal observation.

Question: Most people who achieve success have a combination of many outstanding qualities. Which one of the following qualities do you rate as having contributed most to your success? Which next?

	Most	*Next*
Ability to handle people	30.0%	22.6%
Ability to make decisions	24.5	26.1
Technical or specialized knowledge	18.9	10.4
Great capacity for work	16.2	13.3
Ability to see things through	12.9	18.6
Imagination	10.2	13.4
Other	1.0	1.6

("The Management Poll," *Fortune*, XXXIV (October, 1946), 14. Reprinted by permission.)

In relation to the survey, consider the following questions.
(a) Does the reference to "oral reports" suggest that the meetings are a discussion or democratic conference?

(b) What functions are likely to be served by the "scheduled staff meetings"—for example, decision-making, learning, or motivation?

(c) What does "ability to handle people" mean to you? In what ways can this ability be shown by a leader and by participants in a discussion?

(d) Speech communication is given a high priority in the answers to the two questions. Why do you think speech communication plays the role that it does?

2. The *Apology* is one of the most interesting of the dialogues written by Plato. In this dialogue Plato reports the indictments against Socrates and the defense employed by the famous Greek philosopher.

Read the *Apology* in preparation for a class discussion in which you attempt to analyze and evaluate the basic ideas that are reported. Problem statements for the discussion may be one of the following: How Does Plato Depict Socrates in the *Apology*? What Are the Features of the Dialectical Method Used by Socrates in His Defense? Was Socrates Guilty? If the class is divided into small discussion groups of six to ten persons, each group may select a different type of problem statement.

3. Conduct a class discussion dealing with the differences between a "social and nonsocial" problem. Do you agree with the following remarks?

At the outset of our inquiry it must be noted that there is for our purposes one outstanding difference between social and nonsocial problems. It is this: Frequently a skilled individual can, single-handed, solve a nonsocial problem, be it in engineering, agriculture, or medicine. But no one person can solve a social problem all by himself, precisely because the solution of a social problem is found in coming to agreement of groups of men who have been holding conflicting positions. (E. L. Clarke, *The Art of Straight Thinking*, p. 364. New York: Appleton-Century-Crofts, Inc., 1929. Reprinted by permission.)

4. The three problem situations reported below can be used to experiment with possible qualitative differences between individual and group decisions.

Record your personal solution to each of the problems on a small card or piece of paper. Following this, discuss the problems in small groups composed of six to ten persons. When the members of your group are in general agreement on what is believed to be a good solution, report the solution to your instructor. Keep trying until you reach the correct answer.

(a) On the first day I arrived at the University, I went downtown to buy some books and look around. It all seemed rather confusing, as I didn't know my way around. But I bought the texts I wanted, had something to eat in a drug-store, and took a bus home. As soon as I got inside the house, I found one of the books missing. I was pretty sure I must have left it in the drug-store, but I couldn't remember its name or its location. . . . *Suddenly I remembered seeing a jewelry store next door to the drug-store.* [*Solution?*] (Max Black, *Critical Thinking*, pp. 248–249. New York: Prentice-Hall, Inc., 1946. Reprinted by permission.)

(b) *X-ray technique:* A harmful tumor inside the body of a patient can be eradicated by a sufficient concentration of X-rays. A beam of the required strength would, however, also destroy all intervening tissue. On the other hand, a beam weak enough not to harm the surrounding tissue would be too weak to destroy the tumor. *What method should be used to destroy the tumor?* (*Ibid.,* p. 262.)

(c) A man bought a horse for $60 and sold it for $70. Then he bought it back for $80 and sold it for $90. How much money did he make in the horse business? (Norman R. F. Maier and Allen R. Solem, "The Contribution of a Discussion Leader to the Quality of Group Thinking: The Effective Use of Minority Opinions," *Human Relations,* V (1952), 280. Reprinted by permission.)

Relevant questions are: (a) Did you change your answers to the problems after group discussion? (b) Were group decisions superior to personal solutions? (c) What "helps" in problem-solving have you learned from your experience with these problems? (d) Do you think deliberate training in problem-solving will make you a better conference participant? (Solutions to the problems are given on page 328.)

5. Answer these questions if you feel qualified to do so. Discuss them with others. As your term of study continues, refer to the questions again to see if you have changed your answers.

Leadership

(a) Is leadership in discussion similar to that exercised by the chairman in a parliamentary session? (Explain your answer.)

(b) Is the leader primarily responsible for the success of a discussion?

Participation

(c) Should participants in a discussion ask questions, or should this be a responsibility for the leader?

(d) In what ways are participants responsible for the success of a discussion?

Problem-Solving

(e) Should you know what you think is the best solution to a problem before the discussion is held?

(f) Should you accept the solution of the majority even when you do not feel that it is a good solution?

Interpersonal Relations

(g) Is it important to the success of a discussion to show respect toward others?

(h) How should you react toward a person who tends to monopolize a discussion?

CHAPTER 2

1. In a three-minute speech describe some of the features of a non-classroom discussion in which you have recently participated. Your report might refer to a student organization, club, or committee.

(a) Was the discussion conducted in an informal group atmosphere? Was the level of informality desirable or undesirable?

(b) Was group unity at a high level?

(c) Was freedom of choice apparent during the meeting?

(d) Was the group cooperative?

(e) Was responsibility for decisions shared by all?

2. Analyze a group discussion in terms of levels of cooperation:

(a) Silent Acquiescence

(b) Opposition Followed by Agreement

(c) Compromise

(d) Shared Decision

(e) Integration

3. Write a short paper (300 to 500 words in length) in which you describe a problem situation and tell how the problem was solved. The story "That Tackhead" given in this chapter is an illustration of the type of assignment we have in mind. Explain in what respects your problem-solving plan corresponds with Dewey's steps of reflective thinking.

4. Prepare a list of five problems suitable for group discussion that concern campus or local issues. These possibilities may help you to make your selections:

(a) What Grading System Should Be Followed in Our College?

(b) Is the Semester System of School Terms Better than the Quarter System?

(c) How Can Our Intra Mural Sports Program Be Improved?

(d) What Are the Values and Limitations of the Lecture System in College Teaching?

5. Conduct a series of group discussions on problems selected by the class. The entire class may participate as one group, or the class may

be divided into separate groups, of six to ten persons each, for discussion purposes.

Plan the structure of the discussion so that it conforms in general to the reflective pattern outlined in this chapter. You should, after investigating the facts of your discussion problem, prepare an outline in which you reveal the nature of your knowledge. Submit your outline to your instructor at the time of the discussion in which you are to participate.

A leader, or possibly two leaders who alternate in carrying out the leadership role, should be assigned to each group.

After your discussion, conduct an appraisal session in which you identify the strong and weak points of the discussion.

6. The report that follows has been called a sample of some of the "conferences" between General Motors representatives and representatives of the United Automobile Workers during the 1945–46 strike. The principals here are Walter Reuther of the U.A.W. and Harry Anderson of G.M.C. Discuss this excerpt from the points of view of group unity, freedom of choice, cooperation, and reflective thinking.

Reuther: I will tell you this, gentlemen, if it goes on much longer you make it worse . . . . You turned it on. We have some more panzer divisions to roll out . . . . We have not turned on the full steam yet.

Anderson: Does that mean the goon squads are going to be called out?

Reuther: It has nothing to do with goon squads . . . . It has everything to do with turning on our economic pressure.

Anderson: We are going to give you the demands on the contract changes Monday.

Reuther: We will be prepared to discuss these demands in about the same schedule you were prepared to discuss our wage demands. About six weeks from now we will be prepared to talk about those things . . . . And then we will give you the union's demands. For every one you give us we will give you a counter-demand . . . . Because you ain't fooling anybody.

Anderson: You ain't fooling us, either. (*Time*, XLVI [December 24, 1945], 20–21.)

CHAPTER 3

1. Prepare a list of five discussion problems for each of the four areas: *Personal, School and College, Social and Political,* and *Organization and Business.*

    a. Apply the suggestions given for problem selection and problem statement.

    b. Indicate whether the problems are questions of fact, value, policy, or procedure.

2. Write a case problem (300 to 500 words in length) dealing with school and college situations. Problems that relate to *class requirements, school elections, social restrictions, residence halls,* and *student organizations* are likely to be good choices for the cases you report. (See also Appendix A for illustrative case problems.)

3. Write a case problem that has a bearing upon human relations in business and industry. These topic areas should serve to suggest specific situations or critical incidents that you have experienced.

a. Giving Orders	h. Getting Recognition
b. Using Emotional Words	i. Keeping People Informed
c. Knowing the Facts	j. Consulting Others
d. Feeling Accepted	k. Understanding Others
e. Facing Blocked Goals	l. Being a Good Listener
f. Showing Hostility	m. Using Group Decisions
g. Controlling Boredom	n. Using Non-Directive Skills

Case problems related to the above areas will be more meaningful if they are true descriptions of situations. By keeping case problems factually centered you remove the danger of having others feel that the situation is a hypothetical one and probably could never have happened.

4. Submit the titles of five magazine articles that you believe pose important issues that are suitable for discussion. After your group and group leader have agreed upon the articles to be used for your discussion, hold a pre-discussion meeting to determine a plan for your discussion. The suggestions given in this chapter dealing with the discussion of problems based upon articles and books will help you in designing a format for your discussion.

5. Alternate leadership in a discussion by having a different leader for each fifteen-minute period of the discussion. Do you think the use of several leaders was either helpful or harmful to the discussion? Give reasons for your belief.

6. Conduct a short discussion in which you pool judgments about the suitability of using area problems, problems based on articles or books, and case problems in your group discussions. Present your findings in the form of a written report and distribute the report to all members of your group.

CHAPTER 4

1. Write a brief report on any three discussions you have heard in the past year. Explain the kind of physical arrangements used and the purpose or purposes of the discussion groups.

2. Discuss the effects of different types of physical arrangements on discussions. Do some types of arrangements encourage wide participation, others discourage it? Do some physical arrangements favor the position of the leader, others the position of the participants?

3. By pooling the experiences and information of the members of your group, compile a list of actual examples of each of the types of discussion considered in this chapter.

4. Read the panel discussion on "The Humanities and Higher Education" in Appendix B. Prepare yourself to participate in a discussion in which some or all of the following questions are considered:

(a) How could the topic statement be rephrased as a question?
(b) How would you classify the purpose of this discussion?
(c) Where would you place this discussion on the formality continuum given in this chapter?
(d) What were the main ideas given by members of the panel?
(e) In what respects did the members of the panel agree? Disagree?
(f) What importance do you think should be attached to studies in the humanities?

CHAPTER 5

1. Write a brief evaluation of the preparation of members of a discussion group in which you have taken part. Which members showed evidences of thorough preparation, and which did not? How could you tell whether preparation had been thorough?

2. Indicate where you would go to find information on the following topics:

(a) What form of international organization would best preserve world peace?
(b) Do large or small colleges provide the best education?
(c) What can be done about racial and religious discrimination?
(d) Does a liberal education prepare a person adequately to meet present-day American life?
(e) What is the relationship between discussion and democratic processes?

3. Evaluate the evidence (facts and opinions) in the following news item from the *Detroit Free Press* (October 26, 1952):

Labor Law Violations Pointed Out

Some $10,000,000 in back wages has been paid Michigan employees since 1938 because of the Federal Fair Labor Standards Act, a Government official said Saturday.

But he said, current investigations show that about 50 per cent of employers still violate one or more of the Act's basic provisions—minimum wage, overtime or child labor.

The disclosure was made by Thomas A. Hermansen, supervisor of the United States Labor Department's Wage and Hour Division here.

"Only a few of these violations are found to be willful," Hermansen said.

He pointed out that new businesses and older firms elevating young executives make necessary a "continuous educational program to acquaint these people with the law."

The original minimum wage law called for a 25-cent hourly base and a work week of 44 hours. An amendment raised the wage to 40 cents and cut the hours to 40.

In 1950, the minimum wage became 75 cents.

Said Hermansen:

"When we speak of child labor, many people immediately picture a sweatshop setting. But sweatshops are a thing of the past.

"Only a few years ago, we found 10 and 12-year-old boys in our Michigan forests swinging man-sized axes. Today they are in school where they belong.

"We still find teen-agers doing men's work in the shop, running elevators and driving trucks. We still find youngsters, even 5 and 6-year-olds, in the harvest fields."

Hermansen pointed out that, generally, children 16 and over may be employed in any type of non-hazardous employment. Specific restrictions apply to those between 14 and 16.

Some occupations are exempt from the law, Hermansen said. Among them are newspaper carrier boy, a child working for his parents and juvenile actors. (Reprinted by permission.)

4. Construct a discussion outline for your next discussion.

CHAPTER 6

1. Write two case studies (approximately 300 words each) in which you describe problem situations that illustrate two types of influence in problem-solving. Your case studies should illustrate types of influence discussed in this chapter:

(a) Influence of Intuition
(b) Influence of Initial Choice
(c) Influence of Authority
(d) Influence of Tradition
(e) Influence of Emotion
(f) Influence of Personal Experience
(g) Influence of Reflective Thinking

In writing your paper, depict the *problem situation* and the *solution* that was accepted.

Discuss the case studies. In your discussion groups keep this question in mind: Could the problem have been solved in a better way?

2. Identify the patterns of thinking used in the persuasive appeals of writers and speakers. Fruitful sources you may use for this assignment include:

(a) "Letters to the Editor" section of newspapers
(b) Newspaper and magazine editorials
(c) Printed advertising copy
(d) Radio and television commercials
(e) Speeches by public officials or private individuals representing some cause

Questions you might ask yourself are: What prompted the persuader to adopt the point of view that he advocated? What forms of attempted influence did the persuader use?

Study examples from at least two of the five sources listed above. Plan a three-minute speech in which you report your findings to your class.

3. Discuss the following passage by John Dewey concerning the development of habits of thinking in both childhood and adulthood:

In any case *positive habits are being* formed: if not habits of careful looking into things, then habits of hasty, heedless, impatient glancing over the surface; if not habits of consecutively following up the suggestions that occur, then habits of haphazard, grasshopper-like guessing; if not habits of suspending judgment till inferences have been tested by the examination of evidence, then habits of credulity alternating with flippant incredulity, belief or unbelief being based, in either case, upon whim, emotion, or accidental circumstances. The only way to achieve traits of carefulness, thoroughness, and continuity (traits that are, as we have seen, the elements of the "logical") is by exercising these traits from the beginning, and by seeing to it that conditions call for their exercise. (John Dewey, *How We Think*, p. 66. Boston: D. C. Heath and Company, 1910. Reprinted by permission.)

Key words in this passage include: *hasty, heedless, impatient, glancing over the surface, haphazard grasshopper-like guessing, credulity alternating with flippant incredulity, belief based on whim, emotion or accidental circumstances,* and *suspended judgment till inferences have been tested.* What do these ideas have in common with the patterns of thinking described in this chapter?

4. Evaluate the type of decisions agreed upon in your discussion

groups. One interesting way of doing this is to use a linear scale that permits raters to judge creativeness in decision-making.

Raters may be asked: Do you think your group (or the discussion group if you are an observer) was able to discover an original or creative decision?

(Place a check at a point on the continuum)

1	2	3	4	5	6	7	8	9	10	11

Traditional   Original
or   or
Stereotyped   Creative
Decision   Decision

5. The preferred answers to the problem situations described on page 321 are:

(a) Compare the list of jewelry stores in the classified section of the telephone directory with the list of drug-stores. When two of them are found with the same street address and almost the same number, telephone the drug-store to see if the book has been found.

(b) Several weak beams from different points of origin are made to intersect at the tumor's location.

(c) The correct answer is $20.00.

CHAPTER 7

1. Observe a discussion and keep a record of the time spent on the five major steps of the reflective pattern.

(a) Recognition of the Problem

(b) Description of the Problem

(c) Discovery of Possible Solutions

(d) Evaluation of Possible Solutions and Acceptance of Best Solution

(e) Plan of Action

2. Prepare an outline for your next discussion that is planned in accordance with the steps of reflective thinking. You may omit steps 4 and 5 (evaluation and plan of action) in your outline. By doing this, you will be more likely to reserve your final decision until the problem has been discussed. If, on the other hand, you reveal your choice of "best solution" in your preparation, you may not be willing to consider alternative solutions in the discussion.

3. Study the sample outline below, and follow it as a general guide when you prepare for group discussions.

Preparation Outline *

Specific Problem: What Should Be Our Policy Regarding the Teaching
of Religion in the Public Schools?
I. Recognition of the Problem
  A. Formulation of the Problem as a Question
     1. A question of fact might be: What Types of Religious
        Instruction Are Offered in Our Public Schools?
     2. A question of value might be: Is It Better to Divorce Religion
        and Education in Our Public Schools?
     3. A question of policy might be: What Should Be Our Policy
        Regarding the Teaching of Religion in the Public Schools?
        (*This problem statement best represents the issue faced by
        the American people.*)
  B. Definition of the Problem
     1. "Teaching of Religion"
        (a) It may be defined as instruction in the systems of faith
            and worship having reference to man's relation to God.
        (b) It may be defined as instruction in the specific beliefs,
            doctrines, and creeds of a particular religious group.
        (c) It may be defined as instruction in a system of morals
            or ethics, having no reference to a specific doctrine or
            creed, that is, non-sectarian.
     2. "Public Schools"
        (a) They are defined as those institutions of learning which
            are supported wholly or in part by public funds.
        (b) They are defined, for this discussion, as those institutions
            imparting instruction *at the elementary and secondary
            level.*
     3. "Our Policy"
        (a) It is understood to be a plan that we would recommend
            regarding religious instruction in our public schools.
        (b) It is understood to be a plan that is made with full
            awareness of constitutional and court decisions, but one
            that is not necessarily governed by present interpreta-
            tions.
II. Description of the Problem
  A. History of the Problem
     1. There is a difference of opinion about the meaning of the
        First Amendment of the Constitution, which reads, in part,

---

* Based upon an outline prepared by Paul Huber, Department of Speech,
Arizona State College, Tempe, Arizona.

"Congress shall make no law respecting an establishment of religion or prohibiting the free exercise thereof. . . ."

(a) One interpretation commonly accepted is that the Constitution means that there shall be "a wall of separation between church and state."

    (1) Thomas Jefferson has been credited with the "wall of separation" viewpoint. (See S. K. Padover, *The Complete Jefferson*, p. 518.)

    (2) James Madison vetoed a bill to give public land to a Baptist Church in Mississippi because he felt it was a bill "respecting an establishment of religion." (See I. Brant, *American Mercury*, Vol. 67, 685–692.)

(b) A second interpretation is that the First Amendment refers to a formal union of a single church or religion with the government.

    (1) "An establishment of religion means a state church. . . ." (See E. S. Corwin, *The Constitution—What It Means Today*, p. 154.)

    (2) "The promoters of the First Amendment had no idea of making it a provision for the removal of religion from education. . . ." (See J. M. O'Neill, *Religion and Education Under the Constitution*, pp. 57–58.)

2. A variety of types of Court decisions have been made on the issue of religion and education.

(a) Cochran v. Louisiana Board of Education, 281 U. S. 370. In this case the Court ruled that tax money might be used to provide free textbooks of a non-religious type to students in *both* public and private (church) schools. (See A. W. Johnson and F. H. Yost, *Separation of Church and State*, p. 148.)

(b) Emerson v. Board of Education of Ewing Township et al., 330 U. S. 1. Here the Court ruled that the transporting of parochial school children at public expense was constitutional when New Jersey laws made provision for it. (*Ibid.*, p. 160.)

(c) McCollum v. Board of Education, 333 U. S. 203. The Court ruled that permitting teachers of religion to come into public school buildings during school hours for the purpose of teaching religious matter was *unconstitutional*.

(d) On April 28, 1952, the Court ruled that the released time program of the State of New York was constitutional. Mr. Justice Jackson said, "We find no constitutional requirement which makes it necessary for the government to be hostile to religion and to throw its weight against efforts to widen the effective scope of religious influence." (See P. N. Elbin, *Christian Century*, Vol. 69, 1061.)

B. Effects of the Problem

1. Students show signs of general illiteracy in the field of religion.

    (a) The President of Wellesley College stated that 98.8% of the girls who enter that institution are essentially ignorant of the literature and history of the religious traditions to which they claim allegiance. (See H. E. Fosdick, *School and Society*, Vol. 66, 401–406.)

    (b) ". . . only a small proportion of the children throughout the country have even a brief contact with church influence." (See A. E. Meyer, *Reader's Digest*, Vol. 52, 65–69.)

    (c) "How can we move toward goals . . . if the very foundation of our political and spiritual thinking are left out of what we give our youngsters . . . ?" (See C. P. Taft, *Christian Century*, Vol. 69, 944–946.)

2. Students are likely to believe that religion is of negligible value.

    (a) Religion is looked upon as a "dispensable diversion." (See Cannon B. J. Bell, Editorial, *Christian Century*, Vol. 67, 1287.)

    (b) "Religion is discounted in the eyes of youth." (See G. C. Morrison, *Reader's Digest*, Vol. 49, 127–128.)

3. Students and the public at large show evidence of questionable moral values.

    (a) "There are many signs of a weakening of our moral standards . . . in newspapers, on the radio and in public and private life." (See J. W. Fulbright, *Vital Speeches*, Vol. 17, 386–387.)

    (b) "In this land of plenty, gutted with wealth, we lack the essential ethical currency for its use, and so we are threatened with cultural bankruptcy." (See H. P. Van Dusen, *God in Education*, quoted in *Time*, Vol. 57, 78–80.)

C. Causes of the Problem
    1. Legal decisions and state constitutions have usually discouraged initiative by schools in matters of religious instruction.
        (a) It has been estimated that the McCollum case affected unfavorably the religious instruction of over two million children. (See H. B. Mulford, *School and Society,* Vol. 65, 461–462.)
        (b) A survey conducted among 2,639 schools two years after the McCollum decision revealed that 310 schools had given up their programs in religious instruction. (See Research Bulletin, *N. E. A. Journal,* Vol. 38, 610–611.)
        (c) In twelve states sectarian instruction or influence in the schools is prohibited by state constitutions. (See W. E. Gauerke, *School and Society,* Vol. 75, 401–404.)
    2. The Church and Sunday School have not been successful in their teaching programs.
    3. The home has failed to provide religious instruction.
III. Discovery of Possible Solutions
    A. Conditions to Be Met by an Acceptable Solution
        1. The solution should correct or modify the effects of the problem.
        2. The solution should change one or more of the causes of the problem.
        3. The solution should be one that is consistent with the First and Fourteenth Amendments.
        4. The solution should be one that is acceptable, in varying degrees, to the general public.
        5. The solution should be elective in nature and not mandatory.
    B. Possible Solutions
        1. We might sever any and all relationships between religion and education.
        2. We might ask the states and/or local communities to work out the problem for themselves.
        3. We might have courses in the history of religions.
        4. We might have the schools emphasize ethics and morality to a greater extent.
        5. We might have schools adopt the practice of reading of the Bible and the reciting of prayers.
        6. We might have the schools put into practice the released time program (as adopted in New York) that permits students to receive religious instruction away from the school.

7. We might train teachers to be qualified teachers of religion and to offer sectarian religious instruction.

8. We might have religious instruction by representatives of the various creeds and sects given within the school during school hours.

IV. Evaluation of Possible Solutions and Acceptance of Best Solution

    A. Evaluation of Possible Solutions

    (Solutions No. 1 through 8 and any additional alternative solutions should be evaluated during the discussion.)

    B. Acceptance of Best Solution

    (After evaluation—naming of advantages and disadvantages of all solutions—the group should try to agree upon one or more solutions of the "best solution" type.)

V. Plan of Action

    A. Method of Execution

    B. Action Group to Put Solution into Effect

    (The plan of action must of course be determined after the group has agreed upon how the problem should be solved.)

CHAPTER 8

1. Read an editorial in your daily paper. Analyze the types of reasoning used in the editorial and apply the tests of reasoning to them.

2. Locate the fallacies, if any, in the following statements:

(a) Breaking a mirror brings seven years bad luck.

(b) Brown County is a Republican county. Fred Black is a citizen of Brown County. Therefore, Fred Black is a Republican.

(c) Texas is the largest state in the United States. Houston is the largest city in Texas. Therefore, Houston is the largest city in the United States.

(d) In the late nineteenth century, there were several well-known "rain-makers." Their method of operation was to shoot a cannon in the air. They claimed that any rain that resulted within any reasonable time was the result of the cannon shot.

(e) Voters in the South should vote the Democratic ticket in every election because their fathers and grandfathers voted the Democratic ticket.

3. Observe a discussion group. Take notes on the type of reasoning you see in use. Note also any fallacies you detect. Report on your observation.

CHAPTER 9

1. In his analysis and evaluation of hundreds of leadership studies, Ralph M. Stogdill discovered that eight personal traits commonly associated with leadership have either a *doubtful* or *low* positive correlation. Similarly, he found that eighteen traits have a *significant* or *high* correlation with actual leadership.

(a) Traits having either a doubtful or a low correlation:

1. Chronological Age	5. Appearance
2. Extroversion or Intro-version	6. Dominance
	7. Mood Control
3. Height or Weight	8. Emotional Control
4. Physique, Energy, Health	

(b) Traits having a high correlation:

1. Intelligence	10. Responsibility
2. Scholarship	11. Self-Confidence
3. Knowledge	12. Social and Economic Status
4. Fluency of Speech	13. Integrity and Convictions
5. Judgment and Decision	14. Social Activity and Mobility
6. Insight	15. Bio-Social Activities
7. Originality	(Active)
8. Adaptability	16. Prestige
9. Initiative (Ambition and Persistence)	17. Social Skills
	18. Cooperation

(See "Personal Factors Associated with Leadership: A Survey of the Literature," *Journal of Psychology*, XXV (January, 1948), 35–71.)

Most writers, including Stogdill, say that there is not a universal list of leadership traits. The best we can do is to conclude that, under certain conditions, the traits we have named help to explain personal factors in leadership. But, and this is important, there will always be exceptions.

Plan a discussion in which you use this problem or one similar to it: "What are the similarities and differences in personal traits among men and women who are recognized as leaders?" In preparing for the discussion read several biographical works, articles about people who have distinguished themselves as leaders, and special references on leadership. You may also wish to interview others, and, of course, you should depend in part upon your own knowledge and experiences.

2. We are presenting some statements given by participants regarding personal desires that they hope to satisfy in conferences. Do you agree that as a participant you also feel the need for fulfilling some of

the motives identified? Do you think they are important? Under which style of leadership will they most likely be satisfied?

(a) (*to be liked by others*) Above all, I want to be well liked. I don't think it is fun participating in a discussion, or particularly worth while, if there are people in the group who obviously don't like me. People have to be friendly and like one another to work together most effectively and to get things done. If I am liked, I have the feeling of being wanted or necessary.

(b) (*to receive recognition*) I like to get recognition or credit where credit is due. I believe a certain amount of praise is necessary, either from the leader or the group, in order to make a person feel that his time has been well spent and to keep him from getting discouraged.

(c) (*to contribute*) I feel the need of contributing to a discussion to fulfill what I regard as my responsibility.

(d) (*to be in a cooperative group*) I want to be a factor in the promotion of team-spirit. When "we" are doing it, everyone is more honest with himself and others, and there is little wasted motion on personal prejudices. The group becomes problem-centered, and everyone seems much happier.

(e) (*to have my ideas valued*) I feel the need to have my opinions valued highly by the group. When I voice an opinion or give evidence I want it to be taken for what it is worth, not disregarded because I said it. If Joe Smith doesn't like me, he will disregard my opinion regardless of how sound it is (that is, he will unless he can control his prejudices).

3. Study carefully Appendix C, "Human Relations: A New Art Brings a Revolution to Industry." Write a 500-word paper in which you explain the types of leadership suggested in this article. For instance: (a) What style of leadership does management practice when mechanical efficiency is solely emphasized? (b) What style of leadership is suggested by the theory and practices of Elton Mayo? (c) What were the leadership methods used in the Harwood experiment? (d) In what ways does the article show that fulfillment of wants by workers is dependent upon the style of leadership followed by management?

4. Some of the features of the leadership skill of Frank W. Abrams, formerly Chairman of the Board of Directors, Standard Oil Company of New Jersey, are here briefly described:

He is the kind of man who can walk into a room and put everybody at ease. He never commands or reproaches, but is master of the art of gentle suggestion. Thus he is a great committeeman, with the high talent of getting the right man in the right group and of arriving at a conclusion that is both a consensus and correct. ("The Jersey Company," *Fortune*, XLIV (October, 1951), 102. Reprinted by permission.)

What type of leader, authoritarian, strict supervisory, democratic, non-directive, does Mr. Abrams appear to be?

Plan a three-minute speech in which you identify the characteristics of organizational and business leaders whom you know. In what respects are these leaders similar to, or different from, Mr. Abrams? Would the persons that you depict be better, or less effective, if they practiced different patterns of leadership? The persons you describe may be selected from any field or profession, including student organizations and clubs.

5. Conduct one or more conferences in which the leader deliberately assumes the role of an authoritarian or strict supervisory leader. Preferably the group members, or at least the majority of them, should not know prior to the conference that the leader plans to be an autocratic leader.

An observing group should record the number of times the leader uses the authoritarian conference techniques given in this chapter. Other questions you should try to answer are: Was the atmosphere of the meeting one of friendliness and informality? Was the group a cohesive group? Did the participants display initiative and originality? What were the reactions of the group members toward the leader? Were the decisions of the conference acceptable to the group as a whole?

6. Plan a series of conferences in which the same problem is discussed by groups under different styles of leadership: authoritarian, strict supervisory, democratic, non-directive, and leaderless.

You might, following these discussions, seek answers to these questions: How did the decisions of the various groups compare with one another? How satisfied were the participants with their total experiences in the conference? How satisfied were the participants with the decisions reached in the conference?

7. Conduct a leaderless group discussion in which a group of six to ten persons is given a forty-five minute period to discuss a problem. If you wish, the problem may be assigned to the group only a few minutes before the discussion. Of course, the problem should be one that the participants are qualified to discuss.

A group of evaluators should rate each participant. You might use these factors in your assessment plan (a rating of 10 means *Very High* and a rating of 1 means *Very Low*):

(a) ability to use words to make ideas clear
(b) skill in use of voice and action in speaking
(c) poise and self-control
(d) pleasantness in manner

(e) ability to initiate suggestions
(f) quality of contributions
(g) recognition received from group
(h) ability to support suggestions
(i) ability to evaluate ideas
(j) ability to listen to others
(k) amount of participation
(l) ability to keep to the main issues

Questions: Were procedural and content leadership in the discussion shared by many or by few persons in the group? Did individual participants display authoritarian, supervisory, democratic, or laissez-faire styles of leadership?

CHAPTER 10

1. After you have acted as leader in a discussion, write a 500-word paper describing your experiences. Consider these questions in preparing your report:
   (a) To what degree do you think you achieved the three leadership goals given in this chapter?
   (b) Did you find it unnecessary to execute some of the leadership functions?
   (c) Which leadership functions did you carry out successfully? Were you less successful in performing some of the other leadership functions? Explain.
   (d) If you were in the same situation again, would you do any things differently from the way you did them in this discussion?
2. Observe a discussion and evaluate the effectiveness with which the leader executed the twelve leadership functions.
   (a) Rate the leader on all functions.
   (b) Follow the rating plan described on page 165.
3. Write a 300-word critique of the leader of a discussion. Identify what you believe to be the merits and the weaknesses of the leader. Make your comments as specific as you can.
4. After you have studied the following two references, answer these questions for yourself or discuss them with others. How far should the leader go in attempting to get general participation? Is everyone expected to speak? Should the leader give speaking preferences to participants whose ideas are likely to be superior? Should he insist that superior participants contribute to the discussion?

   (a) "In Cabinet meetings," said Dwight D. Eisenhower, "I always wait for George Humphrey to speak. I sit back and listen to the others talk while he doesn't say a thing. But I know that when he speaks up he will say just what I am thinking." (*Life*, March 16, 1953, p. 63. Reprinted by permission.)

(b) One of his colleagues on Dwight Eisenhower's top strategy board said: "Often I'd look around and see that Brownell's chair was empty. That's the only way I'd know he left the room. Then a little while later, when we were getting near a decision, I would hear a quiet voice speak up—straight to the point. Everyone in the room would stop talking and listen. That's the way I'd find out Brownell was back in the room." ("The Cabinet," *Time*, LXI (February 16, 1953), 23. Reprinted by permission.)

5. In *The Human Use of Human Beings* Norbert Wiener says:

The businessman who separates himself from his employees by a shield of "yes men," or the head of a big laboratory who assigns each of his subordinates a particular problem, and begrudes him the degree of thinking for himself which is necessary to move beyond this problem and perceive its relevance, both show that the democracy to which they pay their respects is not really the order in which they would prefer to live. The regularly ordered state of pre-assigned functions towards which they gravitate is the state of the ants.

In the ant community each worker performs its proper function. There is a separate caste of soldiers. Certain highly specialized individuals perform the functions of king and queen. If man were to adopt this community as a pattern, he would live in a Fascist state, in which ideally each individual is conditioned from birth for his proper occupation: in which rulers are perpetually rulers, soldiers perpetually soldiers, the peasant is never more than a peasant, and the worker is doomed to be a worker. (Norbert Wiener, *The Human Use of Human Beings*, p. 60. Boston: Houghton Mifflin Company, 1950. Reprinted by permission.)

Questions: From the point of view of leadership in a discussion, what inferences can you draw from Wiener's ideas? What pattern of leadership in regard to execution of leadership functions do you think Wiener would recommend for discussions?

6. Keep a record of contributions in a discussion that have to do with the twelve leadership functions. How many times did the assigned leader perform leadership functions? How many times did group members other than the leader perform leadership functions?

7. Conduct discussions in which varied patterns of leadership are followed:

(a) In the first discussion the leader should personally perform all leadership functions.

(b) In the second discussion the leader should perform some functions himself but occasionally ask participants to perform leadership functions.

(c) In the third discussion the leader should ask participants to perform all of the leadership functions.

How did observers of the discussion, participants in the discussion, and the leader himself feel about these discussions? Use rating scales to measure satisfaction with leadership, with decisions, and with the part participants played in the discussions.

8. Conduct a discussion in which no person in the group is assigned nominal leadership. Were leadership responsibilities carried out? Were they carried out by a few persons or by many persons in the group? Was the discussion a success?

9. Plan a discussion centered on this question: What can participants do in a discussion to assist the leader in changing the behavior of troublesome participants or in checking harmful effects created by such participants?

CHAPTER 11

1. Write a 500 word paper about a discussion in which you have taken part or one that you have observed. Describe the actions of the leader, and his effectiveness, in regard to these matters:

(a) Starting the discussion
(b) Structural pattern of the discussion
(c) Problem situations that affected progress
(d) Closing the discussion

2. Conduct discussions in which you follow one of the types of structural patterns described in this chapter.

(a) Reflective Pattern
(b) Modified Reflective Pattern
(c) Vital Issues Pattern
(d) Divisions of the Problem Pattern
(e) Pattern Suggested by Contributions of Members

Questions for discussion: (1) Do you particularly favor any of these structural patterns? (2) Does the problem you are discussing have a bearing upon the pattern you would recommend? (3) What effect do the group members have upon the appropriateness of a particular pattern? (4) What are the values and limitations of each of the structural patterns?

3. Conduct discussions in which you experiment with (a) several different types of introductions and (b) several different types of conclusions.

4. Conduct discussions in which a short intermission period is used in one of these ways: (a) a period of silence in which participants do not leave their seats, (b) a period during which refreshments are served, (c) a period during which participants are free to leave the conference room, or (d) a period during which participants, or an observer, evaluate the merits and weaknesses of the portion of the discussion that has been held. This process is occasionally called "feedback."

What values, if any, resulted from the use of the intermission period? Do you think groups should follow this practice more often?

5. Read "The Quaker Way Wins New Adherents" by Morris Llewellyn Cooke in Appendix E. Do you agree with the ideas advanced in this article? Can they be applied successfully in discussions?

6. Plan discussions in which the leader asks group members to formulate the summary of the discussion. Did the members of the group have difficulty in deciding upon the final summary? Do you think the leader could have given a better summary without consulting the group members?

CHAPTER 12

1. Analyze a group you have been in where interpersonal relations were poor. Describe specific things that happened in the group which indicated that interpersonal relations were bad.

2. Describe some specific measures to improve interpersonal relations that might have been taken by the leader and by individual members of the group you described in Exercise 1.

3. Take part in a group discussion on the subject: "How can group unity be increased in discussion groups?"

4. Write a careful analysis of the cohesiveness of the group in which you took part in (3) above. How could cohesiveness have been improved.

CHAPTER 13

1. Use the sample discussion in Appendix B and analyze the participations in it in the following ways: (a) total number of participations, (b) spread of participation, (c) average length of participations and range in length of participations, (d) the degree of organization of the participations.

2. Find examples in this sample discussion of any five of the seven forms a contribution might take.

3. Keep a record of the frequency of participation per member in your next discussion.

4. Describe the kinds of non-verbal participation you witnessed in the discussion.

CHAPTER 14

1. Two observers reached these conclusions about problem-centered and procedure-centered contributions and percentages of specific contributions given in a discussion.

Problem: How Can We Minimize or Control Narcotic Addiction by Youth?

Types of Contributions Problem-Centered	*Percentage of Total Contributions*
(a) Giving goals, aims, or conditions	4.1
(b) Giving information	28.7
(c) Giving clarification or summary	18.3
(d) Giving suggestion or solution	14.4
(e) Giving evaluation of own contribution or contribution by others	18.2
(f) Asking a question relating to problem	10.2
(g) Giving an irrelevant statement	1.1
Procedure-Centered	
(a) Giving procedural suggestion	3.0
(b) Asking procedural question	2.0

These percentages include contributions by both the participants and the leader.

(a) What do these statistics tell you about the discussion?

(b) Do you think the types of problem-centered contributions (*a* through *e*) show optimum percentages for this problem?

(c) Do you think the 10.2 percentage for questions is unusual? Why or why not?

2. Try to discover the types of contributions that group members give in a discussion by categorizing each individual participation into one or more of the problem and procedure-centered categories.

Do some participants rely heavily upon informative contributions? evaluative? clarification and summary? solution-giving?

3. Write a short paper (300 words) in which you show the good purposes that can be served by the asking of questions in a discussion. Illustrate what you mean by listing some examples of useful types of questions. In the course of your paper, you might also give some

attention to questions that block progress and are therefore harmful to the success of a discussion.

4. Observe a discussion and write a paper (400 words) in which you (a) identify attitudes and contributions that promoted teamwork, and (b) attitudes and contributions that discouraged teamwork. Be as specific as you can in reporting your reactions.

5. The desirable role patterns we mentioned in this chapter are: (a) organizer, (b) fact finder, (c) creator of ideas, (d) critical tester, (e) questioner, (f) energizer, (g) helper of others, and (h) conciliator. After observing a group discussion, place each participant in one or more of these categories. If you think a category is an imperfect description of a participant, indicate that the category is a questionable one. A question you should answer is: Do highly valued participants usually reveal two, three, or more of these role patterns?

6. If your behavior fits any of the fifteen undesirable roles, plan a remedial program for yourself. Write a short paper showing the exact steps you intend to follow in your attempt to become a more competent participant.

CHAPTER 15

1. Record on tape one of the discussions in which you take part. Analyze your own speaking in the conference in light of the factors discussed in this chapter.

2. Make a check-list of your own of additional factors that might be labeled undesirable and desirable traits in conference speaking.

3. Rate the quality of conference speaking of the members of your group as you hear them in conference situations. Use the following five-point rating system, and assign a rating on each of the desirable traits discussed in this chapter:

$$1\ldots\ldots\ldots\text{very good}$$
$$2\ldots\ldots\ldots\text{good}$$
$$3\ldots\ldots\ldots\text{fair—average}$$
$$4\ldots\ldots\ldots\text{poor}$$
$$5\ldots\ldots\ldots\text{very poor}$$

CHAPTER 16

1. Analyze a discussion group with respect to the necessary requisites for good language usage.

2. Discuss methods the listener might use in making contributions from others more understandable to himself such as asking questions, restating contributions of others, and so forth.

3. Analyze one of your own discussions with respect to the use of the stylistic factors discussed in this chapter.

CHAPTER 17

1. Listen to at least one program illustrating each of the four types of radio discussions. Analyze the different techniques used by the leader or the moderator in each of these types. Analyze the different techniques used by the participants.

2. On television, watch programs illustrating each of the four types of discussion considered in this chapter. Analyze different techniques used by the leader or moderator and by the participants in each of the four types.

3. Conduct a discussion on how a radio or television round table differs from other types of discussion and conference.

4. Discuss what you as a viewer or listener expect from radio and television discussions.

CHAPTER 18

1. On the basis of the discussion in this chapter and your own observation, compile a list of desirable and undesirable traits for chairmen of large group meetings.

2. Organize your group into a business session. Use standard rules of parliamentary procedure in the conduct of your meeting. Before the meeting begins, make definite assignments to individual members of the group to perform definite functions—have one member prepared to offer a main motion of business, another prepared to amend the motion, another prepared to move to refer the motion to a committee, another prepared to move adjournment, and so on.

3. Present a panel discussion to your group for thirty minutes. Divide the members of the audience into buzz groups of five or six members as described in this chapter. Each group then should be allowed an opportunity to direct a question to the panel.

4. Discuss specific occasions where the techniques and procedures described in this chapter would be used and specific occasions when the techniques and procedures of more informal conferences described in other sections of this book would be used.

INDEX

A

ABC, 49
Acceptance of solution, 118–119
Acquiescence, 27
Action group, 119–120
Adaptability in discussion speaking, 237
Additive solutions, 29
Adjectives, 244
Adler, Mortimer J., 50
Agenda, 167, 265
Allport, Gordon W., 143
Amberg, George, 79
Ambiguity, 106–107, 131, 246
Americana, 74
American College Dictionary, 74
Analogy, 129–131
  figurative, 130
  literal, 130
  tests of, 130–131
Ansbacher, L., 151
Anti-climactic organization, 208
Apology, 183
Appeals to passion or prejudice, 132
Appeals to tradition or custom, 132
Areopagitica, 10
Atmosphere in group, 17–21, 206, 241
  before discussion, 18–19
  during discussion, 21
  formal, 18
  informal, 17–18
  physical arrangements, 19–21
Attention-seeker, 160, 223
Audibility, 235, 268–269
Audience, 59, 267, 269–270
Auer, J. Jeffery, 69, 82, 204
Authoritarian leadership, 137–142
  techniques of, 140–142
Authorities, 82–83, 93–96, 210
Autocratic leadership (*see* Authoritarian leadership)

B

Backus, Ollie L., 80
Bacon, Francis, 101
Baird, A. Craig, 77
Ballet, The Emergence of an American Art, 79
Bargaining conferences, 21, 64
Bavelas, Alex, 15
Beardsley, Monroe C., 40
Begging the question, 131–132
Beginning the discussion, 168–173
Bell, Laird, 110
Belligerent speaking style, 233
Belongingness, 190
Beside-the-point participant, 160, 223
Bethlehem Steel, 21
Bias, 98–99
Biographical dictionaries, 74
Black, Max, 106
"Blindness" in problem-solving, 90–92
Boak, Arthur E. R., 79
Brevity in participation, 260
Bunche, Ralph, 18
Burtt, Edwin A., 42–43
Buzz groups, 269–270

C

Card catalogue, 74
Carlson, A. J., 94, 103, 144
Case problems, 177–178
Case reports, 88, 91–93, 94–95, 97–98, 99–100, 101–103
Causal reasoning, 127–129
  tests of, 129
Cause-effect reasoning, 128
Causes of the problem, 112–115
Chairman of large group meetings:
  and business meeting, 271–275
  conducting the meeting, 267–271

345